JOURNAL FOR THE STUDY OF THE NEW TESTAMENT
SUPPLEMENT SERIES
117

Sheffield Academic Press
Sheffield

The Sources and *Sitz im Leben* of Matthew 23

Kenneth G.C. Newport

Journal for the Study of the New Testament
Supplement Series 117

For Matthew, Stephen and Sarah

Published by Sheffield Academic Press Ltd
Mansion House
19 Kingfield Road
Sheffield, S11 9AS
England

Printed on acid-free paper in Great Britain
by Bookcraft Ltd
Midsomer Norton, Bath

British Library Cataloguing in Publication Data

A catalogue record for this book is available
from the British Library

ISBN 1-85075-557-4

CONTENTS

ACKNOWLEDGMENTS

Thanks and appreciation are due to many individuals all of whom have in one way or another made a contribution towards the writing of this monograph; I mention just a few. Professor E.P. Sanders provided not only excellent supervision but also valued friendship and support. Professor William Farmer, Dr Harry Leonard, Dr John Baildam and Mr Malcolm Bull read the entire manuscript and offered many valuable suggestions. I feel a particular debt also to Professor M.D. Goulder who similarly offered many valuable criticisms. Particular thanks are due to friends and colleages at the University of Manchester and at Liverpool Institute of Higher Education for constant encouragement and support.

My greatest appreciation, however, must be for my wife Rose-Marie. She has supported me in every possible way over several years. Only those who have experienced such committed and selfless support will know the truth of the old cliche 'without her this book would not have been written'.

Manchester, 1995

ABBREVIATIONS

AB	Anchor Bible
ANRW	*Aufstieg und Niedergang der römischen Welt*
APOT	R.H. Charles (ed.), *Apocrypha and Pseudepigrapha of the Old Testament*
ATR	*Anglican Theological Review*
BAGD	W. Bauer, W.F. Arndt, F.W. Gingrich and F.W. Danker, *Greek–English Lexicon of the New Testament*
BDB	F. Brown, S.R. Driver and C.A. Briggs, *Hebrew and English Lexicon of the Old Testament*
BEvT	Beiträge zur evangelischen Theologie
Bib	*Biblica*
BJRL	*Bulletin of the John Rylands University Library of Manchester*
BJS	Brown Judaic Studies
BNTC	Black's New Testament Commentaries
CBQ	*Catholic Biblical Quarterly*
CTR	*Catholic Theological Review*
EncJud	*Encyclopaedia Judaica*
EvQ	*Evangelical Quarterly*
ExpTim	*Expository Times*
FRLANT	Forschungen zur Religion und Literatur des Alten und Neuen Testaments
GKC	*Gesenius' Hebrew Grammar*, ed. E. Kautzsch, trans. A.E. Cowley
HTR	*Harvard Theological Review*
HUCA	*Hebrew Union College Annual*
IDB	G.A. Buttrick (ed.), *Interpreter's Dictionary of the Bible*
Int	*Interpretation*
JBL	*Journal of Biblical Literature*
JewEnc	*The Jewish Encyclopedia*
JNES	*Journal of Near Eastern Studies*
JQR	*Jewish Quarterly Review*
JSJ	*Journal for the Study of Judaism*
JSNT	*Journal for the Study of the New Testament*
JTS	*Journal of Theological Studies*
LSJ	Liddell–Scott–Jones, *Greek–English Lexicon*
NCB	New Century Bible
NovT	*Novum Testamentum*
NovTSup	*Novum Testamentum* Supplements
NTS	*New Testament Studies*

PEFQS	*Palestine Exploration Fund, Quarterly Statement*
PEQ	*Palestine Exploration Quarterly*
RB	*Revue biblique*
REJ	*Revue des études juives*
SANT	Studien zum Alten und Neuen Testament
SE	*Studia Evangelica* I, II, III (= TU 73 [1959], 87 [1964], 88 [1964], etc.)
SJT	*Scottish Journal of Theology*
SNTSMS	Society for New Testament Studies Monograph Series
SR	*Studies in Religion/Sciences religieuses*
Str–B	[H. Strack and] P. Billerbeck, *Kommentar zum Neuen Testament aus Talmud und Midrasch*
THKNT	Theologischer Handkommentar zum Neuen Testament
TNTC	Tyndale New Testament Commentaries
TynBul	*Tyndale Bulletin*
ZNW	*Zeitschrift für die neutestamentliche Wissenschaft*
ZTK	*Zeitschrift für Theologie und Kirche*

INTRODUCTION

Matthew 23 presents the New Testament scholar with many problems. Not the least of these is the unequivocal affirmation of scribal-Pharisaic authority found in vv. 2 and 3: 'The scribes and the Pharisees sit on Moses' seat,' Matthew's Jesus says, 'so practice and observe whatever they tell you'. Similarly, v. 23 evinces a concern that both the Torah and halakhah should be obeyed; it is proper for mint, dill and cummin to be tithed, even though these particular herbs are not specifically mentioned in the written words of Moses.[1] This apparent confirmation of the authority of the teaching of the scribes and Pharisees is somewhat strange, coming as it does in the book of Matthew;[2] for, as many commentators have pointed out, the struggle between Jesus and the Jewish leaders is one of the most readily identifiable leitmotifs of Matthew's gospel.[3]

The general historical situation presupposed by several of the individual sayings in Matthew 23 has also led to a certain amount of confusion. Beare, for example, thinks that it is 'surprising' that the details mentioned in vv. 16-22—the temple and its decorations, the altar and the sacrifices— meant anything at all to those to whom Matthew was writing.[4] Other commentators, however, have not been so 'surprised', since they have recognized that the chapter contains some of the oldest tradition in the Gospels. Schweizer for one thinks that the voice of Jesus himself can still

1. See further below, pp. 102-103
2. Note for example B.T. Viviano 'Social World and Community Leadership: The Case of Matthew 23.1-12, 34', *JSNT* 39 (1990), pp. 3-21, who thinks that Mt. 23.2 are 'perhaps the most puzzling verses to explain in the Gospel of Matthew' (p. 3).
3. See for example J.D. Kingsbury, *Matthew as Story* (Philadelphia: Fortress Press, 1986), pp. 17-23; *idem*, 'The Developing Conflict between Jesus and the Jewish Leaders in Matthew's Gospel: A Literary-Critical Study', *CBQ* 49 (1987), pp. 57-73; S. van Tilborg, *The Jewish Leaders in Matthew* (Leiden: Brill, 1972).
4. F.W. Beare, *The Gospel according to Matthew* (Oxford: Basil Blackwell, 1981), p. 454.

be heard in Mt. 23.16-22,[1] and Bultmann too suggests that some of Matthew 23 goes back to the preaching of Jesus.[2] Despite these early elements, however, many scholars claim that the chapter as a whole bears the hallmarks of a redactional creation, and witnesses Matthew's own life situation.

If the problem of identifying the *Sitz im Leben* of Matthew 23 is a difficult one, the identification of sources is perhaps even worse. Almost certainly there are sources, for much of the material found in the chapter seems so out of tune with the general thrust of Matthew's gospel that it is highly unlikely that the evangelist has written it himself. It is quite possible, as David Hill has suggested, that Matthew included traditional material with which he did not necessarily agree;[3] but it is much less likely that the evangelist would have created it. The links with Mark are not great, and at best the Marcan priority hypothesis can explain only a few of the total number of verses. Neither is the Q theory of very great help, for comparison with Luke reveals remarkable divergence. There is little verbal overlap, and the order of the material in the two gospels is vastly dissimilar. Multiple source theories such as that of Boismard[4] seem unable to account for the essential unity of the chapter as a whole.

This study seeks to present an understanding of Matthew 23 which is both realistic and historically viable. It argues that the bulk of the chapter is derived from one source, namely an early Jewish-Christian polemical tract (now Mt. 23.2-31). The possible *Sitz im Leben* of this early tract is sketched in and contrasted with the use to which the same material has been put by Matthew. Mention is made of other passages in Matthew's Gospel which seem dependent upon material of the same traditional extraction, most notably the Sermon on the Mount.

This study has six chapters. Chapter 1 examines the most prominent source-critical hypotheses in the context of Matthew 23 and concludes that none is able to account adequately for the material found in that chapter. Chapter 2 then takes up the question of the *Sitz im Leben* of

1.   E. Schweizer, *The Good News according to Matthew* (trans. D.E. Green; London: SPCK, 1975), p. 433.

2.   R. Bultmann, *The History of the Synoptic Tradition* (trans. J. Marsh; Oxford: Basil Blackwell, 1963), p. 147.

3.   D. Hill, *The Gospel of Matthew* (NCB; London: Marshall, Morgan & Scott, 1972), p. 71.

4.   P. Benoit and M-E. Boismard, *Synopse des Quatre Evangiles en Français* (2 vols.; Paris: Cerf, 1972), II, pp. 17-59. All following references are to vol. II of this work.

ch. 23 and argues that there is much in this passage that presupposes a *Sitz im Leben* that is *intra muros vis-à-vis* Judaism. This contrasts with the *Sitz im Leben* of the evangelist which is manifestly *extra muros*. In Chapter 3 it is noted that there is nothing in 23.2-31 which would demand a post-70 CE context: all references to religious practice and halakhic discussion found in this section are explicable in terms of pre-70 CE Palestinian Judaism. Indeed a pre-70 CE *Sitz im Leben* would seem far better able to explain the origin of much of the material in this section than a post-70 one; 23.32-39, on the other hand, seems better explained as later redaction of the earlier source. Chapter 4 contains a verse by verse exegesis of Matthew 23, which puts into exegetical practice the theory regarding the sources and *Sitz im Leben* of the material that has emerged from Chapters 1 and 2. Chapter 5 examines the links between ch. 23 and other parts of the Gospel, attempting to sort out the various layers of tradition and redaction in Matthew, and suggesting other passages within Matthew that may have arisen in a different *Sitz im Leben* from that of the gospel as a whole. Chapter 6 draws the preceding chapters together and offers specific conclusions.

Chapter 1

COMPOSITIONAL THEORIES

The emergence of redaction criticism has doubtless been one of the most significant events in the history of biblical studies. Gospel redaction criticism, and indeed redaction criticism as a whole, is based upon one fundamental assumption: that it is possible to distinguish between original source and later redaction. As a reading of almost any fairly recent commentary on Matthew will show, most Matthean scholars are convinced that such a distinction is possible in the case of the first Gospel.

This current optimism concerning the possibility of tracing the first evangelist's hand, and thus his theological concerns and interests, rests largely, though not exclusively, upon the validity of the two-document hypothesis. Of course, if Matthew really has used Mark and Q, then a comparison of Matthew with Mark and Luke will indeed doubtless reveal the changes to Mark and Q which the evangelist has made. Further, by noting the actual words used to change these sections, an insight into Matthew's own vocabulary may be gained.[1] In the same way, by noting the theological implication of these changes, some rough outline of the evangelist's own theological interests may be drawn up. Once the silhouette of the evangelist is seen in the light of these redaction-critical procedures, his figure may be brought into sharper relief by looking at those passages where the source is not so obvious. Thus the theory of Matthean redaction criticism is born, and thus it is practiced by a large number of modern Matthean scholars.

If the theory of Marcan priority is rejected, however, then the validity of this kind of redaction-critical approach to Matthew loses much of its force. In the same way, if the existence of Q is doubted, or even if the possibility of reconstructing its pre-Matthean form seriously questioned,

---

1. So, for example, M.D. Goulder, *Midrash and Lection in Matthew* (London: SPCK, 1974), p. 476. Goulder does not accept the Q theory, but classifies as 'Matthean' the words that have been 'inserted redactionally by Matthew into an agreed Marcan context or OT citation'.

then the outlook for the Bornkamm–Barth–Held type of redaction criticism is gloomy indeed.[1]

It is not the purpose of this study to challenge directly the Marcan-priority hypothesis (though neither is it assumed). With respect to Q, however, this study is more ambitious. In this and later chapters we shall see that for Matthew 23/Luke 11 at least, the hypothesis which suggests that Matthew and Luke drew on a common written source is far from totally convincing. The substantial unity of the chapter suggests that it is not made up of numerous individual pericopae (i.e. drawn from Q, M and Mark) which have been stitched together by Matthew. Neither can the chapter be explained in terms of its being an *ex nihilo* creation of the Evangelist,[2] for the *Sitz im Leben* of much of the material seems not to be that of Matthew himself. Matthew was writing *extra muros vis-à-vis* Judaism; much of ch. 23, on the other hand, seems to stem from an *intra muros* debate. The chapter is not a mosaic and not from Matthew; thus we must take seriously the possibility that in Matthew 23 we have an extensive pre-Matthean source.

This study, then, seeks to open up once again the question of the sources of Matthew's Gospel. Such an endeavour seems justified, however, since the sources of that gospel may not be as clearly defined as some have argued. Rather confusingly, this becomes apparent when a study of commentaries on Matthew by some alleged two-documentarians is conducted, for it frequently becomes clear that their authors in fact hold to quite complex multi-source theories.[3] Such authors are not prepared to explain the Gospel of Matthew solely in terms of Mark, a single written Q, and the evangelist's own redactional activity and thus are not, in a strict sense, two-documentarians at all, but rather holders of multi-document (or multi-source since some allow for non-written oral traditions) hypotheses. Commentators frequently allow for at least one, and often several, additional sources other than Mark and Q. These sources go by a number of different names such as 'M',[4] 'N',[5] or

1. G. Bornkamm, G. Barth and H.J. Held, *Tradition and Interpretation in Matthew* (trans. P. Scott; London: SCM Press, 1963).

2. Cf. Goulder who suggests that practically the whole of Mt. 23 is the creation of Matthew himself. Goulder's theory is dealt with extensively below.

3. Detailed discussion on this point is found in K.G.C. Newport, 'The Sources and *Sitz im Leben* of Matt 23' (DPhil thesis, University of Oxford, 1988), ch. 1.

4. E.g. G.D. Kilpatrick, *The Origins of the Gospel according to St Matthew* (Oxford: Clarendon Press, 1946), pp. 14-36.

5. So F.W. Green, *St Matthew* (Oxford: Clarendon Press, 1936), p. 12. Green

simply 'Matthew's special source' or *Sondergut*,[1] but all refer to basically the same thing, namely special sources used by Matthew for some sections of his Gospel not paralleled either in Mark or Luke.

Of course, holders of the two-document hypothesis are at liberty to propose sources other than Mark and Q when seeking to explain the material in Matthew that has no synoptic parallel. What is telling, however, is that even where part of Matthew 23 is paralleled in either Mark or Luke, commentators often seek to explain divergence within the parallels by recourse to something other than Matthean or Lucan redactional activity. One such explanation is that there was an overlap between M and Q at this point and that whereas Luke has used Q, Matthew has used the form he found in M.[2] We may note further that several commentators have suggested that the version of Q known to Matthew was not the same as that known to Luke. J.P. Brown argued this case for Matthew generally and in so doing, suggested that M and Q were combined before Matthew to give Mt. 23.1-39. On the other hand, Luke had only the original Q form of the discourse with which to work.[3] Such suggestions highlight the difficulty that holders of the two-document hypothesis face in seeking to explain the relationship between Matthew 23 and Luke 11.

The case of ch. 23 is typical of Matthew as a whole, for in order to explain the actual differences and similarities between Matthew, Mark and Luke, scholars almost invariably resort to complex multi-source theories. We have noted already that many propose 'special sources' or two versions of Q when seeking to unravel the source history of the gospels, and to these complications of the two-document hypothesis could be added several more. Some, for example, propose an 'Ur-Marcus',[4] or a 'proto-Luke'[5] or suggest that Luke knew Matthew and has been

allows also for some 'other non-Marcan sources' in addition to Q and N.

1. E.g. E. Haenchen, 'Matthäus 23', *ZTK* 48 (1951), p. 39.

2. Kilpatrick, *Origins*, p. 30.

3. J.P. Brown, 'The Form of Q Known to Matthew' *NTS* 8 (1961–62), p. 36.

4. X. Léon-Dufour, 'The Synoptic Gospels', in A. Robert and A. Feuillet (eds.), *Introduction to the New Testament* (trans. P.W. Skehan *et al.*; Paris: Desclée, 1965), p. 272, gives a summary of the history of the Ur-Marcus theory. Beare, *Matthew*, p. 394; T.A. Gill, 'The Woes to the Scribes and the Pharisees in Matthew 23' (MLitt thesis, University of Oxford, 1983), p. 11. Bultmann, *History of the Synoptic Tradition*, p. 6.

5. E.g. B.H. Streeter, *The Four Gospels: A Study in Origins* (London: Macmillan, 1926), pp. 201-22.

influenced in his own redaction by his knowledge of Matthew's redaction of Q and Mark.[1] Others allow for the influence of oral sources[2] or a special quotations source[3]. The list of variations on the two-document theme could easily be extended.

Given this uncertainty concerning the sources of Matthew's Gospel, the task of tracing the hand of the evangelist is clearly a highly speculative one, for if we cannot determine sources we cannot sieve out redaction. Neither does the optimism of some scholars, most notably perhaps Goulder, that the vocabulary of Matthew can be used as a guide in sorting out redaction from source, seem warranted. Clearly, some phrases and words are so common in Matthew that there is a clear possibility that they stem from the evangelist's own hand.[4] For the most part, however, the situation is far less clear, and the distinction between source and redaction is not hard and fast. Goulder's confidence that the hand of Matthew can be traced and that it is clearly visible throughout Matthew 23 seems unfounded.

In the pages to follow an attempt is made realistically to assess the possibility of tracing Matthew's own hand in the gospel with special reference to Matthew 23. We will note especially Goulder's work since despite its obvious concern for detail and the clarity and determination with which it is argued his hypothesis has not heretofore received the kind of detailed critical assessment it most certainly deserves.

Suggestions concerning the origin of Matthew 23 range across the

---

1. R.H. Gundry, *Matthew: A Commentary on his Literary and Theological Art* (Grand Rapids: Eerdmans, 1982), p. 5.

2. See for example Hill, *Matthew*, p. 32. According to Hill such oral sources may lie behind some of the special narrative sections of Matthew such as the Petrine stories (14.28-31; 16.17-19; 17.24-27; 18.15-22), the Passion and Resurrection stories and others. It is worth noting also that Hill's Q is in fact extremely complex. For him Q is only a loose term that can be applied to a collection of materials that were common to Matthew and Luke. In fact according to Hill part of Q may not even have been available to Matthew and Luke in the same language. He notes

> It is our opinion then that the basic sources on which the writer of Matthew drew are the Gospel of Mark and that layer of tradition, partly written partly oral, which is conveniently designated Q: the latter circulated in Aramaic, but may have been available in a Greek version before its use by the author of the Gospel (p. 30).

3. See especially R.H. Gundry, *The Use of the Old Testament in St Matthew's Gospel with Special Reference to the Messianic Hope* (NovTSup, 18; Leiden: Brill, 1967).

4. Below, Appendix 1.C.

entire source/redaction-critical spectrum. At one end stands Boismard, who allows for at least four sources in addition to the creative activity of the 'l'ultime Redacteur matthéen' himself,[1] while at the other is Goulder, who argues for the essential unity of the chapter, and sees almost all of the material as stemming from the evangelist's own hand.[2]

Between these two extremes comes the bulk of gospel scholarship. Schweizer,[3] for example, sees Matthew 23 as an intricate web of traditional and redactional material. Matthew has expanded Mark, and in so doing has made use of material from other sources. The evangelist has drawn on Q, and this material itself has undergone redaction and expansion at his hand. Many scholars argue for a special 'M' source.[4] In addition to Q and Mark, Matthew has worked this material into the chapter, but in so doing, his redactional activity has played an important role. In the present chapter these source-critical theories are examined in detail.

1. *Michael D. Goulder*

Goulder's views on the interrelationships between the Synoptic Gospels are now well known. He suggests that Mark's Gospel was the first to be written, and Matthew has used Mark, expanding the material using no source other than the Old Testament. The overlap between Matthew and Luke is explained in terms of Luke's direct dependence upon Matthew. Consequent to this, Goulder argues for the almost completely Matthean origin of Matthew 23. Matthew has simply expanded Mk 12.38-40. All other material is Matthew's own, and is the result of his creative activity. While on a general level many scholars have rejected the views of Goulder,[5] none has attempted to deal thoroughly with his detailed argumentation. As we shall see, Goulder's case is extremely well argued and any attempt to counter it must be based upon the same meticulous concern for the details of the text. Goulder has counted words, and his critics need to do the same rather than attempting to dismiss his work with generalities. In the pages which follow, such an attempt is made.

1. Boismard, *Synopse*, pp. 354-59.
2. Goulder, *Midrash*, pp. 419-30.
3. Schweizer, *Matthew*, pp. 12-13, 427-47.
4. E.g. Streeter, *The Four Gospels*, pp. 253-54; Kilpatrick, *Origins*, pp. 30-32.
5. See for example the reviews of *Midrash and Lection* by A.E. Harvey, *JTS* 27 (1976), pp. 188-95; C.L. Mitton, *ExpTim* 86 (1975), pp. 97-99. D. Catchpole, *EvQ* 47 (1975), pp. 239-40.

Naturally the study is focused primarily on Goulder's source-critical analysis of Matthew 23.

One major and very general objection to Goulder's thesis is obvious: the material within Matthew is simply too diverse to be the product of one mind. For Goulder, the evangelist has created such diverse material as Mt. 10.23 and 24.14; Mt. 23.2-3 and 16.12; and Mt. 8.11 and 18.17, which is scarcely probable. Matthew may have been able to live with contradictory traditions, and may have felt obliged to include what he considered to be authentic traditions about Jesus in his Gospel; but it is less likely that he would have invented such material.

In addition to this general criticism, several more specific ones may be made. Goulder suggests that the evangelist's hand is clearly visible in the redactional material in the gospel. It is no surprise, therefore, that he thinks that the hand of Matthew may be clearly seen in Matthew 23. Goulder points to numerous examples of 'Mattheanisms' in ch. 23, which, he argues, support his thesis of the Matthean authorship of the chapter.

A. *Vocabulary*

Goulder suggests that in Matthew 23 there are numerous words and phrases which are clearly Matthean. Such words are those which, while occurring at least four times in Matthew, are absent from Mark and/or Luke or, alternatively, occur in Matthew at least twice as often as in Mark and Luke combined.[1] Other words Goulder classes as 'semi-Matthean', in that they appear twice as often in Matthew as in Mark *and* are more common in Matthew than in Luke, or they can be seen to have been added redactionally by Matthew into an 'agreed Marcan context or OT citation'.[2]

i. *'Matthean' Words and Phrases*
Goulder's statistics, should they prove correct, would indeed be compelling. Near the end of his discussion of Matthew 23 he notes that 'in the whole chapter there are 646 words, of which 180 are characteristic of Matthew'.[3] Goulder, however, like J.C. Hawkins before him,[4]

---

1. Goulder, *Midrash*, p. 476.
2. Goulder, *Midrash*, p. 476.
3. Goulder, *Midrash*, p. 429.
4. J.C. Hawkins, *Horae Synopticae: Contributions to the Study of the Synoptic Problem* (Oxford: Clarendon Press, 2nd edn, 1909). Extensive remarks on Hawkins's methodology are found in Newport 'Sources and *Sitz im Leben*', pp. 113-30.

has failed to point out that it is frequently the case that a 'characteristically Matthean' word often occurs in only certain sections of the Gospel. Several of the 'typically Matthean' words found by Goulder in ch. 23 are in fact typical only of this chapter and the Sermon on the Mount, and not of the Gospel generally.[1] The clustering of such words in these three sections is not readily explicable by the fact that chs. 5, 6, 7 and 23 primarily contain teaching material and thus of necessity may have a somewhat distinctive vocabulary. According to Goulder's hypothesis all of these chapters stem from the hand of the evangelist. Matthew is responsible also for the bulk of chs. 13, 24 and 25, as well as other sayings material not drawn from Mark, yet these sections do not exhibit the 'characteristically Matthean' words in question.

The weakness of Goulder's (and Hawkins's) word counting approach to the question of Matthean redactoral activity in ch. 23 is perhaps best seen in the example of the figurative use of τυφλός. Both Goulder[2] and Hawkins[3] include the metaphorical use of τυφλός as a characteristic of Matthew's own vocabulary, yet of the six occurrences in the Gospel, five are found in ch. 23 (vv. 16, 17, 19, 24, 26). Metaphorical τυφλός may be characteristic of Matthew 23, but it can hardly be said to be characteristic of the gospel as a whole.

Another example of this kind of weakness in Goulder's methodology is found in his remarks on the occurrences of ὄμνυμι in Matthew. Whether it was customary after 70 CE to swear by 'the temple', 'the gold of the temple', 'the altar' or the 'gift upon the altar' may be impossible to tell, since there may have been vestiges of earlier oath forms, even after the temple had been destroyed. But in any case, Goulder's suggestion that ὄμνυμι is Matthean[4] loses much of its force

---

1. This is a point that is well made in the work of D.G. Tevis, 'An Analysis of Words and Phrases Characteristic of the Gospel of Matthew' (PhD thesis, Southern Methodist University, 1982). Tevis has conducted a careful study of words and phrases in Matthew that seem to be characteristic of the Gospel. However, Tevis does not fall into the same trap as Goulder and Hawkins in equating 'characteristic of the Gospel' with 'from the hand of Matthew'. For example the phrase οὐαὶ δὲ ὑμῖν γραμματεῖς καὶ Φαρισαῖοι ὑποκριταί, ὅτι…is clearly characteristic of the gospel of Matthew, but this does not mean that it is from Matthew's own hand since it appears only in Mt. 23 (see Tevis, 'An Analysis of Words and Phrases', p. 249). Tevis's work is dealt with a some detail below.

2. Goulder, *Midrash*, p. 424.

3. Hawkins, *Horae Synopticae*, p. 8.

4. Goulder, *Midrash*, p. 424.

when we note that of the thirteen occurrences in Matthew ten are found in ch. 23 (two examples in each of vv. 16, 18, 20, 21, 22), two in the Sermon on the Mount (5.34, 36) and only one elsewhere (26.74). This kind of inequality in distribution does not bolster confidence in the claim that the word is Matthew's own.

Another example is the use of θυσιαστήριον.[1] The word appears six times in Matthew, only twice in Luke and not at all in Mark. But θυσιαστήριον is limited in Matthew to the Sermon on the Mount (5.23, 24) and ch. 23 (vv. 18, 19, 20, 35). It is argued extensively in Chapter 5 below that these two sections of Matthew's Gospel are traditional to the first evangelist and are drawn from closely-related sources. This conclusion is primarily reached by noting the similar *Sitz im Leben* of these two sections, a *Sitz im Leben* which seems rather different from that of the Gospel as a whole. However, there are also certain verbal overlaps between these two sections to be noted and in particular the clustering of words and phrases which are otherwise absent of relatively uncommon elsewhere in the Gospel; θυσιαστήριον is one such example and there are numerous others. We have noted already the use of ὄμνυμι above (13 occurrences, 10 in Matthew 23 and two in the Sermon on the Mount) and some further examples are listed below. We might note also that if Matthew is writing at a time subsequent to the fall of Jerusalem (as Goulder himself believes)[2] it is perhaps more reasonable to ascribe these clear references to the altar and the temple to source material than to redactional activity.

Similar to θυσιαστήριον is δῶρον, which occurs nine times in Matthew.[3] Three of these occurrences are in the Sermon on the Mount (5.23, 24 [bis]) and three in ch. 23 (vv. 18, 19 [bis]). Even Bultmann argues that in 5.23-24 Matthew preserves an earlier form of the tradition than does Mark (Mk 11.25); for the saying, in Bultmann's words, 'presupposes the existence of the sacrificial system of Jerusalem'.[4] This

---

1. Goulder, *Midrash*, p. 424.
2. Goulder, *Midrash*, p. 417.
3. Goulder, *Midrash*, p. 424.
4. Bultmann, *History of the Synoptic Tradition*, p. 132. Bultmann's suggestion raises the general question of whether those elements of the Synoptic tradition which are more Jewish are therefore earlier. If this were so, of course, it could be argued that Matthew's Gospel, being considerably more Jewish than Mark's, must be earlier. This is an area of discussion into which this study does not delve. The literature on the topic is vast, but very relevant is E.P. Sanders, *The Tendencies of the*

perhaps highlights the problem, which is taken up in Chapter 2 below, of the *Sitz im Leben* of the Sermon on the Mount, and of ch. 23 *vis-à-vis* the Gospel as a whole.

At first sight it might look as though Goulder is on slightly firmer ground when he suggests that the phrase ὁ πατὴρ ὁ οὐράνιος is a Mattheanism,[1] but even here caution is called for. The phrase appears in four different sections of the Gospel, but even so an imbalance is evident. The phrase appears seven times in Matthew, and yet is absent from the rest of the New Testament. It therefore looks Matthean. Four of the examples are, however, found in the Sermon on the Mount (5.48; 6.14, 26, 32), and one in ch. 23 (v. 9). If Matthew 23 and 5–7 have firm links, the occurrences of the phrase ὁ πατὴρ ὁ οὐράνιος in these sections is readily explicable.

The other two examples of this phrase may also be explained on the basis of the same hypothesis. Hawkins argued that Matthew picked up some nineteen formulae and phrases from his sources, which he then spread throughout the rest of his Gospel.[2] Goulder argues a similar case with respect to the healing of the blind men in Mt. 20.29ff. and 9.27ff., where Matthew has duplicated a story from his source and set it in another context,[3] and Luz says that 'many vocables of Matthew's preferred vocabulary are not new creations of the evangelist but were suggested by his sources'.[4] Is it not equally plausible that the two occurrences of the phrase ὁ πατὴρ ὁ οὐράνιος in 15.13 and 18.35 are likewise an example of the first evangelist utilizing a component of his source material?[5]

Synoptic Tradition (Cambridge: Cambridge University Press, 1969). Also useful is W.R. Farmer, 'Certain Results Reached by Sir John C. Hawkins and C.F. Burney Which Make More Sense if Luke Knew Matthew, and Mark Knew Matthew and Luke'; M. Goulder 'Some Observations on Professor Farmer's "Certain Results"', and W.R. Farmer, 'Reply to Michael Goulder', in C.M. Tuckett (ed.), *Synoptic Studies. The Ampleforth Conferences of 1982 and 1983* (Sheffield: JSOT Press, 1984), pp. 75-109.

1.   Goulder, *Midrash*, p. 423.

2.   Hawkins, *Horae Synopticae*, pp. 170-73.

3.   Goulder, *Midrash*, p. 326.

4.   U. Luz, *Matthew 1–7: A Commentary* (trans. W.C. Linss; Edinburgh: T. & T. Clark, 1989), p. 73.

5.   A point made also by Tevis ('An Analysis of Words and Phrases', p. 11), who states that

It would appear, therefore, that several of those words which Goulder is ready to count as Matthean are characteristic not of the Gospel as a whole, but rather of ch. 23 and the Sermon on the Mount, and it is perhaps better to discount these when attempting to trace the hand of the first evangelist himself.

Other words on Goulder's list are Matthean only by virtue of their appearing unusually often in one or more other sections of the Gospel. One such example is the use of μωρός. Outside of the Sermon on the Mount (5.22; 7.26) and ch. 23 (v. 7), the word is found only in the parable of the wise and foolish virgins.

The above examples—together with several others, all of which have been tabulated in an appendix to this chapter—suggest that the vocabulary of Matthew 23 is not quite as 'Matthean' as Goulder makes out. In all, 24 of those words which Goulder identifies as 'characteristically Matthean' words may be rejected on the basis that they appear only in pockets of the Gospel tradition. (This count includes several of Goulder's 'semi-Matthean' words.) They do not appear with either the frequency or distribution that would demand assent to Goulder's contentions.

Twenty-seven of the words in Matthew 23 which Goulder identifies as 'characteristically Matthean' remain. Of these 27, 19 simply lack conclusive evidence either way, for when their frequency is examined, it appears that any one of them may be a 'Mattheanism'; the evidence is not so strong, however, as to demand that it be interpreted in a way that is supportive of Goulder's thesis. The word οὕτως is one such example;[1] οὕτως appears 32 times in Matthew, 10 times in Mark and 21 times in Luke. The rest of the New Testament gives another 145 examples. Given these figures it is quite clearly impossible to argue conclusively that the one occurrence of the word in ch. 23 (v. 28) is evidence of Matthean authorship. Another example is ἐάν,[2] which occurs some 64 times in Matthew, 36 in Mark and 31 in Luke. The rest of the New Testament gives 220 examples. The word is therefore far from uncommon, and the one example of ἐάν in Matthew 23 (v. 3) can hardly be taken as indicative of the chapter's stemming from the hand of the evangelist himself.

The fact that a phrase is distinctive does not entirely eliminate the possibility that it has been used by more than one writer. One of the Gospel writers may have copied a distinctive phrase from one of his sources and then used that phrase at other points in his own composition.

1.   Goulder, *Midrash*, p. 427.
2.   Goulder, *Midrash*, p. 423.

The evidence in the cases of οὕτως and ἐάν seems neutral. While it may be interpreted as supportive of Goulder's thesis, it is by no means necessarily so. The same is true of 17 other words classified by Goulder as 'Matthean' or 'semi-Matthean'. These have been set out in Appendix 1.b. below.

Eight of Goulder's 'characteristically Matthean' words now remain. It cannot be denied that several of these words do indeed support the thesis of a Matthean redactional element in ch. 23, though the extent of this element is perhaps a good deal less than Goulder imagines. Since it has been admitted that these words do lend some support to Goulder's theory, they must be examined here in finer detail.

At this point it is imperative that we anticipate and state clearly a conclusion reached more firmly later in this study. Close examination of Matthew 23 suggests that the chapter is made up of two principal parts, with the division coming at 23.32. Verses 2-31, it is suggested, are source material, vv. 32-39 redaction. This view seems to account for the substantial unity of the first part of the chapter and the distinct shift in tone from an attack upon the 'scribes and Pharisees' found in vv. 2-31 to a criticism of the Jewish nation as a whole in the latter part of the discourse. Similarly the apparently different *Sitz im Leben* of the first part of the chapter from that of the latter is also explicable on the basis of this hypothesis. These points are discussed at length in the following chapters. However, it should not go unnoticed that the linguistic evidence adds further weight to this view. None of Goulder's 'Mattheanisms' disproves the hypothesis here advanced, and the methodologically similar work of Tevis (surveyed below) positively supports it. It is with this hypothesis in mind, then, that we approach Goulder's strongest arguments for the Matthean origin of Matthew 23.

a. *Words somewhat supportive of Goulder's hypothesis which appear in Matthew 23.2-31.*
1. ἡ βασιλεία τῶν οὐρανῶν. Of all the words classified by Goulder as Matthean in Matthew 23, the ones most likely to be from the hand of the final redactor are ἡ βασιλεία τῶν οὐρανῶν.[1] The phrase ἡ βασιλεία τῶν οὐρανῶν is found in Matthew's Gospel 33 times, yet it is absent from the rest of the New Testament. It is with some justification, then, that Goulder sees the phrase as evidence of Matthew's own work. Goulder, however, is not at liberty to lean too heavily on this

---

1. Goulder, *Midrash*, p. 424.

phrase to support his thesis of the Matthean origin of the material in
Matthew 23. By his reckoning Matthew has changed 'Kingdom of God'
in his Marcan source to 'Kingdom of Heaven' many times (e.g. Mk
4.11/Mt. 13.11), and others have suggested that he has done the same
thing with Q (e.g. Mt. 11.12/Lk. 16.16). It is equally plausible that the
evangelist has replaced 'Kingdom of God' with the circumlocution in
any source he may have used for ch. 23. Matthew may have lightly
edited the source, but as is argued extensively in this study, there is
every reason to suggest that his editing was minimal.

It is quite possible, then, that in Mt. 23.13 we have evidence of
Matthew's own hand. This, however, does not in any way mean that
Matthew was the originator of the verse. Matthew may have changed the
phrase ἡ βασιλεία τοῦ θεοῦ originally found in his source to ἡ βασιλεία τῶν οὐρανῶν. But this is not the only possible explanation. Of
course, if the two-document hypothesis is taken as a starting point, then it
is clear that Matthew has a preference for ἡ βασιλεία τῶν οὐρανῶν
over ἡ βασιλεία τοῦ θεοῦ, for comparison of Matthew with Mark and
Luke reveals that the first evangelist has almost always changed ἡ
βασιλεία τοῦ θεοῦ in his source to ἡ βασιλεία τῶν οὐρανῶν. Why
he has not always done so is not clear,[1] but the fact that he has done it so
often indicates that he preferred the phrase to that found in his sources.
However, if the two-document hypothesis is dropped for a moment, the
situation changes. It is now possible that Matthew simply used what he
found in his sources and did not in fact change them to suit his purposes.
If he found ἡ βασιλεία τοῦ θεοῦ, he let it stand, and if he found ἡ
βασιλεία τῶν οὐρανῶν, he let that stand also. As Tevis notes,[2] in a
Jewish-Christian environment (which is exactly the environment from
which Mt. 23.2-31 seems to have come), the phrase ἡ βασιλεία τῶν
οὐρανῶν might not have been distinctive at all. Matthew may have had
a liking for the phrase, and some of the occurrences of the phrase in
Matthew may be the work of Matthew himself; it does not follow, however, that he was the only one who ever used it. Indeed, it is perhaps just
as reasonable to suggest that Matthew's source for Mt. 23.13 already contained ἡ βασιλεία τῶν οὐρανῶν, as it is to argue that Matthew much
preferred ἡ βασιλεία τῶν οὐρανῶν, to ἡ βασιλεία τοῦ θεοῦ yet
permitted ἡ βασιλεία τοῦ θεοῦ to occur unchanged on four occasions.

---

1. ἡ βασιλεία τοῦ θεοῦ appears at 12.28 (Lk. 11.20); 19.24 (Mk 10.25);
21.31, 43.
2. Tevis, 'Characteristic Words', p. 266.

2. τηρέω. The occurrence of τηρέω in Mt. 23.3 is more difficult to deal with tidily. Among the Synoptic Gospels the word is unusually common in Matthew and appears in such a way as to suggest that it is from the hand of the final redactor. We should note its use in 28.20 especially. This is clearly a redactional passage, where Jesus commands his disciples to teach the nations 'to keep' all the things he has commanded. The word occurs also in 19.17; 27.36, 54; 28.4, but is absent in Luke and Mark (but we may note that τηρέω appears in several MSS in Mk 7.9).

The word τηρέω is hardly an uncommon one however. In addition to its occurrences in Matthew, the New Testament gives 64 others. While its occurrence in Mt. 23.3 might serve to support Goulder if his claim could be established on other grounds, it in no way demands that we assent to the suggestion that Matthew created this verse. The weight of evidence against the Matthean origin of 23.3 is substantial, and the occurrence of one fairly common word cannot in any way counterbalance it.

3. τάφος. The word τάφος appears in Matthew six times, and only once more in the whole of the New Testament (Rom 3.13). The word therefore looks Matthean. It cannot be said with confidence, however, that the word as it appears in Mt. 23.29 is a Mattheanism, for the simple reason that we have here an example of parallelism, and two words for 'tomb' were needed. It is by necessity and not necessarily personal preference that τάφος appears in 23.29; two words were needed and the author used the two available: τάφος and μνημεῖον. The occurrence in 23.27 is more difficult. Here the author could have used μνημεῖον had he so desired. It seems, then, that this word may lend some slight support to Goulder's claims.[1]

4. *Hebraic* υἱός. Goulder thinks that the use of 'Hebraic υἱός' is a characteristic of Matthew's style. Goulder counts eight occurrences of the idiom in Matthew and these would seem to be (8.12; 9.15; 13.38 [bis]; 17.25, 26; 23.15, 31). Such usage is therefore relatively common in Matthew.

The example in 23.31 is slightly ambiguous; the sons here are literal sons, though there seems to be a play on the metaphorical meaning of 'son' also. In 23.15 the situation is clearer and the appearance of the

---

1. There is a slight weakness in Goulder's argument, however, in that according to him Matthew has also created 27.52, 53 and in both places has used not τάφος but μνημεῖον.

'Hebraic υἱός' in this verse (and probably in 23.31 also) certainly supports Goulder's contentions. However, Goulder's conclusion is not necessitated by the facts, since such usage of υἱός could easily have been found in any source stemming from a Jewish-Christian milieu. Matthew was by no means the only one to use this idiom in the New Testament; Mark has two examples and Luke four, and it crops up fairly frequently elsewhere (e.g. Eph. 2.2; 5.6; 2 Thess. 2.3).

5. φαίνομαι. The word φαίνομαι looks Matthean. It appears thirteen times in Matthew and only twice each in Mark and Luke. It is fairly well distributed throughout the Gospel, but not uniformly so. There are four occurrences in the birth story, three in the Sermon on the Mount, two in ch. 23 (vv. 27, 28) and four elsewhere (9.33; 13.26; 24.27, 30). It would be possible, therefore, to argue that the majority of the occurrences of this word are found in sections of Matthew that are quite conceivably source material. However, Goulder's suggestion that the word is from the hand of Matthew looks more plausible (though other explanations are not inconceivable) and the occurrence of the word in Mt. 23.27, 28 lends some support to his theory of the Matthean origin of this chapter.

b. *Words somewhat supportive of Goulder's hypothesis which appear in Matthew 23.32-39.*
1. γεννήματα ἐχιδνῶν. Goulder also cites the use of γεννήματα ἐχιδνῶν as evidence of Matthew's own hand.[1] The phrase occurs three times in Matthew (3.7; 12.34; 23.33), and it is indeed unlikely that it was thought up independently by more than one author. This point is highlighted when we note that the three examples exhibit distinct similarities. In each case it is the scribes and Pharisees who are being attacked, and in each case the rebuke is set in a firmly eschatological context. It is argued extensively in this study that the last eight verses of ch. 23 are not original to their present context, but are rather an appendix added by an eschatologically orientated redactor to a basically non-eschatological source (Mt. 23.2-31). Goulder may be right in ascribing the phrase γεννήματα ἐχιδνῶν to Matthew, for Matthew himself may have been the 'eschatological redactor' concerned. In any case it is clear that the phrase belongs to a layer of tradition in Matthew which is concerned primarily with eschatological matters.

---

1.   Goulder, *Midrash*, p. 428.

2. ὅπως. The word ὅπως lends some slight support to the theory of the Matthean origin of Mt. 23.35. The word is somewhat distinctive in Matthew compared to Mark and Luke (Mt. 17; Mk 1; Lk. 7), but it is common enough in the New Testament (36 examples outside of Matthew) and thus Matthew could easily have found it in any source he had for Mt. 23.35. However, since for other reasons it seems that Mt. 23.35 comes from the hand of Matthew, the occurrence of ὅπως could be used to add some additional, though very slight weight to the argument.

3. ἄρτι. The word ἄρτι appears seven times in Matthew and never in Mark or Luke. The rest of the New Testament gives another 29 examples, 12 of them in John. The word therefore looks like a favorite of Matthew's, although it is not particularly uncommon elsewhere and we cannot with confidence say that its occurrence in Mt. 23.39 means that this section is Matthew's creation. As this study makes clear, there are other reasons for thinking that Mt. 23.32-39 are the work of a redactor, probably Matthew himself, and the occurrence of ἄρτι in this section supports this hypothesis to some slight degree.

c. *Conclusion on those words in Matthew 23 which are somewhat supportive of Goulder's hypothesis.* We are now in a position to summarize the conclusions reached on those words in Matthew 23 which seem supportive of Goulder's hypothesis. Listed above are Goulder's proposed Mattheanisms that seem to come closest to establishing his general case. It will be noted that none of these is particularly impressive; ἡ βασιλεία τῶν οὐρανῶν may well be Matthew's own, but this conclusion falls far short of establishing the Matthean origin of the passage. The word τηρέω may be Matthew's, but it is not an uncommon word and could easily have been found in Matthew's source. The Hebraic use of υἱός to mean 'one like' could easily have existed already in any source that Matthew may have used for 23.15, 31. τάφος and φαίνομαι are stronger, but even these lend only slight weight to Goulder's hypothesis. If Goulder is going to prove his case, he is going to have to do it with evidence other than word statistics.

ii. *Semi-Matthean Words and Phrases*
As might be expected, the 14 words and phrases put forward by Goulder as 'semi-Matthean' support his case for the Matthean authorship of

ch. 23 even less than those he classes as 'Matthean'; ἁγιάζω,[1] for example, occurs only three times in the gospel, and its use is restricted to ch. 23 and the Sermon on the Mount (6.9; 23.17, 19). ὁδηγός[2] can scarcely be used as evidence of the Matthean authorship of Matthew 23 when two of the total of three examples in the Gospel occur in that very chapter (23.16, 24). ὀφείλω[3] appears only in chs. 23 (vv. 16, 18) and 18 and in any case there are many other examples in the New Testament outside of Matthew. The word ναός[4] is another fairly common word (45 occurrences in the New Testament) which could easily have been found in Matthew's source. Matthew may have inserted the particle οὖν[5] into his source (23.3, 20), or it may equally well have been original to it; οὖν is a common enough word (501 examples in the New Testament). Is it really possible to speak of such common words as 'semi-Matthean'?

Goulder is perhaps on slightly firmer ground with ἀμὴν λέγω ὑμῖν.[6] This phrase occurs 29 times in Matthew, 12 times in Mark, and only five times in Luke. The phrase comes in Mt. 23.36, and may indeed be an example of Matthew's redaction of the chapter.[7]

Two words are classified by Goulder as 'semi-Matthean' by virtue of their being inserted into an 'agreed Marcan context'.[8] Two points need to be made here. First, it is far from certain that Matthew has used Mark; the continuing disagreement among eminent scholars suggests that it would be unsafe to rely too heavily upon evidence which is dependent upon the veracity of Marcan priority. Secondly, given that Goulder accepts the hypothesis of Matthew's dependence upon Mark, the two words in question still remain unconvincing. Both κάθημαι[9] and θέλω[10] are common enough words. Matthew may have inserted them into 'an agreed Marcan context', but even so they could quite easily have been found in the source he used for ch. 23. Goulder's semi-Matthean words, then, prove very little, for with the possible exception

1. Goulder, *Midrash*, p. 424.
2. Goulder, *Midrash*, p. 424.
3. Goulder, *Midrash*, p. 424.
4. Goulder, *Midrash*, p. 424.
5. Goulder, *Midrash*, p. 423.
6. Goulder, *Midrash*, p. 429.
7. See further below, pp. 41-42.
8. Goulder, *Midrash*, p. 476.
9. Goulder, *Midrash*, p. 424.
10. Goulder, *Midrash*, p. 423.

of ἀμὴν λέγω ὑμῖν, (a phrase which in any case comes only in 23.36, and which may well be Matthean), none of these appear to be recognizably characteristic of Matthew himself.

iii. *Conclusion on the Vocabulary of Matthew 23*

Goulder's claim that ch. 23 exhibits a vocabulary recognizable as that of the evangelist himself does not stand critical examination. Twenty-four of the examples of 'Matthean' and 'semi-Matthean' words given by Goulder are typical of the Gospel only in so far as they appear frequently in one or two fairly easily definable sections of the Gospel. In particular there seems often to be an overlap between ch. 23 and the Sermon on the Mount. These words cannot be ascribed to Matthew himself with any confidence, for they may equally well be characteristic of any source which he may have used for these sections. Indeed, such an hypothesis may account better for the clustering of these words in these particular passages than does Goulder's.

Nineteen of Goulder's words lack real evidence. While they may be seen as 'Matthean', there is no necessity to view them as such. Any one of them may easily have occurred in a pre-Matthean source. They cannot confidently be said to be typical of the first evangelist himself.

Eight words (five in 23.2-31 and three in 23.32-39) lend some support to Goulder's views, but even here the evidence is far from totally convincing. These words have been dealt with individually above. Matthew may have edited his source lightly in Mt. 23.2-31, but as is noted further in Chapters 3 and 4 below, there is every reason to believe that Matthew's own redactional activity was limited and that he did not radically alter his traditions to suit his own theological purposes. In fact he seems to have included material contrary to his own views, rather than simply suppress it.[1]

In general it is concluded that the use of word statistics is not a very fruitful method of assessing the origin of the material in a passage. Goulder (and Hawkins) may be criticized especially for concentrating upon single words, for it is often the case that the word in question is either not well distributed in the gospel, or else appears elsewhere in the New Testament so frequently as to undermine any claim that the word

---

1. Mt. 23.2-3 seems totally out of tune with Matthew's general view of the Jewish leaders and, despite many attempts to explain how this verse does not conflict with Matthew's extreme rejection of the leaders, the verse continues to stick out in Matthew like a sore thumb (see further below, pp. 119-24).

is definitely Matthew's own. To this extent the work of Tevis is a step forward in that, rather than concentrating upon individual words, he looks for whole phrases, sometimes several words long, that are much more likely to be indicative of an individual's preferred style.

It seems, therefore, that observations on vocabulary are unable to bear the full weight of Goulder's thesis. Mainstays are needed. It is the purpose of the following pages to show that these crucial supports are lacking.

B. *The 'Abusive Vocative'*

Goulder argues that the use of the 'abusive vocative' in ch. 23 is evidence of its Matthean authorship, for such usage is characteristic of Matthew.[1] But Goulder may have overstated his case, and several criticisms are possible.

First, the general tone of the chapter perhaps makes the use of the 'abusive vocative' unavoidable. There is a sharp attack on the scribes and the Pharisees, and a face-to-face confrontation. Given these circumstances any writer would have found it difficult not to use the vocative in a hostile way. Even if it could be shown that Matthew is particularly fond of the 'abusive vocative', he need not necessarily be responsible for its use here.

Perhaps more damaging to Goulder's case, however, is the lack of entirely convincing evidence to support his view that the abusive vocative is a Mattheanism. Goulder counts a total of 23 examples of its use in the gospel, but almost one-half of these occur in ch. 23 itself, and all but one in 23.2-31 (23.13, 15, 16, 17, 19, 23, 25, 26, 27, 29, 33). Four others (6.30; 8.26; 14.31; 16.8) are scarcely in the same league as the harsh ὑποκριταί of ch. 23, and perhaps ought not to be called 'abusive' at all. Similarly the ὦ γενεὰ ἄπιστος of 17.17 may express sadness and disappointment rather than anger. σατανᾶ (Mt. 16.23) is surely abusive, though on Goulder's hypothesis this comes from Mark, and the same is true of the ὑποκριταί of Mt. 15.7. One unparalleled example of ὑποκριταί is found in Mt. 22.18, and the word is found again in Mt. 7.5 (= Lk. 6.42). There are only two other examples of the abusive vocative in Matthew, namely the γεννήματα ἐχιδνῶν sayings of Mt. 3.7 and 12.34, and these may well be Matthew's own.

These figures and pattern of distribution do not support Goulder's contentions. Of the eighteen examples of the vocative in Matthew which

1.   Goulder, *Midrash*, p. 425.

can really be said to be abusive, ten appear in 23.2-31 and one in the Sermon on the Mount. Of the seven remaining examples, two are almost exactly parallel to Mt. 23.33. Thus it appears that, like the use of certain words, the use of the abusive vocative is characteristic not of the Gospel as a whole, but rather of certain sections of the Gospel.

C. *Hyperbole*
'A feature which is rare in Mk and L', Goulder points out, 'is hyperbole'. In Matthew, however, the trait is

> not uncommon... People do not have planks in their eyes, or swallow camels, and the dead cannot bury their dead. When Jesus says, 'If you had faith...', nobody supposed that he should attempt to move Mt. Tabor into the Lake of Galilee; or that Peter was intended to count 490 acts of forgiveness.[1]

According to Goulder, therefore, hyperbolic speech is typical of Matthew himself, and the use of hyperbole in Mt. 23.24 consequently argues in favour of the Matthean authorship of the verse.

It seems, however, that Goulder has accepted some sayings as hyperbolic although they are not really such. Whoever is responsible for the saying 'let the dead bury their dead' (Mt. 8.22), it is quite possible that it was meant to be understood metaphorically. Indeed, it is not really an example of hyperbolic speech at all, but is rather a straightforward metaphor. There may well have been an actual corpse that needed attending to, but those who should do the burying are not the literal dead, but those who are spiritually dead. There is no hyperbole, merely a charge to leave the spiritually dead to take care of their own matters. It is the disciples' business to leave family behind and to follow Jesus. Neither is it altogether certain that the saying found in Mt. 18.22 is an example of hyperbole. It is quite possible that the author of the saying believed in unlimited forgiveness. Goulder is right when he says that Peter was probably not meant to count 490 acts of forgiveness. He was not meant to count at all, but rather was to forgive without limitation. Hyperbole cannot be used to emphasize a concept which is itself infinite.

The faith–mountain saying (Mt. 17.20; 21.21) is an example of hyperbole. On Goulder's thesis, however, it is from Mark and thus ought not to be used as evidence for the hand of Matthew himself. But even if Marcan priority is not assumed, these two examples of 'hyperbole' would not by themselves lead to the conclusion that this

1.   Goulder, *Midrash*, p. 397.

particular literary device was characteristic of Matthew's style. Several other examples would have to be given, but such evidence is lacking.

This leaves only the plank of Mt. 7.4 and the camel of Mt. 23.24. As has emerged already and is made more clear in Chapter Five below, there are several reasons for suspecting that the Sermon on the Mount and parts of Matthew 23 are linked. The use of hyperbole in Matthew perhaps increases this suspicion. Thus, outside of the Sermon on the Mount and Matthew 23, there are only two or possibly three examples of 'hyperbole' (Mt. 17.20; 21.21; [8.22]) and it is therefore not readily identifiable as a characteristic of the first evangelist himself.

D. *The Doubling of 'Jerusalem, Jerusalem'*[1]

Other than Ἰερουσαλήμ, Ἰερουσαλήμ in Mt. 23.37 there are three further examples of the doubling of single words in Matthew. These examples are ναὶ ναί and οὒ οὔ in Mt. 5.37, and κύριε, κύριε in Mt. 7.21. It appears, therefore, that the doubling of single words is a characteristic feature not of Matthew as a whole, but of the Sermon on the Mount where two of the three examples are found. The idiom cannot with confidence be said to be Matthew's own.

E. *The Use of Animal Imagery*

Goulder suggests that further evidence for the Matthean authorship of ch. 23 is the use of animal imagery.[2] This is so, since Matthew 'delights to draw in the whole zoological panorama' though Mark is not strong in such usage.[3] Matthew in fact has added to Mark a further eighteen animals and each one is to him 'symbolic of one aspect of human behaviour'.[4]

Goulder counts a total of 44 uses of animal imagery in Matthew.[5] Since animals appear at least 65 times, it is clear that Goulder does not consider all animal references in Matthew to be symbolic. Unfortunately he gives no complete list of those references to animals in Matthew which, in his opinion, are to be considered as symbolic or of those which are not. It seems, however, that he counts as symbolic some references which possibly are not really such.

1. Goulder, *Midrash*, p. 429.
2. Goulder, *Midrash*, p. 429.
3. Goulder, *Midrash*, p. 101.
4. Goulder, *Midrash*, p. 101.
5. Goulder, *Midrash*, p. 101.

Non-symbolic are the cock in the story of Peter's denial (Mt. 26.34, 74, 75); the pigeons in Mt. 21.12; the fish in the feeding miracles and the temple-tax story (Mt. 14.17, 19; 15.34, 36; 17.27); the donkey and the colt from the triumphal entry scene (Mt. 21.2, 5, 6); the locusts on which John fed (Mt. 3.4); and the swine in the healing of the Gadarene demoniac (8.30, 31, 32). Goulder's count seems to indicate that he omits these references. Almost certainly symbolic are the following: the vipers in the 'brood of vipers' sayings (Mt. 3.7; 12.34; 23.33); the sheep and the wolves of 7.15; 10.6 and 10.16; the dogs and the swine of 7.6 and 15.26, 27; the sheep of 9.36; 18.12; 25.32, 33; 26.31; the birds from the parable of the Sower (13.4); the goats of 25.32, 33; the serpents of 23.33; the hen and the chicks of 23.37; and the camel of 23.24. Possibly symbolic is the gnat in 23.24, but there were real gnats that really did need to be strained.[1] The gnat in this verse is a real one, but it may be symbolic of some other concept as well. To these Goulder seems to add the sheep from 12.11, 12; the moths in 6.19, 20; the fox and birds in 8.20; the sparrows in 10.29, 31; the whale of 12.40; the oxen and calves of 22.4; and the camel of 19.24. He also includes the doves from either 3.16; 10.16, or both; and probably the birds of 6.26; the fish and serpent from 7.10; the fish from the parable of the Dragnet (13.47); and the birds that nest in the mustard tree (13.32).

Goulder may be challenged on the question of which animals in Matthew are to be understood as examples of 'animal imagery'. The oxen and the fatted calf in Mt. 22.4, for example, are said by Goulder to be 'symbolic of wealth',[2] but while the occurrence of these animals in the story indicates to the reader that the king was laying on a feast of some proportion, the beasts can hardly be said to 'stand for' wealth in an allegorical sense. They are perhaps rather an integral part of the story, having no interpretive value of their own. This is to be compared with the hen and chicks in 23.37, and the camel and the gnat of 23.24,

---

1. Below, pp. 103-105.

2. Goulder, *Midrash*, p. 101. Goulder has in fact reworked his animal argument since the publication of *Midrash and Lection*. In his essay 'A House Built on Sand', in A.E. Harvey (ed.), *Alternative Approaches to New Testament Study* (London: SPCK, 1985), pp. 1-24, he concentrates upon pairs of animals in Matthew and counts 10 such occurrences. In part this work indicates a rejection of part of the argument in *Midrash and Lection*, since in the 'House Built on Sand' essay he specifically says that the fatling in 22.4 is 'just part of the scenery' and compares this to his 10 pairs where the animals are 'images in the sense that the traditional character of the animal is made to symbolize some aspect of Jesus' ministry' (p. 19).

where these animals seem representative of some other concept.

A further example of Goulder's tendency to take as symbolic animals that are not really such is found in his understanding of Mt. 19.24. The verse contains a saying in which it is suggested that it is easier for a camel to go through the eye of a needle than for a rich man to enter the kingdom of God. To Goulder, the camel is a symbol of size, but such symbolism is hardly the same as that found in Mt. 23.24, where the camel seems to stand for great omissions in legal duties. The force of Mt. 19.24 depends upon the ridiculous spectacle of a real camel attempting to squeeze through the eye of a real needle; in Mt. 23.24, on the other hand, it depends upon the discernment of the reality behind the symbolism. Similarly, the moth which corrupts in 6.20 is a real moth, and the fox in 8.20, which Goulder sees as a symbol of 'wildlife', is a real fox.

It appears, therefore, that it is possible to sub-divide the use of animal imagery in Matthew's Gospel. On the one hand there are numerous references to animals where it is clear that they are meant to be interpreted symbolically, but on the other there are animals which are to be understood literally. The examples of symbolic animal imagery come in 3.7; 7.6[bis], 15[bis]; 9.36; 10.6, 16[quater]; 12.34; 15.24, 26, 27; 18.12; 23.24, 33[bis], 37[bis]; 25.32[bis], 33[bis]; 26.31, a total of 26 occurrences. Although the use of animal imagery in Matthew is substantial, it may not be as extensive as Goulder suggests, and while Goulder's hypothesis that such use is characteristic of the first evangelist himself may explain the data, such a hypothesis is not necessitated by the facts. It is equally possible that a certain amount of animal imagery was already present in the evangelist's sources. It is in any case worth noting that of the six (or five if the gnat in 23.24 is omitted from the list) occurrences of animal imagery in Matthew 23, four come in the latter part of the chapter (i.e. after 23.31) and thus even if Goulder is right in his observations on the use of animal imagery in Matthew (and he is probably not), his results do not seriously undermine the central thrust of the argument presented here.

F. *Rhythm*

Goulder's discussion of Matthew's poetry is well researched and tightly argued.[1] His conclusion is clear: 'Matthew was the Church's poet'.[2] This

1. Goulder, *Midrash*, pp. 70-94.
2. Goulder, *Midrash*, p. 92.

conclusion rests upon solid evidence, for it is clear that of the Synoptic Gospels, Matthew's is the most poetically presented and that consequently Matthew himself had an ear for rhythmical forms. Not only does the frequency of rhythmical pericopae in the Gospel support this case, but the distribution of such material adds further weight. Rhythm is found throughout all the gospel material.

In the light of these observations, it is with some justification that Goulder sees the pardic[1] rhythm of 23.24, the caesaric[2] of 23.12, the scandalics[3] of 23.8ff., 20ff. and the enchidnics[4] of 23.17, 19, 33 as evidence of the Matthean authorship of the chapter. Several points, however, need to be noted.

The pardic rhythm of 23.24 could be accidental. It is easy to imagine a basically non-poetical mind creating the saying 'blind guides, you strain a gnat and swallow a camel'. In any case, it is not as though pardic rhythm was completely unknown outside of the Gospel of Matthew. On Goulder's own reckoning Luke has added six pardics to his Matthean and Marcan sources, and Mark's Gospel has four. Pardic rhythm could easily have been already present in any source Matthew may have used for this section. Neither is it likely that Matthew had a monopoly on other poetical forms. It is quite possible that the sayings found in Matthew 23 may already have had a poetical format prior to the material being incorporated into the Gospel as a whole. Mark, which contains relatively little teaching material, has, on Goulder's reckoning, some 22 rhythmical forms.[5] Thus, while it can be said that on Goulder's thesis Matthew has changed his Marcan source to a more rhythmical style, is does not follow that all of Matthew's other material, since it shows signs of similar rhythm, stems from the evangelist's own hand. Matthew may likewise have changed any other source to which he had access. Alternatively it is quite plausible, perhaps even probable, that if Matthew did have access to a sayings source upon which he drew for the bulk of ch. 23, then this source may already have had a poetical style. The

---

1.   So called because it is the form found in Jer. 13.23 'Can an Ethiopian change his skin, or a leopard (πάρδαλις) his spots?' (Goulder, *Midrash*, p. 71).

2.   So called after Mk 12.17 'Render unto Caesar (Καίσαρος) the things which are Caesar's' (Goulder, *Midrash*, p. 74).

3.   As in Mk 9.43ff., 'And if your hand offends (σκανδαλίζῃ) you' (Goulder, *Midrash*, p. 81).

4.   After Mt. 3.7, 'You brood of vipers (ἐχιδνῶν)' (Goulder, *Midrash*, p. 79).

5.   Goulder, *Midrash*, pp. 93-94.

presence of the enchidnic in 23.33 may be Matthew's, but this cannot be
stated with absolute confidence.

G. *Inclusio*

Goulder notes that Matthew seems particularly fond of the stylistic
device known as *inclusio*,[1] and in this he is probably right. As far back
as 1923 Lagrange listed some 13 examples of *inclusio* in Matthew,[2] and
to this Butler[3] and Fenton[4] have added several more. There is, according
to Goulder, one example of *inclusio* in Matthew 23, and this is the
saying found in Mt. 23.36 which finds its parallel in Mt. 24.34. If this is
an example of *inclusio*, then, it supports the case presented here that
Mt. 23.33-39 is Matthew's own. However, it should not to go unnoticed
that Lagrange, Butler and Fenton do not include Mt. 23.36/24.34 on
their lists of *inclusio* in Matthew. The reason for this omission is perhaps
plain: Mt. 23.34 is separated from 24.36 by so many verses that it
cannot really be said to be an example of the literary device. This
suggestion is made all the more plausible when it is noted that the
material between Mt. 23.36 and 24.34 cannot be said to form a separate
section, and that Mt. 24.34 does not seem to be a concluding punch line.
It is therefore perhaps more reasonable to see these two verses not as an
example of *inclusio*, but simply as the repetition of a specific formula.

H. *Knowledge of Judaism*

It has long been recognized that the first Gospel is intimately concerned
with Jewish matters. Its author had Jewish concerns and a knowledge of
specific Jewish customs. Goulder appeals to this consensus of opinion
with respect to ch. 23, for this chapter betrays an inside understanding
of the Jewish religion. Since Matthew himself had such an understanding, he may well have been responsible for the creation of the
chapter.

Goulder, of course, is right when he pleads that Matthew knew
enough about Judaism to enable him to compile a discourse such as that
found in ch. 23. He probably knew that it was customary to whitewash

---

1.   Goulder, *Midrash*, p. 87.

2.   M.-J. Lagrange, *Evangile selon Saint Matthieu* (Paris: Etudes Bibliques,
1923), p. lxxxi.

3.   B.C. Butler, *The Originality of St Matthew: A Critique of the Two-Document
Hypothesis* (Cambridge: Cambridge University Press, 1951), pp. 150-51.

4.   J.C. Fenton, 'Inclusio and Chiasmus in Matthew', *SE*, I, 174-79.

tombs so as to prevent accidental incurring of uncleanness, and he could thus be responsible for the appellation of the scribes and Pharisees as 'whitewashed tombs' in 23.27. Matthew was probably sufficiently acquainted with 'Jewish casuistry' to enable him to write 23.25-26, and he perhaps lived in close enough contact with synagogue communities to know that they still swore 'by the temple' or 'by the altar,' even though these had been destroyed; Matthew 23, and especially the woes on the scribes and Pharisees, presupposes a thorough knowledge of several Jewish practices.

But the knowledge of Judaism evident in the bulk of ch. 23 is not only detailed, but also first-hand, and betrays an *intra muros* stance. The author of this pericope believes that the altar sanctifies the gift, and that God is in some sense present in the Jerusalem temple.[1] He knows also of the concern of the scribes and Pharisees to get the best seats in the synagogues and at feasts. In the earlier part of the discourse the author refers to the synagogue as 'the' synagogue (23.6) and not as 'your' or 'their' synagogue as is frequently the case elsewhere in the Gospel (e.g 23.34), and as is argued below, this *Sitz im Leben* is not that of the final redaction of the Gospel.

I. *Conclusions*

Goulder's suggestion that Matthew 23 is largely the work of the evangelist himself has several points in its favour. There is the occurrence of the phrase ἡ βασιλεία τῶν οὐρανῶν, probably a Mattheanism, in 23.13. Likewise there are several other possibly Matthean words and phrases such as τηρέω, φαίνομαι and τάφος. There is also the poetical format, a feature which is widespread elsewhere in the gospel. When drawn together, this evidence does amount to something, and Goulder has certainly made a case for the Matthean origin of Matthew 23.

But the evidence is far from conclusive. Many of the words picked out by Goulder as being characteristic of the evangelist himself, are in fact characteristic only of certain sections of the Gospel. Furthermore, there seems to be a distinct link between Matthew 23 and the Sermon on the Mount. Goulder's thesis does not explain why this should be so. We will explore this link in more detail in Chapter Five below. Similarly, the use of the abusive vocative (which may in fact be explained by the very nature of the material) is not as common in Matthew as Goulder seems to suggest. Neither does the use of animal imagery, nor the use of

1. See further below pp. 137-40.

hyperbole, add real weight to Goulder's contentions. Thus, while Goulder has some points that he can justifiably make in favour of his claim for the Matthean authorship of Matthew 23, the weight of evidence against such an understanding far exceeds it.

At the very least the suggestion made here that Matthew 23 is largely non-Matthean and that it stems from the same source as the material found in the Sermon on the Mount, explains the evidence just as well as that of Goulder. At best it accounts for the evidence far better, for it explains the distinct similarity between ch. 23 and the Sermon on the Mount in terms of vocabulary, idiom, concerns and, perhaps most importantly, *Sitz im Leben.*

This section has raised some serious questions regarding the validity of word counting as an approach to gospel study. In general we might say that the counting of individual words does not serve well as a guide to redactoral activity. Tevis's concentration upon phrases, however, looks as though it will yield more solid results. However, in the final analysis the question of the origin of a passage is perhaps far better dealt with by looking at the presupposed *Sitz im Leben* of the text. It is argued here that the *Sitz im Leben* of Mt. 23.2-31 is that of an *intra muros* debate between one group of Jews (scribes and Pharisees) and another (nascent Christianity). The kind of debate that we see going on there is primarily one of correct halakhah. The author believes that the scribes and Pharisees are authoritative teachers and should be obeyed. He thinks that the altar sanctifies the gift. He knows that the Pharisees love the best seats in *the* synagogue and the best seats at the suppers. Everything suggests a first-hand day-to-day acquaintance with and acceptance of the practices of Judaism. Matthew was not such an author.

2. *Dennis G. Tevis*

As noted above, Tevis has conducted a careful examination of words and phrases in the Gospel of Matthew with the intention of discovering which of them are characteristic of the Gospel. This is not the place to enter into a full discussion of Tevis's statistics, but since his work and this study overlap in several places, some mention of Tevis's study needs to be made. Of course we must note especially the results of Tevis's work as they relate to the composition of Matthew 23. It will be seen that Tevis's work is generally supportive of the source/redaction-critical theory adopted here.

Tevis's study, as yet unpublished but due to appear in the series *New Gospel Studies,*[1] seeks to take a neutral stand *vis-à-vis* the Synoptic problem, and examines the text of Matthew as it now stands for evidence of words and phrases characteristic in the Gospel. Tevis's results are important, for by allowing for the possibility that Matthew has not copied from Mark or Q, he is able to identify a larger number of words and phrases characteristic of the first evangelist than previous word counters have been able to do. Thus, for example, Tevis thinks that the phrase γεννήματα ἐχιδνῶν is likely to come from the hand of one writer[2] and is not the work of Matthew copying Q (cf. Lk. 3.7). It is then possible to develop the argument that since γεννήματα ἐχιδνῶν is a characteristic of Matthew but is found in Luke, the most likely explanation is that Luke had used Matthew. Tevis does not develop such arguments at any length; rather his work consists largely of statistics relating to the occurrences of words and phrases in Matthew's Gospel. Especially important is Tevis's awareness that 'characteristic of the Gospel' and 'from the hand of the evangelist' are not necessarily the same thing. Words and phrases concentrated in just one section of the Gospel are not necessarily from the hand of the evangelist; they may be due to the use of source material.

With regard to Matthew 23 Tevis's work yields very interesting results indeed. To restate the hypothesis once again, it is argued here that Matthew 23 is not made up of a web of traditional and redactional material but is basically one source (23.2-31) which has undergone redaction by an 'eschatological redactor' (23.32-39). Tevis's work is remarkably consistent with this view. The words and phrases noted by Tevis that appear in Matthew 23 are considered below. There is a total of twelve, ten of which are in keeping with the theory advanced here. These are listed below.

A. ἀμὴν λέγω ὑμῖν (σοι)[3]
It has already been noted above that the phrase ἀμὴν λέγω ὑμῖν as it appears in 23.36 is likely to be from the hand of the redactor Matthew,

---

1.   At the time of writing (1994) no date has been set for the publication of Tevis's work. The thesis is, however, available through University Microfilms International, Ann Arbor, MI 48106.

2.   Tevis, 'Words and Phrases', p. 163.

3.   Tevis, 'Words and Phrases', 501 (references to Tevis which do not include 'p' indicate word study number, not page).

though it was noted that the evidence is inconclusive.[1] Tevis's judgment on this phrase is that it is a characteristic of Matthew's Gospel, but he goes on to add that not all occurrences of the phrase necessarily come from the same hand. Tevis seems correct; the phrase stands out in Matthew's Gospel as distinctive, but the possibility that it was found also in one of Matthew's sources cannot be ruled out entirely. Matthew clearly did not have a complete monopoly on this phrase as the frequent occurrence of a close cognate, ἀμὴν ἀμὴν λέγω ὑμῖν (σοι), in John shows. The phrase ἀμὴν λέγω ὑμῖν (σοι) appears in Mt. 23.36, a verse that is in any case within the section composed by the 'eschatological redactor' of the source material.

B. γεννήματα ἐχιδνῶν[2]
The phrase γεννήματα ἐχιδνῶν appears in Mt. 3.7, 12.34 and 23.33. As noted above,[3] in each case the saying appears in an attack upon the Pharisees and in a passage which has eschatological concerns. Tevis thinks that this phrase most probably comes from the hand of a single writer (its occurrence in Lk. 3.7 will then be the result of Luke's use of Matthew at this point), and he may well be right. The alternative, namely that Matthew picked up the saying in a source available also to Luke and then used it twice more elsewhere, is of course possible. In either case Mt. 23.33 seems redactional. Once again, then, it seems that the linguistic evidence is consistent with the argument advanced here that Matthew 23 is made of source (vv. 2-31) and redaction (vv. 32-39).

C. ἐλάλησεν αὐτοῖς + λέγων[4]
Tevis thinks that 'there is a strong possibility that this phrase [ἐλάλησεν αὐτοῖς + λέγων] comes from a redactor'.[5] The words appear in 23.1, which is surely a redactional passage from Matthew himself.[6]

D. ἐν ταῖς συναγωγαῖς + personal pronoun + μαστιγόω[7]
The phrase ἐν ταῖς συναγωγαῖς ὑμῶν is one of the most important ones to note when trying to trace the source and redaction in Matthew 23.

1. See, p. 30.
2. Tevis, 'Analysis of Words', 219.
3. See, p. 28.
4. Tevis, 'Analysis of Words', 49.
5. Tevis, 'Words and Phrases', p. 75.
6. See below, pp. 118-19.
7. Tevis, 'Analysis of Words', 100.

The phrase appears in 23.34 which reads 'διὰ τοῦτο ἰδοὺ ἐγὼ
ἀποστέλλω πρὸς ὑμᾶς προφήτας καὶ σοφοὺς καὶ γραμματεῖς ἐξ
αὐτῶν ἀποκτενεῖτε καὶ σταυρώσετε καὶ ἐξ αὐτῶν μαστιγώσετε
ἐν ταῖς συναγωγαῖς ὑμῶν καὶ διώξετε ἀπὸ πόλεως εἰς πόλιν'. As
Tevis notes, the phrase appears also in 10.17, but the clear links with the
more general phrase ἐν ταῖς συναγωγαῖς αὐτῶν[1] (Mt. 4.23; 9.35;
10.17; 12.9; 13.54) should not be missed. The use of [μαστιγόω] ἐν
ταῖς συναγωγαῖς αὐτῶν is surely the work of a redactor and
importantly it suggests that the writer is not a part of the synagogue
himself. This is to be compared with Mt. 23.6 where we read that the
Pharisees love the best seats ἐν ταῖς συναγωγαῖς and not ἐν ταῖς
συναγωγαῖς **αὐτῶν** (see also Mt. 6.2, 5). The author of Mt. 23.6 is a
part of the synagogue; the author of 23.34 is not. Tevis's work is once
again consistent with the theory advanced here: 23.34 has a redactional
touch.

E. ἡ βασιλεία τῶν οὐρανῶν[2]
The phrase ἡ βασιλεία τῶν οὐρανῶν has been almost universally
judged redactional, and this view seems correct;[3] Mt. 23.13 may betray
light editing on Matthew's part. However, as Tevis correctly notes, it is
quite possible that this phrase was not uncommon in Jewish Christian
circles[4] and it may well have been in any source that Matthew had to
hand. The phrase is, to be sure, characteristic of Matthew's Gospel, but
this does not mean that wherever it is found its use must be put down to
Matthew himself.[5] Accordingly, although Tevis lists the phrase as one
which is characteristic of the Gospel, this does not conflict with the
suggestion made in this book concerning the origin of Matthew 23. As
Tevis notes, the phrase 'is not so distinctive that it seems likely that all
the occurrences of this phrase in Gospel of Matthew come from a single
writer'. As has been noted before, being distinctive of the Gospel and
being the work of one hand are not necessarily the same thing.

---

1. Tevis, 'Words and Phrases', p. 6.
2. Tevis, 'Analysis of Words', 500.
3. See above, pp. 25-26.
4. Tevis, 'Analysis of Words', p. 266.
5. See further above, pp. 25-26.

F. ἰδοὺ ἐγὼ ἀποστέλλω[1]

The phrase ἰδοὺ ἐγὼ ἀποστέλλω appears in Mt. 23.34, a verse we have already noted above. Tevis thinks that the phrase most likely comes from the hand of a redactor and this is consistent with the theory advanced here concerning the origin of Matthew 23. In fact the whole of 23.34 is quite different from 23.2-31 in several ways: first there is the phrase ἐν ταῖς συναγωγαῖς ὑμῶν, quite different from the ἐν ταῖς συναγωγαῖς found in 23.6. More importantly, perhaps, the use of γραμματεῖς in 23.34 is quite different from its use in 23.2, 13, 15, 23, 25, 27, 29. Tevis is probably right then; Mt. 23.34 is redactional and the presence of ἰδοὺ εγὼ ἀποστέλλω adds further support to the theory advanced here.

G. λέγω + *particle* + ὑμῖν οὐ μὴ + *subjunctive verb* + ἀπ' ἄρτι + ἕως[2]

Tevis thinks that the phrase λέγω + particle + ὑμῖν οὐ μὴ + subjunctive verb + ἀπ' ἄρτι + ἕως (Mt. 23.39; 26.29) is redactional and we may agree with this judgment. This is in keeping with the view of Matthew 23 advanced here, for the occurrence of this phrase does not come until v. 39.

H. ὃς ἐὰν θέλῃ ἐν ὑμῖν μέγας γενέσθαι ἔσται ὑμῶν διάκονος[3]

Tevis himself is not sure that Mt. 20.26 ὃς ἐὰν θέλῃ ἐν ὑμῖν μέγας γενέσθαι ἔσται ὑμῶν διάκονος and Mt. 23.11 ὁ δὲ μείζων ὑμῶν ἔσται ὑμῶν διάκονος are from the same hand. He states

> These two occurrences are quite similar. They have a number of common elements. However, there are also enough differences so that there is a significant possibility that both occurrences do not come from the same writer.[4]

This being the case, it is clear that the work of Tevis and that presented here are not in conflict. The saying in Mt. 23.11 could easily have come to Matthew through a source.

---

1. Tevis, 'Analysis of Words', 339.
2. Tevis, 'Words and Phrases', p. 226.
3. Tevis, 'Words and Phrases', 513.
4. Tevis, 'Words and Phrases', p. 280.

I. οὐαί δὲ ὑμῖν γραμματεῖς καὶ Φαρισαῖοι ὑποκριταί ὅτι[1]

Tevis wisely notes that the phrase οὐαί δὲ ὑμῖν γραμματεῖς καὶ φαρισαῖοι ὑποκριταί ὅτι does not appear widely distributed throughout the Gospel. In fact all of the occurrences can be found in close proximity in ch. 23. This being the case, Tevis's remark that it 'seems likely that this phrase comes from a single writer' is surely valid. The identity of that writer is not the main concern of Tevis, but here it is suggested that he was the Jewish Christian responsible for the production of a polemical tract against the Pharisees (Mt. 23.2-31).[2]

J. πρὸς τὸ + *infinitive*[3]

The phrase πρὸς τὸ + infinitive appears five times in Matthew and is counted by Tevis as characteristic of the Gospel. Three of these occurrences appear in either the Sermon on the Mount (5.28; 6.1) or Matthew 23 (v. 5) and thus something of an inequality is noted once again. In fact a very close parallel indeed is noted in 6.1 (προσέχετε τὴν δικαιοσύνην ὑμῶν μὴ ποιεῖν ἔμπροσθεν τῶν ἀνθρώπων πρὸς τὸ θεαθῆναι αὐτοῖς) and 23.5 (πάντα δὲ τὰ ἔργα αὐτῶν ποιοῦσιν πρὸς τὸ θεαθῆναι τοῖς ἀνθρώποις) adding further weight to the suggestion made here that these two sections of Matthew have a very similar if not common origin.

Tevis judges this phrase as characteristic of the Gospel. The phrase does, however, appear elsewhere in the New Testament (e.g. Mk 13.22 [cf. Mt. 24.24]; Lk. 18.1; 2 Cor. 3.13; Eph. 6.11), so Matthew did not have a monopoly on it. Tevis is wise, therefore, to caution that 'it is not distinctive enough that it seems likely that all of the occurrences of this phrase in the Gospel of Matthew come from the same writer'.[4] However, it seems likely that the more extensive parallels in 6.1 and 23.5 do stem from one hand, and this is consistent with the view advanced here.

The work of Tevis, then, is remarkably supportive of the kind of source-critical theory advanced here. There are, however, two exceptions, both of which are listed below.

1. Tevis, 'Words and Phrases', 400.
2. On the more general use of ὑποκριταί see above, p. 32.
3. Tevis, 'Analysis of Words' 503. (Note that his reference to Mt. 8.30 should be 13.30.)
4. Tevis, 'Words and Phrases', p. 270.

A. ὁδηγοὶ + τυφλοί.[1] The characterization of the scribes and the Pharisees as 'blind guides' is unique to Matthew. Tevis has noted this and thinks that it makes it likely that the phrase is from one hand. The occurrences are 15.14, 23.16 and 23.24. The occurrence in 15.14 therefore needs explanation on the basis of the present hypothesis. We have seen above that the view that Matthew may have picked up a distinctive phrase from his sources and used it redaction is not uncommon,[2] and it is at least plausible that this is what has happened with the use of ὁδηγοὶ + τυφλοί as applied to Jewish leaders.

B. ὁ πατήρ + *possessive pronoun* + οὐράνιος.[3] We have already noted above that the phrase [ὑμῶν] ὁ πατὴρ ὁ οὐράνιος is not as obvious a Mattheanism as some have suggested. Tevis also thinks that it is likely that the phrase comes from the hand of a redactor, but this is not the only explanation. There is a very noticeable inequality in the distribution of this phrase which needs some explanation, for it appears in the Sermon on the Mount four times, then in Mt. 23.9, and then only in 15.13 and 18.35. This inequality of distribution is explicable if, as is suggested here, the material in Mt. 23.2-31 and chs. 5–7 comes from very similar, if not the same, sources. On this hypothesis the occurrence of ὁ πατήρ μου ὁ οὐράνιος in 15.13 and 18.35 will be the result of Matthew's own usage of a phrase found in his sources. The suggestion that Matthew picks up phrases from his sources and uses them elsewhere in his gospel is, as has been said, by no means new.[4]

There is, then, a discrepancy between the work of Tevis and the suggestions made here, but this ought not to obscure the fact that in general Tevis's work is remarkably consistent with the theory worked out here.[5] Mt. 23.31-39 frequently betray the work of a redactor; Mt. 23.2-31 do not.

---

1.   Tevis, 'Words and Phrases', 250.
2.   E.g. Hawkins, *Horae Synopticae*, pp. 170-73; Luz, *Matthew 1–7*, p. 73. Those working on the basis of the two-document hypothesis generally make this argument, for example, with respect to the rather distinctive phrase 'weeping and gnashing of teeth' which appears six times in Matthew (8.12; 13.42, 50; 22.13; 24.51; 25.30) and once in Luke (13.28).
3.   Tevis, 'Analysis of Words', 207.
4.   Above, p. 23.
5.   It is perhaps worth pointing out that I became aware of Tevis's work only after the completion of the original thesis upon which this book is based.

Conclusion on Tevis

Tevis's work and that presented in this study are remarkably consistent. In only one case, that of ὁδηγοὶ + τυφλοί, is there anything approaching a serious discrepancy in what Tevis's study has revealed and the hypothesis presented here. Words and phrases which can be positively identified as Matthew's own tend to be clustered in vv. 32-39, whereas vv. 2-31 seems relatively devoid of such phrases. This suggests that further investigation is warranted into the theory that Mt. 23.2-31 is a unit of tradition redacted in 23.32-39 by a person with different concerns from those of his source. This investigation is conducted in the remaining chapters of this study.

3. *M.-E. Boismard*

Boismard's understanding of the sources of Matthew's Gospel differs fundamentally from that of Goulder. To Boismard the chapter is a matrix of source material, much of which has undergone redaction at a pre-final redactor stage. Matthew himself has created some material: vv. 2, 3, 11, 15, 24, 26 and 28, Boismard suggests, come from the evangelist's own hand,[1] but nevertheless the bulk of the material is drawn from either intermediate Matthew, Proto-Luke or, in the case of vv. 16-22, another otherwise unknown source.[2]

On a general level Boismard's hypothesis seems attractive, for it solves many problems. The so-called 'minor agreements' between Matthew and Luke can be explained, as can many other aspects of the synoptic problem which are problematic to other theories. Neither is the complexity of Boismard's theory adequate grounds for its dismissal. As Wink has noted,[3] the history of the gospel tradition may be as complex as Boismard suggests, and, since simpler theories have been tried and found wanting, Boismard's at least deserves a fair hearing.

But Boismard's theory is indeed difficult either to prove or to disprove. One major objection is the almost complete lack of any tangible evidence for the existence of Boismard's hypothetical documents. Two-documentarians may be criticized for their inability to produce a copy of Q, but Boismard's theory asks us to accept the one-time

1. Boismard, *Synopse*, pp. 354-55.
2. Boismard, *Synopse*, pp. 358-59.
3. W. Wink, Review of *Synopse des Quatre Evangiles* by M.-E. Boismard, *CBQ* 35 (1973), p. 225.

existence of not only Q, but also documents A, B, C, Proto-Luke, Intermediate Mark, and Intermediate Matthew.[1] Any theory which pre-supposes so many hypothetical sources without being able to produce any hard evidence for their existence, must surely remain somewhat suspect. As Goulder correctly notes, in Boismard's theory 'lost editions [of the gospels] are multiplied with a contempt for William of Occam which is a wonder to behold'.[2]

Several more concrete criticisms of Boismard's hypothesis may be made. Perhaps the most significant of these is the general observation worked out in detail in below, namely that much of Matthew 23 has a degree of internal unity that would not be expected of the mosaic of material envisaged by Boismard. In vv. 2-31 there seems to be a single mind at work which is seeking to develop the theme of the hypocrisy of the scribes and the Pharisees, who, though they keep part of the law, do not go far enough. Boismard's theory cannot explain the homogeneity within this section.

Furthermore, Boismard's suggestion that vv. 2-3 are the work of the first evangelist himself must be viewed with suspicion.[3] Quite clearly these verses contain an injunction to the crowds and the disciples to obey the teaching of the scribes and the Pharisees. It would be strange indeed if the one responsible for these verses were also responsible for the equally unequivocal warning against the teachings of these leaders found in Mt. 16.12, yet this is exactly what Boismard suggests. Though the bulk of 16.5-12 is, on Boismard's hypothesis, taken over by the final redactor of Matthew from 'Matt-intermediaire', it is 'l'ultime Redacteur matthéen' who has added vv. 11-12.[4]

Thus, on these two points at least, Boismard's theory seems to be found wanting and unable to explain the origin of Matthew 23 adequately. The material looks unified; it looks *intra muros* and it is in tension with what seems to be the *Sitz im Leben* of the evangelist himself. These elements lead us to conclude that there is an extensive pre-Matthean source present, and that it is not a patchwork of individual traditions put together by Matthew himself in a post-70 CE situation.

1.   Boismard, *Synopse*, p. 17ff.
2.   Goulder, 'A House Built on Sand', p. 6.
3.   Boismard, *Synopse*, p. 355.
4.   Boismard, *Synopse*, p. 241.

4. *The Two-Document Hypothesis*

Some time has already been spent discussing the two-document hypothesis and the results of this discussion seem clear: no one actually thinks that the origin of all the material in Matthew 23 is explicable in terms of Mark, Q and the Matthew's redactional activity alone. Furthermore, few scholars would seek to explain even the *overlaps* in the material in terms of the mutual use of two documents.[1] Nevertheless some further discussion of the two-document hypothesis is called for, since the majority of New Testament scholars still claim allegiance to some form of it. The discussion will centre upon two questions: first, does it appear that Matthew has made use of either Mark or an Ur-Marcus in compiling Matthew 23 and, secondly, has the same evangelist made use of a Q document, some form of which was also available to Luke?

A. *The Synoptic Parallels*
i. *Mark*. Marcan parallels to Matthew 23 are slight. Mk 12.37b-39 is parallel to Mt. 23.2-7 in only the very loosest sense. The passages bear virtually no verbal similarity, and indeed the content of these two pericopae seems fundamentally dissimilar. Where Mark has 'and a great crowd heard him gladly, and in his teaching he said, beware of the scribes', Matthew reads 'Then Jesus said to the crowds and to the disciples, "the scribes and the Pharisees sit on Moses' seat..." '. Thus where Mark has a warning against the teaching of the scribes, Matthew introduces a saying designed to encourage obedience to these Jewish leaders.

Closer similarities are found between Mk 12.38b and Mt. 23.5b-7a, though here too several differences may be noted. In Mark the scribes are criticized for their liking of going about in long robes, their receiving of public salutations, and their tendency to seek the best seats at the feasts and in the synagogues. Matthew's scribes and Pharisees are likewise condemned for their public ostentation and desire to be honored by men. In Matthew, however, the order of the salutations–best seats–places of honour, is reversed, and in addition there is a specific condemnation of the scribes and Pharisees for 'making their phylacteries broad and their fringes long'.

---

1. See above, pp. 15-18.

It appears, then, that the only real similarity between Mk 12.38-40 and Matthew 23 is the reference found in both passages to the scribes' desire for public salutations (in the market place), the best seats (in the synagogues) and places of honour (at feasts). Perhaps the 'long robes' of Mk 12.38 and the 'broad phylacteries and long fringes' of Mt. 23.5 are parallel also, though here the wording is quite different.

The situation is further complicated by the occurrence of an almost identical saying in Lk. 11.43, which reads 'οὐαὶ ὑμῖν τοῖς Φαρισαίοις, ὅτι ἀγαπᾶτε τὴν πρωτοκαθεδρίαν ἐν ταῖς συναγωγαῖς καὶ τοὺς ἀσπασμοὺς ἐν ταῖς ἀγοραῖς'. Luke, who parallels Mk 12.38b-39 almost verbatim in Lk. 20.46, is therefore aware of an alternative form of the logion. The form of Lk. 11.43 is in fact remarkably close to Mt. 23.6-7a; both are directed against the (scribes and the) Pharisees who 'Love (Matthew φιλοῦσιν, Luke ἀγαπᾶτε) the best seats in the synagogue and salutations in the market places'. Furthermore, the saying found in Lk. 11.43 has the form of a woe. It hardly needs to be pointed out that the woe formula is characteristic of Matthew 23 as a whole. Neither should the verbal similarity between the two passages go unnoticed. The following parallel shows the extent of agreement:

Mt. 23.6	Lk. 11.43
φιλοῦσιν δε τὴν πρωτοκλισίαν ἐν τοῖς δείπνοις καὶ τὰς πρωτο-καθεδρίας ἐν ταῖς συναγωγαῖς	οὐαὶ ὑμῖν τοῖς Φαρισαίοις, ὅτι ἀγαπᾶτε τὴν πρωτοκαθεδρίαν ἐν ταῖς συναγωγαῖς καὶ τοὺς ἀσπασμοὺς ἐν ταῖς ἀγοραῖς

For the two-documentarian, therefore, the question whether Matthew used Mark or Q in compiling Mt. 23.6-7a arises. Clearly, no simple or conclusive answer is possible and wide disagreement is found among New Testament scholars. Early in his career Streeter sought to explain this confusing state of affairs by suggesting that Mark may have been dependent upon Q at this point.[1] Thus Lk. 20.46 is the result of Luke's use of Mark (who in turn had used Q), while Lk. 11.43 and Mt. 23.6 are dependent directly upon Q. Gundry, on the other hand, thinks that Mt. 23.6-7 are drawn not from Q but from Mark, though Matthew has filled out the Marcan outline. The saying found in Lk. 11.43; 20.46 is also from Mark, though Luke has been influenced by Matthew's

---

1.   B.H. Streeter, 'St Mark's Knowledge and use of Q', in W. Sanday (ed), *Studies in the Synoptic Problem* (Oxford: Clarendon Press, 1911), p. 176. Streeter later changed his views concerning Mark's dependence on Q; see *Four Gospels*, pp. 153-54 where Streeter questions Mark's knowledge of Q.

redaction of the passage.[1] It appears, therefore, that on any hypothesis the amount of Marcan material found in Matthew 23 is very limited. The only real overlap is Mt. 23.6-7a, and even here caution is called for, since it may be that Matthew has not in fact used Mark for this passage but, on the two-document hypothesis, Q. It is suggested here that Matthew has in fact used neither, but that the entire discourse from 23.2-31 comes from an extensive pre-Matthean source.

ii. *Luke*. The general content of Matthew 23 overlaps significantly with Lk. 11.37-52; the wording and structure, however, are noticeably different. The settings too are dissimilar. The Lucan pericope is addressed to an individual Pharisee in whose house Jesus is eating while in Matthew the discourse is far more public, and is for the benefit of the 'crowds' and disciples. The conclusions bear little resemblance to each other: Lk. 11.53-55 reports that the Pharisees asked Jesus many other things in an attempt to trap him; Matthew ends with the lament over Jerusalem as a whole, a passage which appears in an entirely different context in Luke (13.34-35).

Concerning the structure, format and content of the two passages, several observations need to be made. Matthew has seven woes, Luke six. Two of the criticisms found as woes in Matthew, namely crossing earth and sea to make a convert, and incorrect teaching regarding oaths, are absent from Luke. Conversely, two of Luke's woes are not such in Matthew. None of the woes in either of the gospels is in the same place as in the other, and neither do any two come in the same sequence. Of the four Matthean woes found in Luke, two appear in a markedly different form. Three of Luke's woes are addressed to lawyers (νομικοῖς), and three to Pharisees, whereas in Matthew, six are addressed to the scribes (γραμματεῖς) and Pharisees, and one to 'blind guides'. Thus the following picture emerges:

Matthew	Luke
Binding of burdens. Not in the form of a woe. 23.4.	Fourth woe. 11.46.
Chief seats etc. Not in the form of a woe. 23.6-7a.	Second woe. 11.43.

1. Gundry, *Matthew*, p. 457; D.E. Garland, *The Intention of Matthew 23* (NovTSup, 52; Leiden: Brill, 1979), pp. 12-18 gives a summary of the other major solutions proposed for this source-critical problem.

Matthew	Luke
First woe (shutting up the Kingdom of Heaven). 23.13.	Sixth woe. 11.52.
Second woe (Proselytes). 23.15.	Absent.
Third woe (Oaths). 23.16-22.	Absent.
Fourth woe (Tithes). 23.23-24.	First woe. 11.42.
Fifth woe (Purity). 23.25-26.	Not a woe. 11.39-41.
Sixth woe (Whitewashed tombs). 23.27-28.	Third woe. 11.44.
Seventh woe (Tombs of Righteous Men Prophets). 23.29-32.	Fifth woe. 11.47-48.

Further dissimilarities emerge when the individual woes are compared. Garland suggests that Mt. 23.23b/Lk. 11.42b is the point at which Matthew is the closest to the Lucan form,[1] but even here divergences are evident. Where Luke has μὴ παρεῖναι, Matthew reads μὴ ἀφιέναι. Mt. 23.23 differs from Luke in several other ways: Matthew's criticism is that the Pharisees, while correctly tithing ἡδύοσμον, ἄνηθον and κύμινον, have neglected (ἀφήκατε) τὰ βαρύτερα τοῦ νόμου such as κρίσιν, ἔλεος and πίστιν On the other hand, Luke has the Pharisees tithing ἡδύοσμον, πήγανον and πᾶν λάχανον while neglecting (παρέρχεσθε) κρίσιν and τήν ἀγάπην τοῦ θεοῦ.

Matthew's sixth woe (Luke's third) also diverges from its Lucan counterpart. Matthew compares the Pharisees to 'whitewashed tombs' (τάφοις), which are outwardly beautiful, but which within are full of the bones of dead men. Luke's criticism is that the Pharisees are like unmarked graves (μνημεῖα) which defile the unsuspecting. There is virtually no verbal similarity between the two passages.

Examples of such dissimilarity could easily be multiplied, for while it is clear that there is some general overlap between Matthew 23 and Lk. 11.37-52, the two passages disagree on almost every point in structure and detail.

1.   Garland, *Matthew 23*, p. 11.

What may be said, then, concerning Matthew's alleged use of Q for this passage? In view of the very wide divergence between Matthew and Luke, it is clear that if both evangelists were dependent upon a common source, then that source has been changed dramatically by either one or both. Since Matthew's version is by far the longer, it would seem most natural to assume that he rather than Luke has altered Q, and indeed this is the solution adopted by many scholars. But such an hypothesis is not without serious difficulties. Below an attempt is made to show that the bulk of the material found in Matthew 23 belongs to a period in the development of Christianity when the church and synagogue had not yet parted company. There are indications also that the material pre-dates the fall of the temple. Such does not appear to be the *Sitz im Leben* of the final redactor of Matthew,[1] and it is therefore unlikely that the evangelist Matthew is himself the redactor of Matthew 23.

On two counts, therefore, the two-document hypothesis seems unable to give an adequate account of the origin of Matthew 23. The parallels with Mark are only very slight, and even the more substantial overlap between Matthew 23 and Luke 11 is not as great as some have imagined. Furthermore, and most importantly, it does not appear that Matthew himself is responsible for the changes which have been made to the shorter Lucan form of the discourse.

One additional point needs to be made. The two-document hypothesis can at best explain only the material found in more than one gospel, but within Matthew 23 there is much that is unparalleled. This material too needs to be accounted for. Two-documentarians agree that the phenomenon of Matthew 23 cannot be explained on the basis of Mark, Q and Matthean creativity alone. There is widespread agreement, for example, that Mt. 23.2-3 come from another, pre-Matthean source.[2]

5. *The Four-Document Hypothesis*

The four-document hypothesis is largely based upon the two-document hypothesis. It might therefore be expected that the criticisms made above would be sufficient to warrant the rejection of the four-document hypothesis as an adequate explanation of the origin of Matthew 23. Such

---

1.   Below, Chapter 2.
2.   See for example Beare, *Matthew*, p. 448; Schweizer, *Matthew*, p. 430; McNeile, *Matthew*, pp. 329-30; Haenchen, 'Matthäus', p. 40; Garland, *Matthew 23*, p. 52 n. 69 gives several other references.

is not the case, however. Holders of the four-document hypothesis are in fact better able to account for the phenomenon of the chapter than most. Since there is always the possibility that M/Q overlap, four-documentarians may explain the differences between Matthew and Luke in terms of their dependence on differing sources. Streeter, for example, came close to foreseeing the results of the present study when he argued that Matthew's version of the woes looks like a 'Jewish polemical pamphlet'. Matthew himself has conflated this 'pamphlet' (part of the M source) with Q and Mark. Luke, on the other hand, was dependent upon Q alone.[1] A similar suggestion is made by T.W. Manson, who like Streeter suggests that an M/Q overlap is the key to the source-critical problem posed by Matthew 23.[2]

Streeter's solution certainly goes some way in explaining the divergences and similarities of Matthew 23 and Luke 11. As a final solution, however, it is found wanting. The material found in Mt. 23.2-31 evinces a high degree of internal unity which would not be expected of a discourse formed from material of various extractions (i.e. M, Q and Mark plus Matthew's own redaction). The work is much more likely to be from one hand. Similar criticisms may be made of Brown, who has argued for Matthew's dependence upon Q^{mt}, a document which, he argues, combined M and Q to form a longer sayings source.[3] Brown, however, has perhaps pointed in the right direction. In Mt. 23.2-31 (Brown thinks

---

1.   Streeter (*Four Gospels*, p. 253) wrote of Mt. 23:

> We proceed to consider the long discourse of Mt. xxiii., the Woes to the Pharisees. This is, next to the Sermon on the Mount, the longest connected discourse of which both the Matthean and Lucan versions (Mt. xxiii. 1-36 = Lk. xi. 37-52) cannot be referred to a single written source without raising great difficulties. Matthew's is much the longer version, and it reads like an early Jewish Christian polemical pamphlet against their oppressors the Pharisees.

Streeter, then, has come close to identifying Mt. 23.1-36 as a previously redacted source. In his words, it looks like a 'Jewish Christian polemical tract' written 'against their oppressors the Pharisees'. But he cannot follow this observation through, since he is wedded already to a fragmentary understanding of the chapter; parts are from Mark, parts from Q and parts from M. Matthew, who is the overall architect of the chapter, will hardly have written a 'Jewish polemical tract' against the Pharisees, for he is not writing in an *intra-muros* context (pp. 500-27). Thus, despite the fact that the discourse 'looks like a Jewish Christian polemical tract', Streeter cannot accept that this is what it is. Acceptance of his four-document hypothesis has obscured his vision.

2.   T.W. Manson, *The Sayings of Jesus* (London: SCM Press, repr. 1971), p. 23.

3.   Brown, 'The Form of Q Known to Matthew', p. 31.

23.1-39)[1] we have a fairly extensive pre-Matthean unit of tradition.

Numerous other scholars have suggested that Matthew 23 has been created by Matthew himself, who has taken material from Q and M. Grant believes that Matthew has expanded Mark using Q material, also weaving into the discourse material derived from M.[2] Bultmann has similar views: in his estimation Matthew has drawn fairly extensively on M material to fill out Mark and Q. Indeed, according to Bultmann, most of the material of ch. 23 not drawn from either Mark or Q comes from M, with Matthew's own creative activity being only slight.[3] McNeile's explanation is slightly different. For him the differences between Matthew and Luke at this point are due not to Matthew's conflation of M and Q, but rather to his use of a differing recension of Q.[4]

It will be noted that while the above theories improve upon the two-document hypothesis in that they are able to explain the origin of the unparalleled material of Matthew 23, they are still not completely satisfactory, for they do not account for the very wide divergence in the alleged Q material. If Matthew has simply added other material to Q, the Q source should still remain largely intact. Neither do they account for the internal unity found within the chapter.

The fact that so many scholars have sought to explain the phenomenon of Matthew 23 along the lines set out above illustrates one important point: the divergences between the Matthean and Lucan versions of the discourse involved are such as to make dependence upon a common source doubtful. The M/Q overlap theory suggested by Streeter and advanced in various forms by numerous other scholars does, in part, explain some of these differences.

But may not Q be dispensed with altogether? It would appear so. The divergence of Matthew and Luke at this point may be explained, not in terms of their use of different recensions of Q, nor yet by Matthew's conflation of his Q and M sources, but rather by the evangelists' use of different traditions altogether. There seems no good reason why Matthew 23 and Lk. 11.37-52 should not have developed independently from only the barest oral tradition. In the remainder of this study an attempt is made to show that such indeed was the case.

---

1. Brown, 'The Form of Q Known to Matthew', p. 36.
2. F.C. Grant, *The Gospels: Their Origin and their Growth* (London: Faber and Faber, 1957), pp. 145-46.
3. Bultmann, *History of the Synoptic Tradition*, p. 113.
4. McNeile, *Matthew*, p. 329.

Appendix 1

Goulder's Word Statistics

a. *Words concentrated primarily in one or more sections of the Gospel*

Example	Goulder	Matt.	Mark	Luke	SM	23	Other
θυσιαστήριον	424	6	0	2	2	4	0
δῶρον	424	9	1	2	3	3	3
ὄμνυμι	424	13	2	1	2	10	1
γέεννα	424	7	3	1	3	2	2
πρὸς τὸ + infinitive	423	5	1	1	2	1	2
φιλέω	423	5	1	2	1	1	3
ὁ πατὴρ ὁ οὐράνιος	423	7	0	0	4	1	2
Metaphorical τυφλός	424	6	0	0	0	5	1
θεάομαι	423	4	2	3	1	1	2
οἱ ἄνθρωποι	423	25	10	10	11	5	9
μὴ + Aor. Sub.	423	28	9	18	10	2	16
κλείω	424	3	0	2	1	1	1
χρυσός	424	5	0	0	0	3	2
καθαρός	426	3	0	1	1	1	1
ἀνομία	427	4	0	0	1	1	2
ὅστις…μὲν/δὲ	427	4	0	0	0	2	2
φονεύω	429	5	1	1	2	2	1
κρίσις	428	12	0	4	2	2	8
αἷμα = life taken	427	9	1	5	0	3	6
μωρός	424	6	0	0	2	1	3
ἁγιάζω	424	3	0	1	1	2	0
ἀδελφός[1]	423	14	0	5	8	1	5
ὁδηγός	424	3	0	0	0	2	1
ὀφείλω	424	6	0	5	0	2	4

1.   It is only the use of ἀδελφός in a 'transferred' sense that Goulder counts as Matthean (*Midrash*, p. 477). Goulder counts fourteen such uses in Matthew and these seem to be 5.22 (bis), 23, 24, 47; 7.3, 4, 5; 18.15 (bis), 21, 35; 23.8; 25.40. It is possible that 12.48, 49 and 50 should also be included in the count, but Goulder does not include them (pp. 336-37).

b. *Words which lack the evidence necessary for realistic judgment*

Example	Goulder	Matt.	Mark	Luke	SM	23	Other
οὐρανός...γῆ	423	10	2	5	3	1	6
χριστός	423	16	7	12	0	1	15
περιάγω	424	3	1	0	0	1	2
οὕτως	427	32	10	21	8	1	23
ἔμπροσθεν	424	18	2	10	5	1	12
ὅστις	423	29	5	18	6	3	20
πάντα...ὅσα	423	6	2	2	1	1	4
ἐάν	423	64	36	31	10	1	53
οὐ μὴ...ἕως ἄν	430	6	1	3	2	1	3
εἰ...ἄν	427	5	0	4	0	1	4
κατοικέω	424	4	0	2	0	1	3
ναός	424	9	3	4	0	5	4
ἐπάνω	424	8	1	5	1	3	4
θρόνος	424	5	0	3	1	1	3
γῆ	429	43	19	25	6	2	35
οὖν	423	56	6	33	13	2	41
ἔσται	423	39	9	33	0	1	38
δίκαιος	427	17	2	11	1	4	12
μείζων	423	10	3	7	0	3	7

c. *Words somewhat supportive of Goulder's thesis*

Example	Goulder	Matt.	Mark	Luke	SM	23	Other
τηρέω	423	6	0	0	0	1	5
ἡ βασιλεία τ. οὐρανῶν	424	33	0	0	7	1	25
Hebraic υἱός	424	8	3	2	0	2	6
φαίνομαι	427	13	2	2	3	2	8
τάφος	427	6	0	0	0	2	4
γεννήματα ἐχιδνῶν	428	3	0	1	0	1	2
ὅπως	429	17	1	7	7	1	9
ἄρτι	420	7	0	0	0	1	6

d. *Semi-Matthean Words inserted into 'an agreed Marcan context'*

Example	Goulder	Matt.	Mark	Luke	SM	23	Other
κάθημαι	42	42	25	28	3	3	36
θέλω	424	19	11	13	0	1	18
ἀμὴν λέγω ὑμῖν	429	29	12	5	6	1	22

Appendix 2

The use of the 'abusive vocative'

Example	Verse	Notes	Discount?	Parallel?
γεννήματα ἐχιδνῶν	3.7	= 23.33; 12.34		Lk. 3.7
ὀλιγόπιστοι	6.30		yes	Lk. 12.28
ὑποκριτά	7.5	SM		Lk. 6.42
ὀλιγόπιστοι	8.26		yes	nil
γεννήματα ἐχιδνῶν	12.34	= 3.7; 23.33		nil
ὀλιγόπιστοι	14.31		yes	nil
ὀλιγόπιστοι	16.8		yes	nil
σατανᾶ	16.23			Mk 8.33
ὑποκριταί	15.7	Pharisees		Mk 7.6
ὦ γενεὰ ἄπιστος	17.17		yes	Mk 9.19
ὑποκριταί	22.18	Pharisees		nil
ὑποκριταί	23.13	Scribes and Pharisees		[Lk. 11.52]
ὑποκριταί	23.15	As above		nil
ὁδηγοὶ τυφλοί	23.16	As above		nil
μωροὶ καὶ τυφλοί	23.17	As above		nil
τυφλοί	23.19	As above		nil
ὑποκριταί	23.23	As above		[Lk. 11.42]
ὑποκριταί	23.25	As above		[Lk. 11.39]
φαρισαῖε τυφλέ	23.26	As above		nil
ὑποκριταί	23.27	As above		nil
ὑποκριταί	23.29	As above		nil
γεννήματα ἐχιδνῶν	23.33	= 12.34; 3.7		nil
πονηρὲ δουλὲ	25.26			Lk. 19.22

Appendix 3

Animals in Matthew

Animal	Verse	Symbolic?	Symbolic according to Goulder?	Parallel?
Locust	3.4	no	no	Mk 1.6
Vipers	3.7	yes	yes	Lk. 3.7
Dove	3.16	?	?	Mk 1.10
Moth	6.19	no	yes	nil
Moth	6.20	no	yes	Lk. 12.33
Birds	6.26	no	yes	Lk. 12.24
Dogs	7.6	yes	yes	nil
Swine	7.6	yes	yes	nil
Fish	7.10	no	no	Lk. 11.11
Serpent	7.10	no	no	Lk. 11.11
Sheep	7.15	yes	yes	nil
Wolves	7.15	yes	yes	nil
Foxes	8.20	no	yes	Lk. 9.58
Birds	8.20	no	yes	Lk. 9.58
Swine	8.30	no	no	Mk 511
Swine	8.31	no	no	Mk 5.12
Swine	8.32	no	no	Mk 5.13
Sheep	9.36	yes	yes	Mk 6.34
Sheep	10.6	yes	yes	nil
Sheep	10.16	yes	yes	Lk. 10.3
Wolves	10.16	yes	yes	Lk.10.3
Serpents	10.16	yes	yes	nil
Doves	10.16	yes	yes	nil
Sparrows	10.29	no	yes	Lk. 12.6
Sparrows	10.31	no	yes	Lk. 12.7
Sheep	12.11	no	yes	nil
Sheep	12.12	no	yes	nil
Vipers	12.34	yes	yes	nil
Whale	12.40	?	yes	nil
Birds	13.4	yes	yes	Mk 4.4
Birds	13.32	no	yes	Mk 4.32
Fish	13.47	no	yes	nil
Fish	14.17	no	no	Mk 6.38
Fish	14.19	no	yes	Mk 6.41
Sheep	15.24	yes	yes	nil
Dogs	15.26	yes	yes	Mk 7.27
Dogs	15.27	yes	yes	Mk 7.28

Animal	Verse	Symbolic?	Symbolic according to Goulder?	Parallel?
Fish	15.34	no	no	[Mk 8.5]
Fish	15.36	no	no	Mk 8.7
Fish	17.27	no	no	nil
Sheep	18.12	yes	yes	Lk. 15.4
Ass	21.2	no	no	[Mk 11.2
Colt	21.2	no	no	Mk 11.2
Ass	21.5	no	no	nil
Colt	21.5	no	no	nil
Ass	21.5	no	no	nil
Ass	21.7	no	no	Mk 11.7
Colt	21.7	no	no	Mk 11.7
Pigeons	21.12	no	no	Mk 11.15
Oxen	22.4	no	yes	nil
Calves	22.4	no	yes	nil
Gnat	23.24	yes	yes	nil
Camel	23.24	yes	yes	nil
Serpents	23.33	yes	yes	nil
Vipers	23.33	yes	yes	nil
Chicks	23.37	yes	yes	Lk. 13.34
Hen	23.37	yes	yes	Lk. 13.34
Eagle	24.28	no	yes	Lk. 17.37
Sheep	25.32	yes	yes	nil
Goats	25.32	yes	yes	nil
Sheep	25.33	yes	yes	nil
Goats	25.33	yes	yes	nil
Sheep	26.31	yes	yes	Mk 14.27
Cock	26.34	no	no	Mk 14.30
Cock	26.74	no	no	Mk 14.72
Cock	26.75	no	no	Mk 14.72

Chapter 2

THE *SITZ IM LEBEN* OF MATTHEW 23

In the preceding chapter we noted that the material in Matthew 23 is problematic from a source-critical perspective. We have seen how in Matthew 23/Luke 11 the main source-critical hypotheses are put under very serious strain, and we have noted also that Goulder, whose work has not heretofore received the kind of critical assessment it really deserves, has also failed to mount a convincing case for the Matthean origin of Matthew 23. The material remains a problem.

In this chapter Matthew 23 is examined from a different perspective: that of its *Sitz im Leben*. Before looking at it in particular, however, it is imperative that the *Sitz im Leben* of Matthew's Gospel as a whole is first sketched in, for it is only when the contrast been the *Sitz im Leben* of the evangelist Matthew and that of the bulk of material in Matthew 23 is noted that the hypothesis advanced in this study begins to emerge more clearly.

1. *The* Sitz im Leben *of Matthew's Gospel*

The fundamentally Jewish character of Matthew's Gospel has long been recognized. As far back as 1928 Ernst von Dobschütz argued strongly that the work was the product of one rabbinically trained,[1] and this suggestion has found wide acceptance, coming to fruition in the works of W.D. Davies[2] and, more lately, Goulder himself.[3] Indeed, with only a few exceptions,[4] it is now widely acknowledged that Matthew's Gospel

---

1. E. von Dobschütz, 'Matthäus als Rabbi und Katechet', *ZNW* 27 (1928), pp. 338-48 (ET R. Morgan in G.N. Stanton [ed.], *The Interpretation of Matthew* [London: SPCK, 1983]), pp. 19-29.

2. W.D. Davies, *The Setting of the Sermon on the Mount* (Cambridge: Cambridge University Press, 1964).

3. Goulder, *Midrash and Lection in Matthew, passim.*

4. See, for example, K. Clark, 'The Gentile Bias in Matthew', *JBL* 66 (1947),

shows an interest in Judaism that is most readily explicable if the author was himself a Jew. Numerous commentators are supportive of this view; to the names of von Dobschütz, Davies and Goulder might be added those of Bonnard, Green, Hill, Beare and Bacon.[1]

The reason for this widespread agreement is not difficult to find. Within the Gospel of Matthew there is strong if not incontrovertible evidence of the evangelist's intense concern with distinctly Jewish matters. Bacon[2] (and others)[3] may be right in viewing Matthew's division of the Gospel into five distinct sections as a conscious attempt on his part to parallel the Pentateuch. Several other commentators have suggested that Matthew presents Jesus as a New Moses figure. W.D. Davies, for example, discusses the Jesus–Moses parallelism at length, concluding that

pp. 165-72, references here are to the reprint found in K.W. Clark, *The Gentile Bias and Other Essays* (NovTSup, 54; Leiden: Brill, 1980), pp. 1-8; P. Nepper-Christensen, *Das Matthäus Evangelium—ein judenchristliches Evangelium?* (Aarhus: Universitetsforlaget, 1958); G. Strecker, *Der Weg der Gerechtigkeit, Untersuchung zur Theologie des Matthäus* (FRLANT, 82,; Göttingen: Vandenhoeck & Ruprecht, 3rd edn, 1971); W. Trilling, *Das Wahre Israel. Studien zur Theologie des Matthäus Evangeliums* (SANT, 10; Munich: Kösel-Verlag, 3rd edn, 1964). See further G.N. Stanton, 'The Origin and Purpose of Matthew's Gospel: Matthean Scholarship from 1945 to the Present Day', *ANRW* II.25.3, pp. 1890-1951, esp. pp. 1916-21.

1.   P. Bonnard, *L'Evangile selon Saint Matthieu* (Neuchâtel: Delachaux & Niestlé, 1972), p. 10; H.B. Green, *The Gospel according to Matthew* (New Clarendon Bible; London: Oxford University Press, 1975), pp. 30-31; Hill, *Matthew*, p. 43; Beare, *Matthew*, pp. 9-10; B.W. Bacon, *Studies in Matthew* (London: Constable, 1930), p. 81 *et passim*.

2.   B.W. Bacon, 'The "Five Books" of Matthew against the Jews', *Expositor* 15 (1918), pp. 56-66. Davies (*Setting*, pp. 14-25) discusses Bacon's suggestion, and concludes that while Bacon may have somewhat overemphasized the structural parallelism of Matthew and the Pentateuch, such parallelism does indeed exist. And Davies seems correct: there are five blocks of teaching within the Gospel (note the clear closing formulae at Mt. 7.28; 11.1; 13.53; 19.1; 26.1), though as Gundry has noted (*Matthew*, p. 11), the parallelism is not exact. For a discussion of the structure of the gospel see J.D. Kingsbury, *Matthew: Structure, Christology, Kingdom* (London: SPCK, 1975), pp. 1-39. Kingsbury rejects this fivefold division of the Gospel in favour of a threefold 'Christological' division. See further D.R. Bauer, *The Structure of Matthew's Gospel: A Study in Literary Design* (Sheffield: The Almond Press, 1988).

3.   See, for example, Lagrange, *Matthieu*, p. LXXXV; A. Schlatter, *Der Evangelist Matthäus* (Stuttgart: Calwer Verlag, 6th edn, 1963), pp. 125-28; Kilpatrick, *Origins*, pp. 107-108, 135-36; Benoit, *Matthieu*, pp. 7-12; Bonnard, *Matthieu*, pp. 7, 110; Hill, *Matthew*, pp. 44-48. Kingsbury, *Structure*, p. 3 gives several other references.

for Matthew, Jesus is the 'New Moses' who continues (though goes beyond) the work of his predecessor.[1]

The evangelist's evident concern for the Jewish Law has been noted by many scholars,[2] and his knowledge of and interest in the Old Testament has also been seen as firm evidence for Matthew's Jewish origins.[3] The evangelist's knowledge of Hebrew and/or Aramaic[4] also argues for Jewish rather than Gentile authorship. It would seem, then, that despite the presence of some evidence to the contrary, Matthew was a Jew and Matthew's is a 'Jewish' Gospel.[5]

But simply to describe Matthew's Gospel as 'Jewish' is to mask a whole series of problems, for while the Gospel does indeed evince a concern with Jewish matters, this concern is by no means uniform. The statement 'The scribes and the Pharisees sit on Moses' seat; therefore observe whatever they tell you' (Mt. 23.2, 3) seems possible only for one who was intimately connected with Judaism and who thought that these individuals were the authoritative leaders of the people. In

---

1.   Davies, *Setting*, especially pp. 25ff., 51ff., 78ff., 85ff., 96ff. On the Jesus–Moses parallelism see also R.T. France, *Matthew* (TNTC; Leicester: InterVarsity Press, 1985), p. 85; Hill, *Matthew*, pp. 85-86, 102; F.V. Filson, *The Gospel according to Matthew* (BNTC; London: A. & C. Black, 2nd edn, 1971), p. 29; G. Bornkamm, 'End Expectation and Church in Matthew', in G. Bornkamm, G. Barth and H.J. Held, *Tradition and Interpretation in Matthew* (trans. P. Scott; London: SCM Press, 1963), p. 35; J.D. Crossan, 'From Moses to Jesus: Parallel Themes', *Bible Review* 2 (1986), pp. 18-27; D.C. Allison, 'Jesus and Moses', *ExpTim* 98 (1987), pp. 203-205; *idem*, *The New Moses* (Edinburgh: T. & T. Clark, 1993).

2.   E.g. G. Barth, 'Matthew's Understanding of the Law', in Bornkamm, Barth and Held, *Tradition*, pp. 58-164; France, *Matthew*, pp. 48-50; E. Schweizer, 'Matthew's Church', in Stanton (ed.), *The Interpretation of Matthew*, p. 129.

3.   E.g. Gundry, *Use of the Old Testament*; K. Stendahl, *The School of St Matthew and its Use of the Old Testament* (Philadelphia: Fortress Press, 2nd edn, 1968); W. Rothfuchs, *Die Erfüllungszitate des Matthäus-evangeliums* (Stuttgart: Kohlhammer, 1969); G.N. Stanton (ed.), *A Gospel for a New People* (Edinburgh: T. & T. Clark, 1992), pp. 346-63.

4.   E.g. J. Jeremias 'Die Muttersprache des Evangelisten Matthäus', *ZNW* 50 (1959), pp. 270-74. Based largely upon an examination of the Shema' (Deut 6.5; cf. Mt. 22.37), Jeremias comes to the conclusion that the language used by Matthew in prayer was Hebrew, though his mother tongue was Aramaic. See further J.H. Moulton, W.F. Howard and N. Turner, *A Grammar of New Testament Greek* (4 vols.; Edinburgh: T. & T. Clark, 1908–76), IV, pp. 31-44.

5.   This is a point discussed at greater length in ch. 3 of Newport 'Sources and *Sitz im Leben*'.

Mt. 16.5-12, however, a fundamentally different attitude from the Pharisees is evinced, for here the advice is not to 'do whatever the Pharisees tell you', but rather to 'watch out for their teaching'. Likewise, although Matthew's Jesus seems thoroughly 'Jewish' when he limits his activity and that of his disciples to the 'lost sheep of the house of Israel' (Mt. 10.5, 6), he also sends his disciples to 'all nations' (Mt. 28.19, 20). Neither is it to go unnoticed that while Matthew seems concerned to establish some degree of continuity between the Jewish religion and the community he is addressing (witness the formula quotations), there is also discontinuity. Being a son of Abraham is not enough to guarantee God's beneficence (Mt. 3.9). Indeed, being a member of Israel may even be detrimental to one's fate at the final judgment, for while many shall come from Gentile lands and participate in the eschatological supper, the 'Sons of the Kingdom' stand a real chance of being thrown into outer darkness (Mt. 8.11, 12).

The attempts made to solve this confusing state of affairs are complex and a full discussion of these attempts need not be entered into here.[1] Suffice it to say that, while scholars are generally agreed that Matthew was a Jew, most would go on to say that by the time he wrote his Gospel this Jew was no longer a participating member of the synagogue. Matthew has left the faith to which he once belonged. Indeed, it would seem that Matthew has not only left the synagogue, but now views his former co-religionists and compatriots with the utmost suspicion. He portrays the Jewish people as a whole as a wicked race which has killed the messiah and failed to respond to his call. Gaston put the point succinctly when he wrote 'More than any other gospel, Matthew emphasises Jesus' messiahship. More than any other gospel, Matthew emphasises the utter rejection of Israel. These two emphases are not unrelated.'[2] Gaston's comment falls short only in that he perhaps underestimates the extent to which John emphasizes these two themes; but he is right to note that Matthew most certainly stresses Jesus' messiahship, and at the same time clearly portrays Israel as a nation which has consciously rejected him. The three parables of Mt. 21.28–22.14 seem intent on underlining this fact, and the ominous cry of 'his blood be on

1. The argument is taken up in Newport, 'Sources and *Sitz im Leben*', ch. 3 and see further S.H. Brooks, *Matthew's Community: The Evidence of his Special Sayings Material* (Sheffield: JSOT Press, 1987).

2. L. Gaston, 'The Messiah of Israel as Teacher of the Gentiles', *Int* 29 (1975), p. 32.

us and on our children' (Mt. 27.25) seems to seal the fate of the Jews.

Further examples of this concern to underline Jewish guilt for the death of Jesus and the nation's rejection of the Messiah could easily be adduced; Mt. 11.2-24 clearly castigates Israel for rejecting the messiah. The controversy narratives of Mt. 12.1-50 are also most probably designed to underline Israel's guilt. Mt. 13.53-58 explains how the Jews took offence at Jesus, asking 'Is not this the carpenter's son? Is not his mother called Mary?' In the Birth Narrative we are told that it was not only Herod who was 'troubled' (ἐταράχθη) by the Magis' announcement that 'the King of the Jews' had been born, but 'all Jerusalem with him' (Mt. 2.3); and in the story of the healing of the centurion's servant, Jesus says that he has not found the faith manifested by this non-Jew to be paralleled by that of Israel (Mt. 8.5-13).[1] This very negative portrayal of the Jews by Matthew has been an embarrassment to many Christian scholars, for there is no doubt some truth in Gaston's suggestion that it was Matthew who taught the Church to hate Israel.[2]

Matthew's harsh castigation of the Jewish nation is surely indefensible, though it is somewhat understandable. Despite the apparent contradiction, Matthew was, it seems, both a Jew and anti-Jewish. Religious polemics often bring forth tirades of abuse and arouse the bitterest of feelings. Religious ties are often stronger than racial or family ones, and Matthew is by no means alone in rejecting family and race in favour of religion. Indeed, Saldarini seems correct when he notes that although the harsh verbal criticisms found in Matthew 23 may seem malevolent and offensive to the modern western mind, such acidity is hardly unusual in religious polemics and Matthew 23, even with its charges of blindness, hypocrisy, corruption and murder, does not surprise the historian of religion.[3] We could think, for example, of such figures as Johannes Pfefferkorn (1469–1522), the Jewish convert to Lutheranism, who demanded the suppression of the Talmud and other Jewish books, since

---

1. See further E. Buck, 'Anti-Judaic Sentiments in the Passion Narrative According to Matthew'; and B. Przybylski, 'The Setting of Matthean Anti-Judaism', in P. Richardson (ed.), *Anti-Judaism in Early Christianity* (2 vols.; Ontario: Wilfred Laurier University Press, 1986), I, pp. 165-80, 181-200.

2. Gaston, 'The Messiah of Israel', p. 40.

3. A.J. Saldarini, 'Delegitimation of Leaders in Matthew 23', *CBQ* 54 (1992), p. 659. Saldarini draws attention also to the work of L.T. Johnston ('The New Testament's Anti-Jewish Slander and the Conventions of Ancient Polemic', *JBL* 108 [1989], pp. 419-41), who seeks to set the polemics of Mt. 23 within a broader historical framework.

these in his view contained certain blasphemous elements.[1] Furthermore, as Stanton points out, Matthew's Gospel is not the only 'Jewish' work that at times speaks harshly of the Jews; similar attacks are found in *5 Ezra*.[2] Schulz also notes several similarities between Matthew 23 and the accusations made by the author of the *Ass. Mos.* 7.1-10.[3] Thus, it seems, Matthew may have been a Jew who had converted to Christianity and now bitterly attacked his former co-religionists.[4]

No doubt Matthew carried over much of his Judaism into his version of Christianity and did, to some extent, put new wine into old skins (cf. Mt. 9.17). Many of those for whom he was writing were doubtless converts from Judaism who understood some of the language and technical jargon of that religion. His community probably kept the Sabbath (Mt. 24.20)[5] and insisted upon the observance of the law (as interpreted by Jesus). However, the extremely bad light in which the Jews are portrayed in Matthew, coupled with his very obvious pro-Gentile stance, indicates that Matthew no longer viewed Israel as a whole as God's people.

It would seem, then, that Matthew and the community to which he belonged had separated from the synagogue, and viewed the rest of the Jews as a rebellious and hard-hearted race whose chances of salvation were slight. But if this is so, how are we to explain the clear affirmation of scribal-Pharisaic authority found in Mt. 23.2-3? Did Matthew really think that mint, dill and cummin should be tithed (Mt. 23.23)? And what

1.   For a brief summary of the career of Pfefferkorn see L. Poliakov, *The History of Anti-Semitism* (4 vols.; London: Routledge & Kegan Paul, 1966–84), I, pp. 214-15. See also H.A. Obermann, *The Roots of Anti-Semitism in the Age of Renaissance and Reformation* (trans. J.I. Porter; Philadelphia: Fortress Press, 1983), pp. 32-37.

2.   G.N. Stanton, '5 Ezra and Matthean Christianity in the Second Century', in *A Gospel for a New People: Studies in Matthew* (Edinburgh: T. &. T. Clark, 1992), pp. 256-77.

3.   S. Schulz, *Q: Die Spruchquelle der Evangelisten* (Zürich: Theologischer Verlag, 1972), pp. 97-100.

4.   See also M. Kelly, 'The Woes Against the Scribes and Pharisees in Matthew 23.13-36. What Did They Mean for the Author? and What Do They Mean in the Gospel Today?' (MA thesis, University of Bristol, 1972). In ch. 1 Kelly notes that bitter dispute between sects within Judaism was widespread. She notes especially the conflict between the Qumran Community and their opponents and the conflicts evidenced by the rabbinic literature.

5.   See G. Stanton 'Pray That Your Flight May Not Be in Winter or on the Sabbath', *JSNT* 37 (1989), pp. 17-30 for a discussion of the various possible interpretations of this verse.

of the reference to the temple and the altar found in Mt. 23.16-22, where the altar is said to sanctify the gift, seemingly betraying a belief in the efficacy of the Jewish cult system? Are these verses simply stray sayings which have crept into Matthew's gospel from his source Q? Or are they, as Goulder has argued, from Matthew's own hand? It is the contention of this study that such an understanding of Matthew 23 is not entirely convincing and that a better explanation is possible. Rather, it seems, Matthew has taken a fairly extensive source (now Mt. 23.2-31) to which he has added his own appendix (Mt. 23.32-39). This source stems from a different *Sitz im Leben* from that of the Gospel as a whole. It is the burden of the remainder of this study to show that this hypothesis is better able to explain the material.

The Sitz im Leben *of Matthew 23*

Naturally, most commentators see the whole of Matthew 23 as a Matthean creation. Matthew has taken material from various sources and woven them together to form the discourse as it now stands. In this editorial activity, Matthew's own interests become clear and his *Sitz im Leben* begins to emerge. Commentators who take this view are therefore concerned to give an account of the evangelist's purpose in this section of the gospel. They see the *Sitz im Leben* of Matthew 23 as being that of Matthew himself.

In an apparent attempt to soften the very harsh tone of Matthew 23 and to make it more applicable to Matthew's own community, many commentators interpret the chapter paradigmatically. The thinking behind this view is simple and not entirely unreasonable. Matthew is writing sometime after 85 CE, that is after the adoption by the Jews of the *Birkath ha-Minim.*[1] Matthew's community no longer associates with the Pharisees and scribes who are, after all, blind guides leading the blind and are best left to their inevitable fate (Mt. 15.14). But if Matthew has created Matthew 23, it must in some way address his post-85 CE *extra muros* situation and is therefore at least in part paradigmatic. According to this interpretation, the scribes and Pharisees are held up in Matthew 23 as mirror images of the Christian church and its leaders. Garland, and others, also emphasize the extent to which Matthew 23 is an attempt by

---

1. E.g. Kilpatrick, *Origins*, pp. 109-11; Schweizer, *Matthew*, p. 430. But see R. Kimelman '*Birkat-ha-Minim* and the Lack of Evidence for an Anti-Christian Jewish Prayer in Late Antiquity', in E.P. Sanders (ed.), *Jewish and Christian Self Definition* (3 vols.; London: SCM Press, 1980–82), II, pp. 226-44 for a discussion of this topic.

the author to elucidate the problem of God's apparent rejection of Israel; this is more plausible, but even here the exegesis is often strained.

In this study it is argued that Mt. 23.2-31 stems from a Jewish-Christian milieu in which the traditional 'pillars' of Judaism, namely the law, the temple, the synagogue and the leadership, were still held in high regard. Furthermore, vv. 2-31 form a complete unit, having a high degree of internal unity. This entire section is most at home when seen in the context of pre-70 CE Judaism. The *Sitz im Leben* of this section is to be found within Judaism, though some concept of a separate identity was beginning to emerge (Mt. 23.8-12). To be sure, the evangelist has partly covered his tracks by giving Mt. 23.2-31 a different setting and by adding an appendix to it, but the material refuses to come wholly into line with his theological purpose and religious standpoint, and, in the last analysis, Mt. 23.2-31 cannot be fitted convincingly into the Matthean scheme. The *Sitz im Leben* of Mt. 23.2-31 is not that of the evangelist himself.

Matthew, however, was no fool and while he sometimes seems to have felt obliged to include material that it would have suited his purposes better to leave out (e.g. Mt. 10.23), in Matthew 23 he manages to pull off a partial transformation of the material so that it suits his own purposes. This he does by adding his appendix (Mt. 23.32-39) and by placing the material carefully in the context of his material about the Jewish rejection of the Messiah found in Matthew 21 and 22. What, then, was Matthew's purpose in Matthew 23?

2. *The Intention of Matthew in Matthew 23*

The most extensive study of Matthew 23 is that of David E. Garland, whose final conclusions are adequately summed up in the following words:

> the intention of Matthew in his composition of chap. 23 is considered to be two-pronged: he attempted to elucidate the problem of the rejection of Jesus by the Jews and God's rejection of Israel in the catastrophic war with Rome in order to clarify that Israel no longer had special status with God but had been replaced by a nation which is to produce the fruits of the kingdom in due season. He also intended it to be a warning to the church not to go the way of "this generation" of Israel, for what had happened to them may also happen to "you". Therefore, the Christian is to see himself potentially mirrored in the scribe and the Pharisee as a type and to recognise that the same judgment which befell the leaders of Israel awaits

the unfaithful leaders of Christ's community. In this matter Matthew would probably wish to say to the Christian leaders, who embody everything which is condemned in this chapter all too much and who live out everything which is commended in this chapter all too little, "Do you not see all these things?"[1]

Garland's suggestions were not entirely new. In 1971 Simon Legasse similarly suggested that Matthew's 'anti-Judaism' was primarily didactic and designed to warn Christians against hypocrisy on their own parts. The Jewish opponents had indeed shown themselves to be 'hypocritical', that is 'impious', and had rejected the Messiah, but Matthew's interest is as much in holding them up as a bad example before the Christian church, as in attacking the Jews *per se*.[2] For Legasse, as for Garland, the *Sitz im Leben* of Matthew 23 is located not within Judaism, but within the early Christian church.[3] The material is more homiletical than historical; it is Matthew's sermon illustration. Schweizer makes a similar observation when he suggests that Matthew 23 was as much an attack upon the evangelist's own community as it was a rebuke of Pharisaic piety. Matthew's intention was, in part at least, to 'call men to self knowledge and repentance'. It was to serve as a warning for those who try to 'evade' God.[4] Sjef van Tilborg similarly suggests that it was part of Matthew's purpose in composing his Gospel to warn his readers not to follow the bad example that the Jews had set, lest they too fall under the same condemnation.[5]

This 'paradigmatic' understanding of Matthew 23 may be homiletically useful, but it is not entirely convincing as an explanation of the whole chapter. Verses 8-10 may address the Christian community with the words 'but you are not to be called Rabbi', but this is little more than a *sotto voce*, and cannot be taken as determining the central thrust of the whole chapter. Neither is the fact that the passage ends on an eschatological note sufficient evidence to warrant reading the chapter

1. Garland, *Intention*, p. 215.
2. S. Legasse, 'L'antijudaïsme dans L'Evangile selon Matthieu', in M. Didier (ed.), *L'Evangile selon Matthieu: Rédaction et Théologie* (Gembloux: Duculot, 1971), pp. 417-28.
3. See also S. Freyne, 'Vilifying the Other and Defining the Self: Matthew's and John's Anti-Jewish Polemic in Focus', in J. Neusner and E.S. Frerichs (eds.), *'To See Ourselves as Others See Us': Christians, Jews, 'Others' in Late Antiquity* (Chico, CA: Scholars Press, 1985) who adopts a similar viewpoint.
4. Schweizer, *Matthew*, p. 446.
5. Van Tilborg, *Jewish Leaders*, pp. 168-69.

simply as a warning to the Christian community to take seriously the message of Jesus or else face final judgment. The judgment which comes is a judgment upon the Jews; it is their house that is left desolate. The chapter does not end with a generalized warning to all those who do not do God's will, but to Jerusalem in particular. The city has rejected God's call and must now face the consequences. There is nothing in this final section to suggest that this is anything more than a straightforward attack upon the Jews. The hypothetical Christian audience to which, according to some, this chapter is addressed seems absent at this point.

However, as Garland notes,[1] the chapter is introduced by the evangelist as a speech of Jesus directed to the crowds and the disciples (Mt. 23.1), and the first part of the discourse does indeed seem to be directed towards these individuals. To this extent the chapter may have a didactic intent and be aimed at the evangelist's own community, but if so this intention has been forgotten by the time we reach the real substance of the chapter, namely the seven woes, which are addressed not to the crowds and disciples, but directly to the scribes and Pharisees themselves. In Mt. 23.13 the speech is addressed to the scribes and Pharisees themselves, who are 'hypocrites' and 'blind guides', who lock up the kingdom, and who turn proselytes into children of hell. This section of the chapter at least cannot be regarded as a warning to the Christian community. It is a direct attack on the scribes and Pharisees for failing to do the law of God.

The audience changes again in Mt. 23.32-39, for from Mt. 23.32 on the attack seems to be not upon the scribes and Pharisees alone, but rather upon all Jews in general. This section is the work of Matthew himself and it is here that he shows his hand. The section is an attack upon those who, in the evangelist's mind, have rejected God's call, perverted his word, and committed the ultimate sin of killing the Christ himself. The lessons which the 'disciples and crowds' of Mt. 23.1 are supposed to learn, then, may in part be that they are to guard against hypocrisy in their midst and to refrain from calling their leaders 'Rabbi', but it is also Matthew's intention to point out that the Jews are totally wicked because they have rejected Christ and persecuted his followers. Matthew is not simply drawing some spiritually useful lessons based upon some Christological anecdotes; he is issuing a scathing attack upon

---

1.   Garland, *Intention*, p. 120.

and condemnation of an entire nation which he considers to be wicked and rebellious and now without hope.

Garland, then, is perhaps wrong to suggest that Matthew 23 has a distinctly paradigmatic intent. In this, however, he is in good company, for, as has been noted, several other commentators have a similar understanding of the chapter. In part, this tendency for many Christian scholars to interpret Matthew 23 in this way may be due to their concern to exculpate either Jesus, the evangelist, or both from the charge of anti-semitism. Schweizer, for example, probably betrays his own motivation for interpreting the passage in the way he does when he notes that 'any other interpretation turns it into an un-Christian judgment upon others'.[1] Has a desire to defend Matthew (or, more serious still, Jesus) against the charge of such 'un-Christian' behaviour led Schweizer to gloss over the most obvious reading of the text?

Similar questions could be asked of other scholars. Garland suggests that the 'unremitting acrimony' of ch. 23 seems 'out of character for Jesus',[2] and similarly Beare, when concluding his discussion on this chapter, advises his readers that

> it should be clear that there is very little in this chapter that can be regarded as language ever used by Jesus, or in accordance with his spirit. It is manifestly impossible to imagine him as delivering such a scathing denunciation in the temple.[3]

Jesus, then, in Beare's view, is not to be seen as the originator of this discourse; but who is? Beare faces a problem greater than that of Garland, for, whereas the latter is prepared to understand the chapter as largely paradigmatic, as a discourse aimed not at Jews, but at Christians, Beare recognizes that the material as it now stands is primarily polemical in its intention, blatantly unfair and, in the last analysis, anti-Jewish, and it is perhaps for this reason that he seems so sure that the material is not authentic Jesus tradition. Thus, while Beare thinks that 'a Christian expositor is under no obligation to defend such a mass of vituperation',[4] the same commentator is anxious to draw the fire away from Jesus by using the evangelist as a decoy.

But even Beare cannot leave the evangelist totally undefended. After pointing out that the material of Matthew 23 is vituperative and unfair,

---

1. Schweizer, *Matthew*, p. 446.
2. Garland, *Intention*, p. 1.
3. Beare, *Matthew*, p. 461.
4. Beare, *Matthew*, p. 461.

he goes on to suggest that 'the words may be taken as a warning addressed to the church and its leaders against allowing the hypocritical attitudes here denounced to develop in their own ranks'.[1] In any case, the level of animosity evident in the discourse may, perhaps, be excused to some extent in Matthew by virtue of the fact that Matthew's community has the 'inflamed hostility of the persecuted'.[2]

Numerous other scholars could be mentioned here who display concerns similar to those of Beare, Schweizer and Garland. As Garland points out,[3] Montefiore thought the chapter the most 'unchristian' in the Gospels, expressing the hope that little of the material was traceable to Jesus himself,[4] and H. B. Green states that 'the extreme bitterness of this chapter is out of character with what we can recover of the historical Jesus'.[5] These and other such remarks highlight the level of embarrassment felt by many modern day Christian scholars when confronted with Matthew 23.

This embarrassment has not always been felt, however. John Chrysostom, for example, understood the chapter as being an accurate reflection of the state of the Jews, who were known to be 'murderous and deceitful, and having much guile, and surpassing their fathers in their outrages'. And indeed, Mt. 23.37 contains a statement by Jesus who, realizing that the Jews 'hated Him, and so hated as to kill Him', left them with the words 'How often would I have gathered your children together, and ye would not?'[6]

Similarly, Luther indicated his own understanding of the chapter when he wrote:

> My boast is that I have injured no one's life or reputation, but only sharply reproached, as godless and sacrilegious, those assertions, inventions, and doctrines which are against the Word of God. I do not apologize for this, for I have good precedents. John the Baptist [Lk. 3:7] and Christ after him [Mt. 23:33] called the Pharisees the 'offspring of vipers'.[7]

1.   Beare, *Matthew*, p. 461.
2.   Beare, *Matthew*, p. 461.
3.   Garland, *Intention*, p. 1.
4.   C.G. Montefiore, *The Synoptic Gospels: Edited with an Introduction and Commentary* (2 vols.; London: Macmillan, 1927), I, p. 296.
5.   H.B. Green, *Matthew*, p. 187.
6.   P. Schaff (ed.), *The Nicene and Post-Nicene Fathers* (14 vols.; Grand Rapids: Eerdmans, repr. 1969), XIV, p. 246.
7.   J. Pelikan and H.T. Lehmann (eds.), *Luther's Works* (55 vols.; Philadelphia: Fortress Press, 1958–86), XXXII, p. 141.

The words of Calvin are also worth noting in this context. Commenting on Mt. 23.15 he wrote

> The scribes had also won popular esteem for their zealous efforts to win foreigners and uncircumcised to the Jewish faith. If their tricks and other devices had thrown the wool over someone's eyes they got a marvelous reception for their so-called increase to the Church... Christ on the contrary declares that their enthusiasm is so far from laudable that it increasingly calls down God's vengeance, since they pull down to greater destruction any who join their sect. Note how corrupt their condition was, how dissipated their religion. To bring disciples to God would surely have been a holy and splendid thing, yet to attract gentiles to the Jewish worship of those days (so degraded, so chock-full of wicked profanity) was nothing but leading them from Scylla to Charybdis.[1]

Such an understanding of Matthew 23 has now largely died out, for modern scholars generally recognize that the picture of Judaism painted in Matthew 23 is unfair and inaccurate. This unfairness cannot have originated with Jesus, some such as Beare argue, and they therefore shift the blame over to Matthew. Others seek to exculpate both Jesus and the evangelist by interpreting the chapter paradigmatically.

However the material will not simply go away: Matthew 23 is, it seems, an unfair, unjust, biased, scathing and bitter attack upon the perceived opposition. But such animosity and unfairness is hardly unusual in religious polemics. One need think only of the literature of the reformation to appreciate the level of feeling aroused by religious debate. Matthew 23 represents real friction,[2] and the chapter cannot be watered down to an insubstantial paradigm held up by the evangelist as the hypothetical antithesis of true Christianity. It must be taken with the historical seriousness it deserves. What is the conflict here? What are the sides? What are the issues? This study seeks to answer these questions realistically.

Garland is on much firmer ground when he suggests that part of Matthew's intention in composing ch. 23 was 'to elucidate the problem of the rejection of Jesus by the Jews and God's rejection of Israel'.[3]

---

1. D.W. Torrance and T.F. Torrance (eds.), *Calvin's Commentaries* (12 vols.; Edinburgh: Saint Andrew's Press, 1972), III, p. 54.

2. G.N. Stanton in 'The Gospel of Matthew and Judaism', *BJRL* 66 (1984), pp. 264-84 has urged the same point. For Stanton the polemic in Mt. 23 is '*real*' (his italics) and must not be subjugated to Matthew's Christology or ethics' (p. 273).

3. Garland, *Intention*, p. 215.

Matthew does indeed face a problem similar to that tackled by Paul in Romans 9–11. The evangelist knows that salvation comes through obedience to Jesus' words and his sacrificial death (Mt. 19.16-30; 26.28), and he knows also that the Jews as a nation have rejected Jesus-Messiah, and have, therefore, forfeited the right to the kingdom (Mt. 21.33-43 *et passim*). Matthew, living as he does in the post-70 CE period, knows also of the terrible catastrophe that has hit Jerusalem.

Hill too argues that Matthew's purpose in his Gospel was partly one centred upon matters of *Heilsgeschichte*. He writes:

> The Matthean church was concerned to know about the history out of which it came, and the evangelist offers this. The story of the events, how-ever tragic, must be told. Nothing was more certain than that Jesus was crucified. To answer the questions 'Why?' and 'By whom?' meant that the sad tale of Israel's rejection (and especially the attitude of her religious leaders) had to be told, and, in the telling, attitudes towards the Jews which had been created by the first half century of the Church's life found expression... The Matthean church was intensely aware of being the heir of God's promises and purposes. This is unmistakably clear in its under-standing of the Law and of Scripture. The refusal of Israel, the chosen race, to receive her Messiah becomes the decisive reason for the Kingdom passing to the Church: it is the new creation built upon the foundations which unbelieving Jews were unwilling to accept.[1]

Has God therefore rejected his people? Matthew's answer (unlike Paul's) is affirmative, but this response is qualified by theological explanation. The rejection of Israel did not start with God, for his action was only reciprocal. Israel first rejected God, and this caused God to act in the way he did. The birth narrative and the parables of the Two Sons (Mt. 21.28-32), the Wicked Tenants (21.33-43), and the Wedding Feast (22.1-14) all drive home this point. And if a final blow were needed, it is surely delivered in Matthew's account of the passion. It is not just the Jewish leaders who have rejected Jesus, but the 'crowds' too, for in Mt. 27.22-23 it is they who, at the instigation of the chief priests and the elders, call for Jesus' crucifixion, and acknowledge their own guilt with the words 'His blood be on us and on our children' (27.25). Throughout the Gospel the Jews are portrayed as an evil and wicked generation who have set themselves in constant opposition to God.

Clearly Matthew 23 plays an important part in the development of

---

1.   Hill, *Matthew*, p. 71.

this Matthean leitmotif. The latter part of the chapter may well stem from the hand of Matthew himself, and it is in this latter part that Matthew's own intention is seen. The so-called 'lament over Jerusalem', found in Mt. 23.37-39, strongly suggests that the redactor of this whole section was seeking to explain the destruction of Jerusalem. The temple has been left desolate because Israel, like disobedient chicks who fail to respond to their mother's call, have declined the offer of safety and protection. They have rejected God's messengers; first his prophets, and now even his own Son (see Mt. 21.35-40; 22.6). As a result of these actions Jerusalem has been sacked, the temple burnt, and the religion of the Jews left in tatters. Judaism is now defunct. This has happened not because God suddenly changed his mind and decided not to favour Israel after all, but because the Jews have rejected the Christ whom God has sent.

Garland's work is therefore useful, for he is almost certainly right to emphasise the fact that Matthew 23 ends on a note of judgment, and that consequently the material which has gone before the concluding few verses may, on a Matthean-redactoral level, be understood as an attempt by the evangelist to explain why it was that the Jewish nation had incurred the wrath of God. This is not to say that this was the original intention of the material, for on a pre-Matthean level Mt. 23.2-31 had an entirely different function from that which it now has in the Gospel. Matthew has taken source material and has modified it to serve his own purposes.[1] This modification is not the result of the evangelist's tampering with the actual text, for signs of Matthew's own redactoral hand are relatively slight in Mt. 23.2-31. Rather, the modification is effected by the position given to the chapter by the evangelist within the basic structure of the Gospel as a whole and by the ending he has given it.

---

1. It is worth pointing out here that the contention of Stanton that Matthew consistently heightened the anti-Judaism found in his sources seems basically correct. If, as it is suggested here, Mt. 23.2-31 once formed a polemical pamphlet which was written against the scribes and Pharisees, it seems that Matthew has taken this source and added to it the eschatological material of Mt. 23.32-39. In so doing Matthew has broadened the whole context of the debate, for although in 23.2-31 it is the scribes and Pharisees who are in view, in Mt. 23.32-39 it is the whole of the Jewish nation symbolized by Jerusalem itself. See further Stanton, 'Matthew and Judaism', pp. 267-71.

These observations are important, for they reinforce the suggestion made by critics such as Kingsbury,[1] Cope,[2] Thompson[3] and Garland himself, that the context in which the individual pericopae are placed in the gospels must be noted carefully. When studied on the level of Matthew himself, ch. 23 must be set firmly within the context of the entire Gospel. The evangelist is in a real sense an author; he is out to tell a story and to develop a plot. But it seems that much of what is found in Matthew 23 is subjugated source material. This material, though it jars historically if understood as representing Matthew's own situation, fits reasonably well into the general plot of the evangelist's gospel story. But if Mt. 23.2-31 is taken from its Matthean context, it is seen to form an integral unit. What is more, this unit may be placed in another, altogether different *Sitz im Leben*, and be seen to fit into place like a piece of a jigsaw puzzle. In other words, Mt. 23.2-31 as a unit is not entirely parasitic on its Matthean context and continues to live even when separated from its adopted host.

3. *The Original* Sitz im Leben *of Matthew 23.2-31*

General Observations

Above the most probable *Sitz im Leben* for Matthew's gospel as a whole has been sketched in and an attempt has been made to show how Matthew develops ch. 23 in line with his overall purposes. It is against this general background that the more original *Sitz im Leben* of Mt. 23.2-31 needs to be placed and it is immediately obvious that there are several major differences. First, it was noted above that the final edition of Matthew's Gospel almost certainly stems from a period after the destruction of the Jerusalem temple. The debate over oath forms contained in Mt. 23.16-22, however, fits best into a pre-70 CE *Sitz im Leben*. This is true whether or not phrases such as 'by the temple', and 'by the altar' were used as oath forms even after the temple's destruction, for the statement 'he who swears by the temple, swears by it and him who dwells in it' (23.21) assumes that God does indeed dwell in the Jerusalem temple, which would surely have been an unlikely

1.   Kingsbury, *Story*, p. 2.
2.   O.L. Cope, *Matthew: A Scribe Trained for the Kingdom of Heaven* (Washington: Catholic Biblical Association, 1976), p. 7.
3.   W.G. Thompson, *Matthew's Advice to a Divided Community: Matthew 17,22-18,35* (Rome: Pontifical Biblical Institute, 1970), p. 13.

assumption for anyone writing after it had already been burnt down.[1] So, too, the argument 'which is greater the gift, or the altar which sanctifies the gift?' (23.19) betrays the author's belief in the efficacy of the Jewish sacrificial system. The logic is obviously non-Matthean, and this saying too seems most at home in a pre-70 CE *Sitz im Leben.*[2]

It is also apparent that in Matthew 23 there are certain pericopae which seem to have originated at a time when there was close contact between the author of the passages and Judaism. The author has accurate knowledge on some of the finer points of the Jewish law such as the tithing of mint, dill and cummin (which ought to be done according to 23.23) and the straining of gnats (23.24). Of course, as a converted Jew, and perhaps even a former rabbi, Matthew certainly knew enough about Jewish law and custom to enable him to have written the passage from an *extra muros* standpoint. However, the kind of knowledge of and attitude towards such practices evident in this chapter does not suggest that it was written by an outsider. There is no question that gnats need to be strained or that phylacteries need to be worn; mint dill and cummin need to be tithed and oaths need to have the right form; converts need to be won and cups need to be cleaned; the scribes and Pharisees rightly sit upon the seat of Moses in the synagogue and need to be obeyed. The altar sanctifies the gift and God dwells in the temple. What is in question here is not the efficacy or correctness of the Jewish way of life in general, but the form that way of life should take in individual cases.

---

1. The force of this argument is somewhat weakened by the story of Elisha ben Abuya as recounted in *y. Hag.* 77b. According to the Talmud passage, Elisha (c. 100–150 CE [*EncJud*, VI, p. 668]) was riding past the temple (i.e. the place where the Temple had once stood) on the day of atonement (which was also a Sabbath) when the voice of God came out proclaiming 'Return, O faithless children, except for Elisha b. Abuya, who knew my strength and rebelled against me'. But even though it is possible (though perhaps unlikely) that the saying found in Mt. 23.16-22 was created after 70 CE, its reasoning seems not to be that of Matthew himself, and it is surely in conflict with Mt. 23.38. See further E.P. Sanders, *Paul and Palestinian Judaism* (London: SCM Press, 1977), p. 180.

2. On the suggestion that the sacrificial cult continued even after 70 CE (though in a much reduced form) see K.W. Clark, 'Worship in the Jerusalem Temple after A.D. 70', *NTS* 6 (1960), pp. 269-80. Clark's arguments, even if accepted, do not seriously affect the observations made here, for as we have noted, the logic of Mt. 23.16-22 is certainly not that of Matthew. The passage might, with a certain amount of shoving and pushing, be squeezed into a post-70 CE hole; but it fits far better into pre-70 CE one.

It was noted above that Matthew's community had separated from the synagogue community, as is clearly seen by the evangelist's use of the phrase 'their synagogues'. This observation brings with it another, for in Mt. 23.6 we read 'and they love the place of honour at feasts and the best seats in *the* synagogues'. Here there is no hint of a separation between the author and the Jewish community at large. He speaks simply of 'the synagogues' and not, as is the case elsewhere, of 'their synagogues'. The author sits in a lesser seat in the same synagogue.[1]

Conclusions

If the arguments outlined above are accepted, it appears that there is a stark contrast within the Gospel of Matthew. On the one hand it is reasonably clear that there are several passages which speak in unequivocal terms of the rejection of the messiah by Israel and consequently of Israel's rejection by God. These passages are often harsh in the extreme (e.g. Mt. 27.15-23) and seem to indicate a belief that Israel is no longer the chosen nation of God. On the other hand, the Gentiles, who were not God's first choice, have now inherited the kingdom by default (Mt. 8.11; 21.33–22.10). Thus Clark is certainly right to point out a distinct Gentile bias in Matthew. But within the same gospel there are several passages which seem to point in the opposite direction. Matthew's Jesus is sent only to the house of Israel, a mission which will not be completed before the coming of the apocalyptic Son of Man (Mt. 10.5, 23, cf. Mt. 24.14; 28.19). The scribes and Pharisees need to be obeyed and tithe needs to be paid on garden produce (Mt. 23.2, 23). The altar sanctifies the gift and God dwells in the temple (Mt. 23.16-22). Material such as this is distinctly *intra muros*, though the author behind such sayings seems to have had a clear conception of the existence of his own smaller community within the mother faith (see also Mt. 23.8-12). In other places, too, there seems to be no real distinction between the author's community and Israel. While some of this material is dotted throughout several parts of the gospel, it is in the main concentrated in two large sections: the Sermon on the Mount and Matthew 23.

On the basis of this evidence an hypothesis suggests itself. Is it the case that at least part of Matthew 23 (i.e. vv. 2-31) stems from a *Sitz im*

---

1.   This is a point apparently missed by Saldarini in his 'Delegitimation of Leaders', for although he correctly notes that in Matthew generally the use of 'their synagogues' seems to suggest separation (from the synagogue at least) he fails to note that use of 'the' synagogue in Mt. 23.6.

Leben which is different from that of the final redaction of the whole Gospel? In this chapter a partial, tentative and affirmative answer to this question has already been given. In the next chapter an attempt is made to show that all the references to specific religious practice mentioned in Mt. 23.2-31, such as the wearing of 'tassels' and 'phylacteries' and the calling of religious leaders 'Rabbi' and 'master', are explicable in terms of a pre-70 CE *Sitz im Leben*. In Chapter 4 the hypothesis is tested further by offering a detailed exegesis of Matthew 23; and in Chapter 5 an attempt is made to tie together Matthew 23 and the Sermon on the Mount even more closely on the basis of linguistic and other evidence.

Chapter 3

PRE-70 CE JEWISH CUSTOMS AND PRACTICES IN MATTHEW 23

In Chapter 1 of this study we noted that for several reasons the material in Matthew 23 is problematic for the source critic. The passage is not easily explained either in terms of the standard source theories, or in terms of those theories which are not so standard. In Chapter Two we noted that the *Sitz im Leben* of the bulk of the chapter appears not to be that of the evangelist himself. Rather the passage seems to bear the marks of being the creation of a mind which was working in an *intra muros* context *vis-à-vis* Judaism; the temple still sanctifies the gift that is put upon it, mint is to be tithed, and the scribes and Pharisees (who love the best seats in *the* synagogues) are to be obeyed.

In an attempt to solve these problems, it has been suggested that Mt. 23.2-31 is composed of a single source. This source would appear to stem from a pre-70 CE *Sitz im Leben*, and in this it has close links with parts of the Sermon on the Mount. These links began to emerge when we looked at the occurrences of individual words, but they become even more apparent when the *Sitz im Leben* of Mt. 23.2-31 and that of the Sermon are compared. This single-document hypothesis seems able to explain not only the basic unity of the chapter, a feature for which the most common multiple-source theories seem unable to account, but also the apparent *intra muros* stance of the chapter *vis-à-vis* Judaism. The present chapter seeks to test this hypothesis further by closer examination of those practices and customs mentioned in Mt. 23.2-31. Are the references to 'Moses' Seat', the 'straining of gnats' and the tithing of 'mint, dill and cummin' explicable in terms of known pre-70 CE practice? And what of the 'scribes and Pharisees'? Is the place afforded to these individuals by the author of Mt. 23.2-31 plausible in the light of the historical evidence?

1. *Moses' Seat*

Scholarly opinion is divided as to whether the 'seat of Moses' mentioned in Mt. 23.2 is to be understood literally or figuratively. Beare, for example, thinks that the saying is metaphorical, and is merely a foil for what follows.[1] Hill, on the other hand, takes the saying literally: the reference is to a real seat upon which the Jewish leaders sat.[2]

In support of his position Hill refers to the work of E.L. Sukenik, who indeed has done much to make the possible context of Mt. 23.2 clearer. In his *Ancient Synagogues in Palestine and Greece*, Sukenik gives several examples of 'Chairs of Moses' found by archaeologists.[3] The first to be unearthed was that at Hammath-by-Tiberias; this seat was carved from a single block of white limestone and measures 94cm by 60cm. As might perhaps be expected, the chair was found with its back towards Jerusalem, meaning that the one who sat upon it would be facing the congregation.[4]

A better preserved 'seat of Moses' than that of Hammath-by-Tiberias comes from Chorazin. This seat too was carved from a single block of stone. The chair stands 56cm high and is 76cm wide. It originally had arm rests and a back.[5] On the front of the chair is an inscription which reads, according to Sukenik's translation, 'Remembered be for good Judan b. Ishmael, who made this στοά and its staircase. As his reward may he have a share with the righteous'.[6]

A third example comes from Delos, where, according to both Josephus (*Ant.* 10.8, 14) and first Maccabees (1 Macc. 15.23), a Jewish community was well entrenched. Belle Mazur has strongly argued that

1. Beare, *Matthew*, p. 448. See also France, *Matthew*, p. 324; Walter Grundmann, *Das Evangelium nach Matthäus* (THKNT, 1; Berlin: Evangelische Verlagsanstalt, 4th edn, 1975), p. 483; Lagrange, *Evangile selon Saint Matthieu*, p. 437.

2. Hill, *Matthew*, p. 310. See also Schlatter, *Matthäus*, p. 663; Fenton, *Matthew*, p. 366; Green, *Matthew*, p. 189; K. Stendahl in M. Black and H.H. Rowley (eds.), *Peake's Commentary on the Bible* (London: Thomas Nelson & Sons, 1962), p. 792; W.F. Albright and C.S. Mann, *Matthew* (AB; Garden City, NY: Doubleday, 1971), p. 278; Gundry, *Matthew*, pp. 453-54; Benoit, *Matthieu*, p. 139.

3. E.L. Sukenik, *Ancient Synagogues in Palestine and Greece* (The Schweich Lectures of the British Academy; London: Oxford University Press, 1934).

4. Sukenik, *Ancient Synagogues*, p. 58.

5. See the photographs accompanying J. Ory, 'An Inscription Newly Found in the Synagogue of Kerazeh', *PEFQS* (1927), pp. 51-52.

6. Sukenik, *Synagogues*, p. 60 n. 2.

the building uncovered at Delos is not in fact a synagogue,[1] and her arguments have convinced, among others, Cecil Roth.[2] Mazur points out that the building does not face Jerusalem but rather the northeast.[3] This factor alone, however, is not a sufficient support for Mazur's contentions, for as Andrew Seager has noted, not all synagogues faced Jerusalem.[4] More importantly, Mazur has failed to explain the numerous religious inscriptions found in the building.[5] Sukenik believes that the Delos building is a synagogue, and that it is probably one of the earliest known, perhaps dating back to the end of the second century BCE.[6] The marble seat found in the ruins may, therefore, be one of the oldest known examples of a seat of Moses and may help to set the context of Mt. 23.2.[7]

Whether these chairs were actually called 'seats of Moses' is not entirely clear. The literary evidence is thin indeed, for outside of Mt. 23.2 itself, the expression 'seat of Moses' seems not to be used in early Jewish sources. The earliest reference outside of the New Testament comes from *Pesikta de Rab Kahana*, which many authorities class amongst the earliest of the Midrashim, perhaps dating back to the fourth century CE.[8] The Pesikta passage in question refers to a Palestinian scholar by the name of Rabbi Aha, who, when explaining the biblical description of Solomon's throne, said that it was 'like the *Kathedra* of Moses' (קתדרא דמשה כהדא).[9] The suggestion made by M. Ginsburger that the reading of the Pesikta needs drastic emendation and that consequently

1. B. Mazur, *Studies on Jewry in Greece* (Athens, 1925), pp. 9, 15-22.

2. C. Roth, 'The "Chair of Moses" and its Survivals', *PEQ* 81 (1949), pp. 100-11.

3. Mazur, *Studies on Jewry*, p. 20.

4. A.R. Seager, 'Ancient Synagogue Architecture: An Overview', in J. Gutmann (ed.), *Ancient Synagogues: The State of Research* (BJS, 22; Chico, CA: Scholars Press, 1981), p. 41 and fig. 5.

5. P. Jean-Baptiste Frey, *Corpus Inscriptionum Judaicarum: Recueil des Inscriptions Juives qui Vont du IIIe Siècle avant Jésus-Christ au VIIe Siècle de notre Ère* (2 vols.; Rome: Pontificio Instituto di Archeologia Cristiana, 1936–52), I, pp. 525-26.

6. Sukenik, *Ancient Synagogues*, p. 40.

7. Sukenik, *Ancient Synagogues*, p. 61 gives a diagram of the seat.

8. *EncJud*, XIII, pp. 333-34; *JewEnc*, VIII, pp. 559-60.

9. S. Buber (ed.), *Pesikta de-Rab Kahana* (1868), § i., p. 12 (trans. W.G. Braude and I.J. Kapstein, *Pěsikta dě-Rab Kahǎna*; Philadelphia: Jewish Publication Society of America, 1975), p. 17.

the 'seat of Moses' never existed,[1] has not found favour among scholars, and, in the light of the archaeological discoveries made since Ginsburger's article appeared, his suggestion does indeed seem unnecessary.

It appears, therefore, that by the fourth or fifth centuries at the latest, 'the seat of Moses' was the name given to some actual artifact of Jewish life. But was this seat reserved for the leaders of the Jewish community, and did these teachers sit upon it in a literal sense?

Cecil Roth answers these questions in the negative, and his suggestions need careful examination. He points out that there exists in Rome a community of Jews which claims a continuous tradition going back to classical times, and that this community has a practice which may throw some light upon the problematic 'chair of Moses' mentioned in Mt. 23.2.[2] There are times during the synagogue service when the scroll of the law is not in use. The general custom among Jews is that when this is so, the scroll is held by an individual who has been appointed to this task. Roth points out that this custom is not followed in Rome, however. Instead, whenever the scroll of the law is not in direct use, it is placed upon a 'chair' which has been especially designed for this purpose, having holes drilled into the seat into which the staves of the scroll may be inserted in order to keep it in place. Roth is, of course, fully aware that the present Great Synagogue of Rome was built at the beginning of this century, and this particular seat can therefore hardly be used to illuminate the practices of first-century Judaism.[3] What must be noted, however, is that the basement of the present building houses several earlier examples of such chairs (the oldest bearing an inscription dated 1594),[4] all of which have similar holes bored in them and were therefore probably used for the same purpose.

Further evidence for Roth's hypothesis comes from the eighteenth-century Jews of China. In 1704 a Jesuit priest by the name of Jean-Paul Gozani visited a community of Jews at Kai-Feng-fu and published a description of their synagogue.[5] Among other details, Gozani mentions a 'chair of Moses'. The relevant passage reads as follows:

1. M. Ginsburger, 'La "Chaire de Moïse"', *REJ* 90 (1931), pp. 161-65.
2. Roth, 'Chair of Moses', pp. 103-104.
3. Roth, 'Chair of Moses', p. 104.
4. Roth, 'Chair of Moses', p. 104.
5. Roth, 'Chair of Moses', pp. 105-106; and see also M. Sulzberger, 'Encore Le Siège De Moïse', *REJ* 35 (1897), pp. 110-111.

Il y a au milieu de leur synagogue une chaire magnifique et fort élevée, avec un beau coussin brodé. C'est la Chaire de Moïse, dans laquelle les samedis (ce sont leurs dimanches) et les jours les plus solennels, ils mettent le Livre du Pentateuque, et font la lecture.[1]

This evidence does not stand alone, for Roth also notes that a later Jesuit priest, Gabriel Brotier (c. 1770), also recorded that it was the practice of the Jews of Kai-Feng-fu to place 'the Scriptures' on the chair after they had been read to the people.[2]

Roth's observations are important, though they may not prove decisive. We cannot be sure that the Jews of the Kai-Feng-fu synagogue themselves called this 'chair' the seat of Moses. Both the Jesuit priests may have been influenced in their understanding of the synagogue ornamentation by the passage from Matthew presently under discussion. It does, however, seem at least possible that in some Jewish communities some form of seat, possibly known as the 'chair of Moses', was used not as a place from which the law was read and expounded, but as a stand for the law-scroll itself. Whether this was the practice in first-century Palestine cannot be determined with certainty. It would be unwise to base any understanding of Mt. 23.2 on the data available from sixteenth-century Rome and eighteenth-century China. Furthermore, Roth himself notes that the 'chair of Moses' now evident in Rome is scarcely wide enough to enable anyone to sit upon it comfortably.[3] This is not the case, however, with the much larger chairs found at Chorazin, Hammeth-by-Tiberias and Delos.[4]

Finally, on an exegetical level, Roth's suggestion that the words of Mt. 23.2 are symbolic and that the phrase 'they sit on Moses' seat' merely points to intellectual arrogance,[5] must be viewed with suspicion, for, if such is the case, what do the words 'therefore do all that they tell you' mean? Is the meaning of Mt. 23.2 really that 'the scribes and the

---

1. Sulzberger, 'Le Siège', p. 110.
2. Roth, 'Chair of Moses', p. 106. For a much more complete account of the Jews of Kai Feng fu, including a discussion of the 'Seat of Moses' found in the synagogue (pp. 8, 13-15, 40, 43, 128), see W.C. White, *Chinese Jews: A Compilation of Matters relating to the Jews of K'ai fêng Fu* (Toronto: University of Toronto Press, 2nd edn, 1966), and M. Pollak, *Mandarins, Jews, and Missionaries: The Jewish Experience in the Chinese Empire* (Philadelphia: Jewish Publication Society of America, 1980).
3. Roth, 'Chair of Moses', p. 104.
4. See description in Sukenik, *Ancient Synagogues*, pp. 57-61.
5. Roth, 'Chair of Moses', p. 110.

Pharisees are intellectually arrogant, therefore you should obey them'? Is it not more probable that at one time the 'chair of Moses' was a seat at the front of the synagogue upon which teachers sat, and that the author of Mt. 23.2, believing that these characters were in some way authoritative expounders of the Torah, genuinely thought it the duty of all believers to obey their words? It may be that Mt. 23.2, and its context within the chapter, is itself the best evidence to support the literal understanding of the phrase 'chair of Moses' adopted here, though, as noted above, there is a certain amount of other data to support this understanding.

2. *Phylacteries*

In Mt. 23.5 the criticism is made of the scribes and the Pharisees that they 'make their phylacteries broad'. This criticism is perhaps best understood literally, and evinces the author's dislike of the scribes and the Pharisees who, in his opinion, make a show of their religion by unnecessary ostentation.[1]

It has become standard to equate 'phylacteries' with '*tefillin*', the small, usually black leather boxes which were bound to the left hand and to the forehead.[2] These boxes contained certain passages of Scripture (usually Exod. 13.1-10, 11-16; Deut. 6.4-9; 11.13-21, though there is evidence from Qumran that other passages were sometimes also included).[3] The wearing of *tefillin* was certainly an old institution by Rabbinic times, being based ultimately upon Exod. 13.9, 16; Deut. 6.4-9; 11.13-21. Already by the time of the Letter of Aristeas (dated variously between 200 BCE and 33 CE),[4] these commands were being interpreted literally, for v. 159 of this document states 'and upon our hands, too, he expressly orders the symbol to be fastened'[5] and perhaps also the book of Proverbs (dated c. 500–400 BCE)[6] contains allusions to *tefillin* (see Prov. 1.9; 3.3; 6.21; 7.3).

---

1.   See further below, pp. 127-29.

2.   E.g. Beare, *Matthew*, p. 449; Fenton, *Matthew*, pp. 366-67; Schlatter, *Matthäus*, pp. 668-69; Green, *Matthew*, p. 189.

3.   See S. Safrai and M. Stern (eds.), *The Jewish People in the First Century: Historical Geography, Political History, Social Cultural and Religious Life and Institutions* (2 vols.; Amsterdam: van Gorcum, 1974–76), II, pp. 799-800.

4.   *APOT*, II, pp. 85-87.

5.   *APOT*, II, p. 109.

6.   For a discussion on the date of the book of Proverbs see *IDB*, III, pp. 939-40.

There is evidence also from literature roughly contemporary with the New Testament. In *Ant.* 4.213 Josephus probably speaks of *tefillin* (and *mezuzoth*) when he refers to the practice of the wearing on arms (and the inscribing on doorposts) of 'the greatest of benefits which they [the Jews] have received from God'. Still further evidence may be gleaned from the findings at Qumran. These are not limited to the numerous examples of the parchments which were placed in the *tefillin*; boxes too have been discovered. This evidence is now widely available as a result of the work of J.T. Milik[1] and Karl Georg Kuhn.[2]

The practice of wearing *tefillin* was, therefore, certainly a part of the religious life of many first-century Jews. This being the case, it is hardly surprising that numerous references to *tefillin* are found in the Mishnah: *m. Ber.* 3.3 exempts women and slaves from the duty of wearing *tefillin*; *m. 'Erub.* 10.1 gives rulings concerning correct conduct should *tefillin* be found in a field on the Sabbath, and *m. Men.* 3.7 declares that each one of the four portions of Scripture placed in the *tefillin* may impair the validity of the others (see also *m. Ber.* 3.1; *m. Šab.* 6.2, 8.3, 16.1; *m. Shek.* 3.2; *m. Ned.* 2.2 *et al.*)

Thus if the φυλακτήρια of Mt. 23.5 does indeed refer to *tefillin*, the criticisms made in the verse are quite explicable in terms of an intra-Jewish debate. There is no question that *tefillin* should be worn, but they should not be made unnecessarily large.

John Bowman, however, has challenged the practice of equating Phylacteries with *tefillin*.[3] According to him 'this identification of phylacteries with Tefillin is quite wrong',[4] and he suggests rather that the Phylacteries of Mt. 23.5 are *qeme'in*, that is, 'amulets'.[5] George Fox has made similar remarks,[6] and I. Abrahams pointed out that it is

---

1. *Discoveries in the Judean Desert vi: Qumran Grotte 4*, pp. 33-37 and plates 6-25.

2. K.G. Kuhn, *Phylakterien aus Höhle 4 von Qumran* (Heidelberg: Abhandlungen der Heidelberger Akademie der Wissenschaften, 1957). See also J.M. Allegro, *The Dead Sea Scrolls* (Harmondsworth: Penguin Books, 1956), p. 175.

3. J. Bowman, 'Phylacteries', *SE*, I, pp. 523-38.

4. Bowman, 'Phylacteries', p. 523.

5. Bowman, 'Phylacteries', p. 532.

6. G.G. Fox, 'The Matthean Misrepresentation of Tephillîn', *JNES* 1 (1942), pp. 373-77. Fox suggests that Matthew has misunderstood the purpose of *tephillin*, thinking of them as little more than magical amulets, and thus uses φυλακτήρια a word not used by other authors to describe these components of Jewish religious regalia.

difficult to imagine how the criticism 'they make their phylacteries broad' could be applied to *tefillin*.[1]

Bowman's comments are certainly worth noting. He is right, for example, to point out that nowhere in early Jewish literature are *tefillin* called phylacteries. He is probably right also to note that the fact that Jews now call *tefillin* 'phylacteries' proves nothing, for it may be that this is simply an example of the Christian understanding of Mt. 23.5 influencing Jewish parlance.[2] Bowman claims that 'Rabbinic works from the Mishnah down, carefully distinguish between *tefillin* and phylacteries, which latter were called *qeme'in*. *Qeme'in* were phylacteries in the proper sense of the word, that is, 'amulets'. Bowman further points out that 'though Tefillin and $Q^e me'in$ are mentioned side by side in *m. Šab.* 6, 2, *m. Mik.* 6, 4, *m. Kel.* 23, 9, a clear distinction is made between them'.[3]

Concerning *m. Šab.* 6.2 Bowman is indeed correct. The text states that 'a man may not go out with...phylacteries [*tefillin*] or with an amulet [*Qame'a*] that has not been prepared by one who was skilled'. Bowman's other texts similarly support his general contention, since they too make a clear distinction between 'amulets' (*qeme'in*) and 'phylacteries' (*tefillin*), and one might note also *m. Šab.* 8.3, which states that 'he is culpable that takes out leather enough to make an amulet, or vellum enough to write on it the shortest passage in the phylacteries'. It seems highly likely, therefore, that the practice of wearing *tefillin* and that of wearing *qeme'in* developed independently from each other, and Bowman's contention that the phylacteries of Mt. 23.5 are *qeme'in* and not *tefillin* is at least possible.

However, several criticisms of Bowman's hypothesis need to be made. The most obvious of these is that just as no early Jewish source calls *tefillin* 'phylacteries', so too the same body of literature lacks any example of *qeme'in* being called by this Greek term. Those who think that the phylacteries of Mt. 23.5 refer to *tefillin* may at least claim some support, slight though it may be, from the use of the word 'phylactery' in later Judaism. Bowman, however, would have to suppose that although 'phylactery' was once used among early Greek-speaking Christian communities to refer to *qeme'in*, this terminology was later

1. I. Abrahams, *Studies in Pharisaism and the Gospels* (Cambridge: Cambridge University Press, 2nd series, 1924), pp. 203-205. Abrahams argued that the reference is to the straps of the *tephillin* rather than the boxes themselves.
2. Bowman, 'Phylacteries', p. 523.
3. Bowman, 'Phylacteries', p. 529.

dropped, and the word 'phylactery' reapplied to another part of the Jewish religious regalia, namely *tefillin*. This is possible, but unlikely.

It must also be noted that all the examples of *qeme'in* given by Bowman are late. The Mishnah provides his earliest evidence, and even here the references are not copious. No examples of *qeme'in* seem to have emerged from the caves of Qumran, and neither Philo nor Josephus makes any mention of them. Further, not only are the examples of *qeme'in* examined by Bowman late, but they are also Samaritan. Bowman states that there is 'every reason to believe that the Pharisees had phylacteries similar to those of the Samaritans', though he does not make clear exactly what these reasons are.[1]

All this having been said, it is still possible that Bowman is right. The 'phylacteries' of Mt. 23.5 may refer to some form of amulet worn by the Jews of the period, and not to *tefillin*. Amulets were a common enough feature of the ancient world,[2] and it is possible that they were known also to first-century Palestinian Judaism. The contention is purely hypothetical, however, and Bowman has almost certainly failed in his attempt to show that the identification of phylacteries with *tefillin* is 'quite wrong'. It might finally be noted that although no early Jewish source unequivocally calls *tefillin* 'phylacteries', a fairly early Christian source does call phylacteries *tefillin*. The Peshitta version of the New Testament (c. 450 CE) translates φυλακτήρια αὐτῶν in Mt. 23.5 as *tephlaihon*.

Thus it seems that Mt. 23.5 is quite explicable in terms of a pre-70 CE *Sitz im Leben* and that it is best understood as a literal condemnation of an actual practice. *Tefillin* should be worn, and there is no condemnation of this religious act. But they should not be over large.

3. *Tassels*

In Mt. 23.5 it is said that the scribes and the Pharisees 'make their tassels long'. To what does the word 'tassels' (κράσπεδα) refer, and was the wearing of these religious insignia a part of the religious life of the first-century Jew?

---

1.   Bowman, 'Phylacteries', p. 531; For further arguments against the views of Bowman and Fox see J.H. Tigay 'On the Term Phylacteries (Mt. 23.5)', *HTR* 72 (1979), pp. 45-53.

2.   See further G. Wissowa (ed.), *Paulys Real-Encyclopädie der Classichen Altertumswissenschaft*, I (Stuttgart: J.B. Metzlerscher Verlag, 1894), pp. 1984-89.

The wearing of 'tassels' (צִיצִית) is based upon the commandment of Num. 15.37-41 which states 'the Lord said to Moses "Speak to the people of Israel, and bid them to make tassels [צִיצִית, LXX κράσπεδα] on the corners of their garments throughout their generations..." '; Deut. 22.12 has similar injunctions.

Verse 158 of the Letter of Aristeas probably refers to *tsitsiyyot* in the words 'moreover, upon our garments he has given us a symbol of remembrance',[1] and there is some evidence also from the caves of the Judean desert that *tsitsiyyot* were worn by the Jews of the first century. Further evidence comes from the cave of letters, some of the contents of which have been dated to the bar-Kokhba period, where among other objects actual *tsitsiyyot* have been found.[2]

Extensive reference to *tsitsiyyot* is made in the talmudic literature. In *b. Men.* 43b, for example, we read 'Our Rabbis taught: Beloved are Israel, for the Holy One, Blessed be He, surrounded them with precepts. *Tefillin* on their heads, *tefillin* on their arms, *zizith* on their garments and *mezuzoth* on their door posts', and *b. Men.* 44a reports how a certain Jew was saved from committing a sin by the wearing of *tsitsiyyot*, and how this same act led to the conversion of a Gentile harlot. Other references to *tsitsiyyot* are found in *b. Men.* 43a, *b. Ber.* 47b, *b. Sot.* 22a.

Earlier than these talmudic references are those found in the Mishnah; *m. Men.* 3.7–4.1 is largely taken up with the question of whether the condition of one *tsitsith* can impair that of the others (see also *m. Kat.* 3.4, *m. 'Ed.* 4.10, *m. Mik.* 10.3.)

References to κράσπεδα are also found in the New Testament. Mark reports that wherever Jesus went in the villages and cities the sick were brought to him, beseeching him in order that they might touch his κράσπεδα and be made well (Mk 6.56 = Mt. 14.36), and Mt. 9.20 (= Lk. 8.44) tells of a certain woman who had been suffering from a haemorrhage who came up behind Jesus and touched the 'fringes' (κράσπεδα) of his garment. Mark does not have this particular detail, stating rather that the woman touched Jesus' ἱματίον (Mk 5.27, 28).

This evidence makes it reasonably clear that the practice of wearing *tsitsiyyot* was firmly entrenched in Judaism. The Letter to Aristeas and the Old Testament show that the origin of the practice pre-dates the fall of the temple. Mk 6.56, too, may lend further support, though naturally

---

1.   *APOT*, II, p. 109.
2.   Y. Yadin, *Judean Desert Studies: Finds from the Bar Kokhba Period in the Cave of Letters* (Jerusalem: Israel Exploration Society, 1963), pp. 182-88.

this depends upon the extent to which Mark's Gospel may be historically trusted. It is quite possible, therefore, that the criticism of Mt. 23.5
originated in a pre-70 CE context. Once again it may be noted that there
is no implicit or explicit condemnation of *tsitsiyyot per se*. *Tsitsiyyot*
should be worn, but the scribes and the Pharisees err in making them
too long, therefore, in the mind of the author, making a hypocritical
outward show of their religion.[1]

4. *Rabbi*

In Mt. 23.7 it is said that the scribes and the Pharisees love to be called
'Rabbi' by their contemporaries. In the context of the hypothesis
regarding Mt. 23.2-31 presented here, then, the question of whether the
title 'Rabbi' was in use before 70 CE is clearly of importance. As we
shall see, this question is difficult to answer either way.

The evidence from the New Testament itself is not to be discounted.
In addition to the two occurrences of 'Rabbi' in ch. 23, Matthew gives
two further examples (Mt. 26.25, 49); in both, however, the title appears
on the lips of Judas, and this may be the evangelist's own doing, a way
of avoiding Judas use 'Kyrios'. In any case, in both places the word
could be translated as 'Sir', and may not therefore have the pedagogical
connotation which the title seems to have in Mt. 23.7.

Luke does not use the word 'Rabbi' at all. There are three occurrences in Mark (Mk 9.5; 11.21; 14.45), but here too the word is somewhat ambiguous, and it would not be possible to argue on the basis of
the Marcan evidence alone that 'Rabbi' was a title of religious honour
used at the time of the production of Mark's Gospel. What may be said,
however, is that 'Rabbi' was known to Mark at least as a polite form of
address.

John is clear, however: for him 'Rabbi' means 'teacher', as he is careful to point out at Jn 1.38 where he translates ῥαββί with διδάσκαλε.
Furthermore, John has seven other occurrences of the word (1.49; 3.2,
26; 4.31; 6.25; 9.2; 11.8), suggesting that to him at least, if not to those
for whom he was writing, this title was already fairly well known. In Jn
3.2 Jesus is addressed as 'Rabbi' by a Jew who, we are told, knows that
Jesus has come 'as a teacher', and in Jn 9.2 the disciples ask Jesus
'Rabbi, who sinned, this man or his parents, that he was born blind?'
The clearly didactic intention of this passage suggests once again that

---

1.   See below, pp. 127-29.

John understands the word to mean 'teacher'.

The date of John is a matter of great debate, however. J.A.T. Robinson in *Redating the New Testament*[1] suggests an early date for John, perhaps as early as 65 CE, a position which he restates in his more recent book *The Priority of John*.[2] Less radical scholars place the Gospel somewhere between 85 CE and 100 CE.[3] Obviously this disagreement over the dating of John is of consequence here, and until this disagreement is resolved the fourth Gospel cannot be cited as evidence for pre-70 CE Jewish practice. What may be said, however, is that by at least 100 CE, 'Rabbi' was a title of honour given to those held to be important teachers.

But the New Testament evidence may perhaps be pressed a little harder, and in this context Hershel Shanks has made several important observations. First, he points out that the frequency with which the title 'Rabbi' appears in the gospels is itself strong evidence for its pre-70 CE use. He writes

> Surely this frequent appearance of the term [Rabbi] in the Gospels is more persuasive evidence that the title was in fact used at the time of Jesus than the absence of the term in pre-Destruction tannaitic literature is evidence that it was not used.[4]

And he may well be right, though he has been vigorously opposed by Solomon Zeitlin.[5] However, a major weakness of Zeitlin's counter argument is that it is largely based upon the fact that the early Tannaitic literature fails to call several important Jewish leaders and teachers 'Rabbi'. Strictly speaking this is not an argument from silence, for the Mishnah and other rabbinic literature do indeed mention individuals like Hillel and Shammai, but do not call them 'Rabbi'. However, this silence cannot by itself nullify the New Testament witness, for, as Shanks points out,[6] the Dead Sea Scrolls excepted, there is virtually no surviving

---

1. Robinson, *Redating the New Testament*, p. 307.

2. J.A.T. Robinson, *The Priority of John* (London: SCM Press, 1985), p. 67.

3. E.g. B. Lindars, *The Gospel of John* (NCB; London: Marshall Morgan & Scott, 1972), p. 42; W.G. Kümmel, *Introduction to the New Testament* (trans. H.C. Kee; London: SCM Press, rev. edn, 1975), p. 246.

4. H. Shanks, 'Is the Title "Rabbi" Anachronistic in the Gospels?', *JQR* 53 (1963), p. 342.

5. S. Zeitlin, 'A Reply', *JQR* 53 (1963), pp. 345-49. See also *EncJud*, XIII, p. 1445.

6. Shanks, 'Title Rabbi', p. 340.

Hebrew or Aramaic literature between the period c. 167 BCE and 130 CE; consequently it is difficult in the extreme to assess any development in the use of the term 'Rabbi' that there might have been during this period.

Zeitlin's reply to Shanks is perhaps somewhat high-handed; it is also unconvincing. Zeitlin maintains that Shanks has 'lost his way'[1] among the forest of Rabbinic literature, and is in fact in a state of 'total confusion'.[2] Shanks's statement that 'there is no original extant Hebrew or Aramaic literature between c. 167 B.C. and c. 130 C.E.', displays, according to Zeitlin, 'an utter lack of knowledge',[3] as does his remark that Rabban Gamaliel the Elder 'was active in the last decades before and shortly after the destruction of the Second Temple'.[4]

It cannot be denied that Shanks was almost certainly wrong to suggest that Rabban Gamaliel the Elder was alive after 70 CE.[5] Zeitlin's other criticisms, however, seem less sound, and in general Zeitlin has failed to undermine the central thrust of Shank's arguments. Zeitlin seeks to deny the evidence from the gospel of John by stating that 'it is a historical fact...that the gospel, according to John, was composed not earlier than the middle of the Second Century C.E.'.[6] It hardly needs to be pointed out that few scholars would agree with this rather dogmatic statement, especially since many would date $\mathfrak{P}^{52}$, a MS which contains a fraction of John's Gospel, to the first half of the second century.[7] Consequently, the evidence from John deserves a hearing.

On a redaction-critical level, too, the use of the term 'Rabbi' in the

---

1. Zeitlin, 'A Reply', p. 349.
2. Zeitlin, 'A Reply', p. 348.
3. Zeitlin, 'A Reply', pp. 348-49.
4. Zeitlin, 'A Reply', p. 348.
5. Shanks, 'Title Rabbi', pp. 338-39, 339 n. 7. In a later article Shanks objected that he had not stated as an historical fact that Gamaliel lived after 70 CE, but had merely taken this position for the sake of the argument. (See 'Origins of the Title "Rabbi"' *JQR* 60 [1969], pp. 152-57). But Shanks's statement that 'the first person to bear the title "Rabban" was Gamaliel the Elder (traditionally a son or grandson of Hillel), who was active in the last decades before and shortly after the destruction of the Seond [*sic*] Temple' ('Title "Rabbi"', pp. 338-39) does not look like a position taken *arguendo*. See further the discussion in R.E. Brown, *The Gospel according to John* (AB; 2 vols.; Garden City, NY: Doubleday, 1966–70), I, p. 74.
6. Zeitlin, 'A Reply', p. 347.
7. For a brief discussion of $\mathfrak{P}^{52}$ and other early MSS of John see Brown, *John*, I, pp. LXXXII-LXXXIII.

Gospels is difficult to understand unless the title was indeed used at some time before the final redaction of the Gospels. Is it really the case that John inserted into his text a title which apparently was unknown to at least some of his proposed audience (see Jn 1.38; 20.16)? Similarly, why should John, convinced as he was that the gospel was now for the Gentiles (the Jews having through their own hardness of heart lost their place of primacy in God's plan for salvation) invent material in which Jesus was referred to as 'Rabbi', a Hebrew/Aramaic term likely to confuse some Gentiles, if not cause offence to others?

Brown notes that the use of the title 'Rabbi' in John follows a distinct pattern, the term being used almost exclusively in 'the Book of Signs' (Jn 1–12), while in 'the Book of Glory' (Jn 13–20) the title '*Kyrios*' comes to the fore.[1] But this observation does not mean that 'Rabbi' in John is purely redactional, for at the resurrection, the point at which the reader might expect to find an emphatic statement of faith on the part of Mary, Jesus is referred to ('in Hebrew') as 'Rabboni' (Jn 20.16). Has John really invented this saying, which he knows many will not understand? Or is it more probably the case that he found it already in his tradition? And even if John is ignored, there is still the evidence, thin though it may be, from Matthew and Mark. Zeitlin has made no convincing response to Shanks's arguments *vis-à-vis* these texts. On balance, therefore, it seems that Shanks is correct. Certainly, the title 'Rabbi' could not have been common among first-century Jews, and neither, perhaps, was it official. But the New Testament itself strongly suggests that it was known. The fact that none of the early first-century sages such as Hillel and Shammai are ever referred to as 'Rabbi' in the Tannaitic material, does not totally exclude the possibility that the title was used unofficially.

Shanks's discussion is somewhat more ambitious than the present study requires, for, whereas he seeks to show that 'Rabbi' was a title used in Jesus' day, the concern here is to show only that it was in existence before the destruction of the temple. To this extent one further point needs to be made.

Zeitlin was probably right to discount the tenth-century letter written by Sherira Gaon to the community of Kairwan in which Sherira recounts the history of the title 'Rabbi', 'Rabban' and 'Rab'; for, as Zeitlin notes, a tenth-century letter is hardly to be used as evidence of

---

1. Brown, *John*, I, p. 75.

first-century practice.[1] Nevertheless, the letter may provide one further clue, a clue which is supported by the Mishnah. In the letter, Sherira states that the first person to be given the title 'Rabban' was Gamaliel the Elder[2] who, as noted above, probably died before 70 CE. It may be impossible to tell whether Rabban Gamaliel the Elder received his title during his life, or whether it was added to his name posthumously. According to Danby's index, Rabban Gamaliel the first appears in the Mishnah several times (*m. Pe'ah* 2.6; *m. 'Or.* 2.12; *m. Shek.* 3.3; 6.1; *m. Roš Haš.* 2.5; *m. Yeb.* 16.7; *m. Soṭ.* 9.15; *m. Giṭ.* 4.2, 3; *m. Ab.* 1.16), but these references may simply reflect later accretion of the title to Gamaliel's name. Alternatively, the Mishnah may indicate that Gamaliel the Elder was one of the first to be called 'Rabban', and that he was known by this title during his life. It is therefore quite possible that 'Rabban' was known before 70 CE, and if 'Rabban', then probably also 'Rabbi', since the two titles are plainly interdependent.

Neither is it necessary for us to establish that 'Rabbi' was used as a special religious title reserved for ordained scholars, for as Brown has noted,[3] and as seems obvious from the text itself, the use of 'Rabbi' in Mt. 23.8 may mean simply 'teacher' (as in Jn 1.38; 20.16). This may be the sense in which it is used also in Mt. 23.7.[4]

Finally, there is also a certain amount of archaeological evidence that needs to be taken into consideration. From the end of the first century CE, 'Rabbi' appears on numerous Jewish inscriptions. A second-century inscription from Joppa, for example, reads. 'This is the tomb of Youdan, son of Rabbi [בירבי) Tarphon the teacher. Peace to his soul, what a blessing is his remembrance! Peace'.[5] A further example comes from El-Hammeth, where the shorter form 'Rab' is used. According to Frey's reconstruction, the inscription reads. 'And blessed be the memory of Rab Tanhum, the Levite, son of Halipha'.[6]

1.　Zeitlin, 'A Reply', p. 345.

2.　Shanks, 'Title Rabbi', p. 338.

3.　Brown, *John*, I, p. 74.

4.　On the suggestion that none of the uses of 'Rabbi' in the Synoptic Gospels reflects its use as a title at the time of Jesus, see also J. Donaldson, 'The Title Rabbi in the Gospels-Some Reflections on the Evidence of the Synoptics', *JQR* 62 (1972–73), pp. 287-91. Donaldson's argument is that all examples may be simply polite forms of address, though, conceivably, the later evangelists may have understood 'Rabbi' as found in their sources as a title.

5.　Frey, *Corpus*, II, p. 120.

6.　Frey, *Corpus*, II, p. 97.

Further evidence may come in the form of an ossuary found by E.L. Sukenik on the Mount of Olives, though here, since the inscription is in Greek, the case is more difficult to judge.[1] The ossuary, which Sukenik dates before the destruction of the temple, has upon it an inscription which clearly uses the Greek word διδάσκαλος as a title. Shanks reminds his readers that this Greek word is the exact one used by John in his explanation of 'Rabbi' ('Rabboni') in Jn 1.38 and 20.16, and this fact should not go unnoticed. If διδάσκαλος was known as a title before 70 CE, as seems highly likely, then 'Rabbi' may well also have been, since, at least to John, and possibly to other gospel writers, the two titles were somewhat synonymous.

Thus it seems that it is quite possible that the title 'Rabbi' was known, although its use as a title of religious honour was not widely used before 70 CE (neither Josephus nor Philo uses the word). The evidence is far from unequivocal, however, but while we cannot be certain that the title 'Rabbi' was used before 70 CE, we likewise cannot be certain that it was not. The silence of the Mishnah, Josephus and Philo must be taken into account. The New Testament, however, seems to pull in the opposite direction. In fact Mt. 23.7 may itself be one of the earliest examples of the use of this appellation. Indeed, the criticism may in part be motivated by an innate conservatism, and a reaction against the increasing use of this new title of honour.

5. *Father*

The very title of tractate Aboth provides evidence for the use of 'Father' as a title of esteem in later rabbinic Judaism. In addition to this general observation *m. 'Ed.* 1.4 needs to be noted, for here both Shammai and Hillel are called 'fathers of the world'. Neither should it go unnoticed that several important figures in first and second-century Judaism regularly had 'Abba' prefixed to their names: Abba Eleazer ben Dolai (Dulai) (c. 10–80 CE),[2] appears in *m. Mik.* 2.10, and other persons such as Abba Hilkiah (first century CE)[3] and Abba Saul Ben Batanit (first century CE)[4] are also known. The use of 'Abba' as an

---

1. Shanks, 'Title Rabbi', pp. 343-45.
2. Dates according to Danby, *Mishnah*, p. 799.
3. *EncJud*, II, p. 35.
4. *EncJud*, II, pp. 40-41.

epithet of these men is not, Dalman argued,[1] interchangeable with the proper name 'Abba', and in this he has the support of Jastrow, who gives as one explanation of אבי 'a title of scholars (less than Rabbi), as A. Saul, A. Yudan etc'.[2]

The New Testament itself may also be of some help. Luke obviously knew the title 'Father', for he reports both Stephen and Paul as using it of earthly persons (Acts 7.2; 22.1). But the roots may go back still further, for in *4 Maccabees*, a book which most scholars date pre-70 CE,[3] Eleazer is unequivocally referred to as 'Father' in several places, (*4 Macc.* 7.1, 5, 9). The Old Testament too furnishes a few examples: in 2 Kgs 2.12, for example, אבי (LXX πάτερ), is found upon the lips of Elisha who calls out after Elijah 'My Father, my Father' (see also 2 Kgs 6.21 and 13.14).

On balance, therefore, it seems that 'father' was known as a title of honour in first-century Judaism. And indeed, as *4 Maccabees* and the Old Testament show, the title almost certainly predates the fall of the temple.

6. *Master*

The third title prohibited to the disciples is that of 'Master' (καθηγητής). As with 'Rabbi' and 'Father' we must ask the question whether this title was in use in the pre-70 CE period.

The word καθηγητής does not appear elsewhere in the New Testament, nor in the LXX, Josephus or Philo; καθηγητής is, however, found in classical literature; Plutarch (first/second century CE) uses it of Aristotle;[4] Numenius Apamensis (second century CE) also gives one example;[5] and the form καθηγονος appears in earlier writers such as Herodotus (fifth century BCE), Polybius (second century BCE) and Philodemus (first century BCE).[6] Most recently Bruce Winter has drawn

---

1.   G. Dalman, *The Words of Jesus Considered in the Light of Post-Biblical Jewish Writings and the Aramaic Language* (trans. D.M. Kay; Edinburgh: T. & T. Clark, 1902), p. 339 n. 1.

2.   M. Jastrow, *A Dictionary of the Targumim, the Talmud Babli and Yerushalmi, and the Midrashic Literature* (2 vols.; New York: Judaica Press, 1975), I, p. 2.

3.   *APOT*, II, p. 654; H. Anderson in J.H. Charlesworth (ed.), *The Old Testament Pseudepigrapha* (2 vols.; New York: Doubleday, 1983–85), II, p. 533.

4.   BAGD, pp.388-89.

5.   LSJ, p. 852.

6.   LSJ, p. 852.

attention to P. Oxy. 2190 (first century CE), where the term is found with the meaning of 'tutor', a meaning to which, according to Winter, the occurrence in Mt. 23.10 also testifies.[1]

The title καθηγητής was, therefore, certainly known in the ancient world prior to the destruction of the temple of Jerusalem, and thus its use in Mt. 23.10 is not contradictory to the thesis presented here that this section of the gospel predates 70 CE. Possible Hebrew and Aramaic equivalents of the Greek word are known to have been used as titles in rabbinic Judaism. Dalman,[2] for example, argued that the word translates רבי and that Mt. 23.10 is in fact another recension of Mt. 23.8. Strack and Billerbeck make several other suggestions such as פרנס (פרנסא) and מנהיג, (see *b. Ber.* 28a; *b. Bat.* 91a).[3]

C. Spicq makes an interesting point when he suggests that Mt. 23.10 is, in part at least, an allusion to the Teacher of Righteousness known to the Qumran sectarians.[4] Spicq's suggestion remains little more than justifiable speculation, but his observation that the followers of the Teacher of Righteousness called him 'Master' (מורה)[5] may perhaps throw some light upon the possible context of Mt. 23.10. One should not call any teacher by an honorific name, for such appellation detracts from the greatness of God and the authority of Christ.

In this context a passage from the *Antiquities of the Jews* is also worth noting, for in this passage (18.23-25), Josephus speaks of a fourth 'philosophy' known among the Jews which had a certain Judas the Galilean as its leader.[6] This φιλόσοφος, which agreed in many of its tenets with the Pharisees, had 'a passion for liberty that is almost unconquerable'. The adherents of this 'philosophy', Josephus reports, were convinced that God alone was leader (ἡγεμόνος) and master (δεσπότην), and consequently they thought 'little of submitting to death in the unusual forms and permitting vengeance to fall on kinsmen and friends if only they may avoid calling any man master (δεσπότην)'. Such records show how seriously some Jewish sectarians took the

1.   B.W. Winter, 'The Messiah as the Tutor: The Meaning of καθηγητής in Matthew 23:10', *TynBul* 42 (1991), pp. 152-57.

2.   Dalman, *Words of Jesus*, p. 340. Dalman is not alone in this suggestion, Garland, *Matthew 23*, p. 60 n. 99 gives several other references.

3.   Str–B, I, pp. 919-20.

4.   C. Spicq, 'Une Allusion au Docteur de Justice dans Matthieu, XXIII,10?', *RB* 66 (1959), pp. 387-96.

5.   Spicq, 'Une Allusion?', p. 393, CD 20.28.

6.   Died c. 6 CE (*EncJud*, X, pp. 354-55).

question of whether earthly powers should be referred to by using titles of honour normally reserved for God. It appears that the author of Mt. 23.10 had similar scruples.

7. Proselytes[1]

Mt. 23.15 reads: 'Woe to you scribes and Pharisees, hypocrites! for you traverse sea and land to make a single proselyte, and when he becomes a proselyte, you make him twice as much a child of hell as yourselves'. It is argued below that this woe is to be taken literally, and that the scribes and the Pharisees come under attack for ruining their good work of proselytizing by turning their converts into 'sons of hell'.[2] Was proselytization an activity engaged in by these Jewish religious groups prior to 70 CE?

There are numerous references to proselytes (גר) in the Old Testament: Exod. 12.48, for example, reports that any 'stranger' who sojourns in the land of Israel and desires to keep the passover should be circumcised. Once this has been done, the stranger is to be thought of as a 'native of the land'. Similarly, Isa. 14.1 foretells of a time when 'The Lord will have compassion on Jacob and will again choose Israel...and aliens (הגר) will join them and will cleave to the house of Jacob'; Esther 8.17 records how 'many from the peoples of the country declared themselves Jews' (see also Isa. 56.3, 6; Ruth 2.11-12).

In the New Testament too several references to 'proselytes' and also to 'God-fearers' occur, most notably in the book of Acts. Acts 13.43 perhaps provides the clearest example in stating that after a synagogue meeting had broken up 'many Jews and devout converts to Judaism (προσηλύτων) followed Paul and Barnabus, who spoke to them and urged them to continue in the grace of God'. Furthermore, Acts 10.22

---

1.   See generally M. Simon, *Verus Israel: A Study of the Relations between Christians and Jews in the Roman Empire (135–42)* (trans. H. McKeating; Oxford: Oxford University Press, 1986), ch. 10. His n. 1 on p. 271 gives several further bibliographical references. Simon argues that Judaism was and remained a pros-elytizing religion even after the fall of the temple. The chapter is littered with refer-ences to primary sources. The present task is less ambitious than Simon's, for whereas he seeks to show that proselytism took place in the period after 70 CE, the concern here is only with the pre-70 CE situation. In fact, as Simon notes (p. 271), those who argue that later Judaism did not actively engage in proselytism, see the fall of Jerusalem as marking the point at which the religion began to withdraw into itself.

2.   Below, pp. 135-37.

speaks of a certain man named Cornelius who was 'a centurion, an upright and God-fearing man, who is well spoken of by the whole Jewish nation' (see also Acts 2.10-11; 6.5; 10.2; 13.16, 26).

Josephus also speaks of proselytes and God-fearers: in *Apion* 2.123, for example, he reports that many Greeks adopted the Jewish laws, of whom some remained faithful, while others who lacked endurance reverted to former ways. Further information regarding proselytes to Judaism is found in *Apion* 2.282 which reads

> The masses have long since shown a keen desire to adopt our religious observances; and there is not one city, Greek or barbarian, nor a single nation to which our custom of abstaining from work on the seventh day has not spread, and where the fasts and the lighting of lamps and many of our prohibitions in the matter of food are not observed.

As is well known, the royal family of the Herods was, to the embarrassment of many, descended from proselytes, and Josephus records how a certain court historian, Nicholas of Damascus, tried to cover up this lineage and give Herod Jewish ancestry (*Ant.* 14.9).

Roman historians too mention Jewish proselytes: Juvenal (died c. 127 CE) speaks of them rather disdainfully, saying that certain of his fellow Romans had adopted the ways of the Jews. Consequently they think it a great crime to eat pork, and they 'get themselves circumcised, and look down on Roman law, preferring instead to learn and honour and fear Jewish commandments'.[1] Similarly, there are numerous references to proselytes in rabbinic literature (see for example *m. Pe'ah* 4.6; *m. Dem* 6.10; *m. Šeb.* 10.9; *m. Hal.* 3.6).

It would seem, therefore, that proselytizing was an activity engaged in by the Jews of the first century, but recently Martin Goodman has seriously challenged this hypothesis.[2] He points out that the acceptance of proselytes is not the same thing as actively seeking them out and maintains that all the material amassed by those who seek to show that

---

1. Juvenal, *The Sixteen Satires* (trans. P. Green; Harmondsworth: Penguin Books, 1976), p. 266. For further Roman references see Simon, *Verus Israel*, pp. 280-82.

2. M. Goodman 'Jewish Proselytizing in the First Century', in J. Lieu, J. North and T. Rajak (eds.), *The Jews among Pagans and Christians* (London: Routledge, 1992), pp. 53-78. See also S. McKnight, *A Light among the Gentiles: Jewish Missionary Activity in the Second Temple Period* (Minneapolis, MN: Fortress Press, 1991).

the Jews of the first century were a proselytizing race is explicable in terms of passive acceptance.

It is not necessary for us to attempt to counter the arguments of Goodman here, for Goodman himself offers a convincing exegesis of Mt. 23.15, which is both in keeping with his overall comments and consistent with the work presented in this study. Certainly, Mt. 23.15 seems to be at odds with Goodman's proposals, for it clearly states that the scribes and Pharisees cross 'land and sea' to make a convert, which seems to imply great missionary zeal. Unlike some other scholars, Goodman does not seek to explain this as a reference to one single incident,[1] but rather presents the much more plausible hypothesis that it refers to the practice of the Pharisees in seeking Jewish converts to pharisaism. As he notes, this view was proposed briefly by Munck,[2] but Goodman himself deals with the topic much more thoroughly.

Whether we accept the arguments of Goodman or the majority is of little direct relevance here. The conclusion is the same: Mt. 23.15 is quite explicable in terms of pre-70 CE Jewish practice.

8. *Oath Forms*

Mt. 23.16-22 contain what may be described loosely as a 'squabble' over oath forms. The scribes and the Pharisees say that an oath taken by the temple or by the altar is not to be considered absolutely binding, but to swear by the gold of the temple or the gift upon the altar is a valid oath form and the one who takes it is therefore bound by his oath. The author of the passage, on the other hand, is stricter; oaths taken by any one of a number of different objects are binding upon the individual. Is this passage consistent with pre-70 CE Jewish practice?

Once again the Mishnah may be of help, for it contains several references to debates such as the one witnessed in Mt. 23.16-22. No exact parallels are found, but the following are clearly in the same vein.

> If a man said, 'I adjure you', or 'I command you', or 'I bind you', they are liable. But if he said, 'By heaven and by earth', they are exempt. If he adjured them 'by *Aleph-Daleth*' or 'by *Yod-He*' or 'by Shaddai' or 'by Sabaoth' or 'by the Merciful and Gracious' or 'by him that is long-suffering and of great kindness', or by any substituted name, they are liable (*m. Šeb.* 4.13)

1.   Cf. J. Munck, *Paul and the Salvation of Mankind* (trans. F. Clarke; London: SCM Press, 1959), p. 266.

2.   Munck, *Paul*, p. 267; the suggestion was also made by Allen, *Matthew*, p. 246.

If [a man] vowed by any of the utensils of the Altar, although he did not utter the word *Korban*, an offering, it is a vow as binding as if he had uttered the word *Korban*. R. Judah says: If he said, 'May it be Jerusalem!' he has said naught (*m. Ned.* 1.3)

Garland makes several interesting and important points regarding the halakhic context of Mt. 23.16-22.[1] His work is based largely upon that of Lieberman, who has himself made an extensive study of oaths and vows in rabbinic literature.[2] Lieberman concludes that the rabbis made every effort to correct the misunderstanding and malpractice of the unlearned masses. The populace tended, he argues, to view all oath forms as binding, regardless of the object by which they were taken. He gives the example of an oath being taken 'by the life of a fig-picker'.[3] The rabbis maintained that only oaths involving the word שבועה or the Divine Name were truly binding.[4] The question to be asked when considering the validity of an oath was, then, whether it contained the name of the Lord. Thus an oath taken 'by the altar' did not have legal force for it did not involve the name of the Lord. The same was true of an oath taken 'by the temple'.

There was one exception to this general rule. An oath taken by '*Korban*' was considered valid, and the one who swore 'by *Korban*' was consequently bound by his oath.[5] This perhaps helps to explain the background to Mt. 23.16-22. The teaching of the scribes and the Pharisees is completely understandable against the kind of background sketched in by Lieberman, for, as Garland notes

in vv. 16 and 18 the Temple gold and the altar gift were binding as part of an oath because they were connected with the term *Korban*, while the Temple and the altar, though holy objects, were illegitimate substitutes in an oath formula.[6]

Thus the context of Mt. 23.16-22 seems reasonably clear. It is an early outbreak of an argument over oath-formulas between the scribes and the Pharisees (who limited the number of binding oath formulas to those

1. Garland, *Matthew 23*, pp. 132-36.
2. S. Lieberman, *Greek in Jewish Palestine: Studies in the Life and Manners of Jewish Palestine in the II-IV Centuries CE* (New York: Jewish Theological Seminary of America, 1942).
3. Garland, *Matthew 23*, p. 134.
4. Garland, *Matthew 23*, p. 134.
5. Garland, *Matthew 23*, p. 135 n. 43 for the main references.
6. Garland, *Matthew 23*, p. 135.

which specifically mentioned God or 'Korban') and a stricter group who felt that any oath was binding. This argument continued, as is evidenced by its appearance in rabbinic texts, into later Judaism.

9. Tithing

Many commentators have drawn attention to Mt. 23.23, suggesting that the statement 'you tithe mint and dill and cummin' evinces the actual practice of the scribes and Pharisees who go further than the written law actually requires.[1] Hill, for example, states that 'tithing of vegetables and spices was probably over and above what was required by the Law (Dt. 14.22-23)'.[2] In Lev 27.30-33, however, a very extensive tithing law is found. According to this passage, 'all the tithe of the land, whether of the seed of the land or of the fruit of the trees, is the Lord's...and all the tithe of the herds and the flocks, every tenth animal of all that pass under the herdsman's staff, shall be holy to the Lord'. Similarly, the command found in Deut. 14.22 'you shall tithe all the yield of your seed, which comes forth from the field year by year', naturally led to debate over which plants exactly fell under the category of 'your seed'.

It is argued below that the criticism of Mt. 23.23 is not that the scribes and Pharisees tithe, since tithing is an ordinance of God and should be obeyed. Rather, the scribes and Pharisees come under attack for their negligence of even more important matters of the law such as justice, mercy and faith.[3] Is it the case then that the scribes and Pharisees of the first century CE tithed 'mint, dill and cummin'?

The Mishnah may be of help here, though as always the extent to which it reflects the practices of the first century is debatable. In *m. Ma'as.* 4.5 the statement 'from dill the seeds, plant, and pods, must be tithed' is attributed to Rabbi Eliezer (c. 90 CE), though on this point 'the sages' disagree, thinking that both seeds and plant are tithable only in the case of pepperwort and eruca. Cummin is mentioned in *m. Dem.* 2.1, which reads, 'tithe must everywhere be given from these things as being *demai*-produce; fig-cake, dates, carobs, rice and cummin'. That this was a matter of some debate is indicated in *m. 'Ed.* 5.3 where Rabbi Simeon (vl. Ishmael) states that those of the school of Shammai were

---

1.   E.g. Hill, *Matthew*, pp. 312-13; Beare, *Matthew*, p. 455; Fenton, *Matthew*, p. 373; Green, *Matthew*, p. 191.

2.   Hill, *Matthew*, pp. 312-13.

3.   Below, pp. 140-42.

more lenient than the school of Hillel in three particular matters, one of which concerns black cummin, which the school of Shammai declared insusceptible to uncleanness and thought that it was not liable to tithing. The school of Hillel, on the other hand, thought black cummin both susceptible to uncleanness and subject to tithe law.

Nothing is said directly concerning mint, though the disagreements concerning tithes found in the Mishnah suggest that laws governing this aspect of Jewish life were far from settled. This uncertainty makes it quite possible that mint was tithed, at least by some. The scribes and the Pharisees, being strict in matters pertaining to the law, may well have practiced the tithing of even mint.

It is also worth noting that the whole debate is most explicable within a Palestinian context, for, it seems, the tithe laws were not generally applied outside of the holy land. There is some evidence that this geographical limitation was occasionally overlooked with respect to some tithes; thus the Old Testament prophets held that tithing was necessary also in Babylon, and some of the earlier rabbis thought that certain tithes should be paid also in Egypt, Ammon and Moab, and also on produce sold in Syria.[1] There is no way of knowing, however, if these opinions were followed.

The criticism of Mt. 23.23 is, therefore, quite explicable within a firmly Jewish context, though the rebuke cannot be pinned down as definitely pre-70 CE. The scribes and the Pharisees have a conservative understanding of Deut. 14.22, and consequently tithe even mint, dill and cummin. This practice is laudable and ought to be done (Mt. 23.23b), but the scribes and the Pharisees err in neglecting other, more important, matters.

10. *Gnat-Straining*

Mt. 23.24 makes the further criticism of the scribes and Pharisees that while straining out gnats, they swallow camels. Both of these creatures were unclean, according to Levitical law (see Lev 11.4, 41), and the

---

1. According to *m. Yad.* 4.3, for example, Rabbi Tarphon (c. 120–140 CE) thought that Ammon and Moab must pay the poor man's tithe in the seventh year. Rabbi Eleazer b. Azariah (c. 80–120 CE) thought that the same countries must pay the second tithe. So, too, *m. Dem.* 6.11 states that if a man sold produce in Syria it ought to be tithed, even if he said 'It is of my own growing'. See further *JewEnc*, XII, p. 151.

intention of the woe seems to be to highlight the failure of the scribes
and Pharisees to do all that the law required. They correctly strain out
real gnats, but swallow metaphorical camels.

That gnats (κώνωψ) were common enough in the ancient world is
indicated by the numerous references to them in classical literature.
Aristotle mentions them several times, as do Aschylus and Herodotus.[1]
Little wonder, therefore, if those who were strict regarding matters of
the law should take the precaution of straining liquids before drinking
them. Indeed, it may well have been the case that the scribes and the
Pharisees had strainers always to hand, for according to Lev. 11.32-35 if
the carcass of an unclean animal came into contact with a liquid, then
the liquid was rendered unclean. Should a gnat fall into a wine, then, the
gnat had to be extracted before it died. Straining dead gnats would not
have been enough, for once it had been in contact with the corpse of a
gnat, the wine would be unclean.

This biblical law is expanded somewhat in the Mishnah. In *m. Makš.*
1.1-2, for example, we read that there was particular discussion
concerning when the regulation 'If he put water on...' applied. In Lev.
11.37 it is stated that if seed were dry and the body of an unclean animal
fell upon it, the seed would still be clean. If, however, water had been
put on the seed and the same body should fall upon it, the seed would
then be contaminated.

According to the Mishnah passage, the crucial question was whether
the seed had been made wet intentionally. Thus if a person was shaking
a tree with the specific intention of bringing down fruit, and if in this
process water should fall upon the fruit, the law 'If he put water on...'
did not apply. If, however, the intention in shaking the tree was to bring
down drops of rain, then the rule 'If he put water on...' does indeed
apply. Thus fruit which had been shaken down from a tree and which
had accidentally become wet in the process and had then come into
contact with the body of an unclean animal, was not considered unclean.
Fruit which had fallen as a by-product of a man's effort to shake down
water would be counted as unclean, however, if it then came into
contact with a corpse. This discussion shows a distinct interest in the
Levitical laws pertaining to contact between animal corpses and liquid,
and it may safely be assumed that the same rabbis knew that dead gnats
made wine unclean. The saying 'you strain gnats' may, therefore, quite
plausibly refer to actual practice.

1.   BAGD, p. 462.

The Mishnah also refers to the practice of straining wine through a 'napkin' or 'basket', presumably to remove impurities (*m. Šab.* 20.2), and *b. Hor.* 11a specifically states that eating a flea or a gnat constitutes a transgression of the Torah, as does *b. 'Abod. Zar.* 26b. 'Strainers' are mentioned in *b. Šab.* 137b and *b. B. Bat.* 97b, though it is unclear what exactly such strainers were designed to strain.

It is therefore at least possible, perhaps even probable, that the practice of straining liquids to avoid accidental consumption of unclean insects and to prevent the liquid itself becoming unclean by corpse contact was one known to stricter members of Jewish society in the first century CE. The evidence does not require that the saying of Mt. 23.23 be dated post-70 CE, and thus the verse is not in conflict with the view presented here that Mt. 23.2-31 predates the fall of the temple.

11. *Cup-Cleaning*

Mt. 23.25 reads 'Woe to you scribes and Pharisees, hypocrites! for you cleanse the outside of the cup and of the plate, but inside they are full of extortion and rapacity'. This saying, like the one it follows, is perhaps at once both literal and metaphorical. The scribes and the Pharisees really do wash the outside of cups and plates, but inside they (the scribes and the Pharisees) are full of greed and uncleanness. Was the washing of the outside of cups and plates a feature of first-century Jewish life?

Rabbinic literature from the Mishnah onwards bears substantial witness to the practice of utensil washing. Much of tractate *Kelim* deals with the ritual uncleanliness of vessels, and elsewhere in the Mishnah, passages are found which discuss the way in which this uncleanliness may be removed. In *m. Mik.* 10.1, for example, we read

> If a vessel was immersed mouth downwards it is as though it had not been immersed at all. If it was immersed and held in its usual way without immersing the handle, it does not become clean unless it is turned on its side...A bottle whose mouth is turned downwards does not become clean unless a hole is made at the side...

and in *m. 'Abod. Zar.* 5.12

> If a man brought utensils from a gentile, those which it is the custom to immerse he must immerse, those which it is the custom to scald he must scald; those which it is the custom to make white-hot in the fire he must make white-hot in the fire...

It would appear, therefore, that by the time of the Mishnah at least, the practice of cleansing utensils was well established as part of the religious life of the stricter Jews.

In this context, the work of Jacob Neusner needs to be noted.[1] He suggests, probably correctly, that the practices of utensil washing and the division of utensils into 'inner' and 'outer' parts pre-date the fall of the temple.[2]

The main-beams of Neusner's argument are drawn from the Mishnah, especially tractate *Kelim*. Neusner suggests that here the tradition of dividing vessels into 'inner' and 'outer' surfaces at several places. In particular we might note *m. Kel.* 25.1, which clearly states that 'In all utensils an outer and an inner part are distinguished', a statement attributed to Rabbi Judah (c. 150 CE). According to Neusner, however, an even earlier tradition is found at *m. Kel.* 25.7-8, where it is said that vessels are divided not into two parts, but three; the 'inner', the 'outer', and the 'part by which they are held'. Concerning the application of such classification, however, there was some disagreement, for whereas Rabbi Tarfon said that such division applied 'only to a large wooden baking-trough', Rabbi Akiba said it applied only to cups. Both Tarfon and Akiba flourished towards the end of the first century;[3] therefore, provided that these sayings are correctly attributed, it appears that the distinction of 'inner' and 'outer' parts was known at least by 100 CE. The fact that Matthew and Luke have a saying in which a distinction is made between two parts of a vessel supports the Mishnaic evidence.

It may well be that the saying of Mt. 23.25 comes from within the heart of first-century Judaism. The author of the saying knew of the division of vessels into inner and outer parts, and was able to play on this distinction to drive home a stinging criticism of those he considered in the wrong. The evidence does not allow us to say with confidence that the saying found in Mt. 23.25 was formulated before 70 CE, but neither does it contradict this conclusion. What may be said with more certainty, however, is that the author of this saying was well versed in the ways of the Pharisees. He knew not only that they 'washed pots'

1. J. Neusner, ' "First Cleanse the Inside" The "Halakhic" Background of a Controversy Saying', *NTS* 22 (1976), pp. 486-95.

2. Even H. Maccoby ('The Washing of Cups', *JSNT* 14 [1982], pp. 3-15), who challenges Neusner on almost every other point, does not deny this pre-70 distinction between the 'inner' and 'outer' parts (p. 10).

3. *EncJud*, II, pp. 488-92; XV, pp. 810-11.

(cf. Mk 7.4), but also that they divided the pot into various parts and considered that the state of one of these parts affected the state of the other. This is not the criticism of an idle onlooker; it is the sarcasm of an informed co-religionist.

12. *Tombs*[1]

Tombs are mentioned twice in Matthew 23: v. 27 reads 'woe to you scribes and Pharisees, hypocrites! for you are like whitewashed tombs, which outwardly appear beautiful, but within are full of dead men's bones and uncleanness'; and v. 29 has 'woe to you scribes and Pharisees, hypocrites! for you build the tombs of prophets and adorn the monuments of the righteous'. Are these criticisms explicable in terms of pre-70 CE Jewish practice?

That the Jews took much care over the burial of the dead has now been widely demonstrated by archaeological discoveries. One of the most ornate tombs so far uncovered is that known as 'the tomb of Zechariah', which belongs to the Second Temple period. According to Yadin, the base of this monument, which is in the form of a rough cube, measures $5 \times 5.5 \times 7.5$ metres and is cut entirely from one block of rock.[2] All four sides of this block are decorated with ionic style columns, and the corner pillars support an Egyptian cornice. On top of this block is a pyramid top which stands over four and a half metres high. The whole tomb therefore measures almost twelve and a half metres high.[3]

Another example is 'Absalom's tomb'. The base of this tomb is cut from bedrock, and, like that of Zechariah, is in the form of a cube.[4] On top of this base is a cylinder, on the top of which there is a cone. The whole monument rises to a height of twenty metres. G. Foerster describes this tomb as 'the most complex monument in the Kidron valley',[5] and Yadin gives an impressive summary of the tomb's appearance.

---

1. See generally J. Jeremias, *Heiligengräber in Jesu Umwelt (Mt. 23,29; Lk 11,47): Eine Untersuchung zur Volksreligion der Zeit Jesu* (Göttingen: Vandenhoeck & Ruprecht, 1958). Also P. Figuras, *Decorated Jewish Ossuaries* (Documenta et Monumenta Orentis Antiqui; Leiden: Brill, 1983).

2. Y. Yadin, *Jerusalem Revealed: Archaeology in the Holy City 1968–74* (Jerusalem: Israel Exploration Society, 1975), p. 18.

3. Yadin, *Jerusalem Revealed*, p. 18.

4. Yadin, *Jerusalem Revealed*, p. 18.

5. G. Foerster in Safrai-Stern, *The Jewish People*, II, p. 1101.

Most of the square structure is carved out of bedrock, to a height of 8 m; it terminates in a course of large ashlars and is ornamented on all four sides with engaged Ionic columns, with a Doric frieze of triglyphs and metopes (containing rosettes) and an Egyptian cornice above...The round structure is built entirely of ashlars. It comprises a drum and a concave conical roof, crowned by a stone carved in the form of a multi-petalled flower.[1]

Quite clearly, then, 'Absalom's Tomb' is a highly-decorated structure. On the basis of the style, Yadin ascribes this particular edifice to the beginning of the first century CE.

Also from the Kidron Valley is the sepulchre of the Sons of Hezir. This monument is probably earlier than the tombs of either Absolom or Zechariah, dating to the beginning of the first century BCE .[2] Like its neighbours, this tomb is decorated; the facade, which leads into the burial chambers, is cut into rock, and the entrance comprises two doric pillars capped by a doric frieze. The architrave above the columns has the inscription 'This is the tomb and monument of Eleazar, Hania, Joezer, Judah, Simeon (and) Johanan, sons of Joseph son of Obed; Joseph and Eleazer, sons of Hania, priests of the Bene Hezir'.[3]

Also worthy of note are the so-called 'Tombs of the Sanhedrin'. This is a general name given to a number of rock-cut tombs found to the north of the Old City. Yadin explains that the main entrance to these tombs is 'crowned by a gable with acroteria... Stylized acanthus leaves fill the entire triangle, with pomegranates and other fruit scattered among them'.[4] The catacomb has two rows of niches cut into the walls, enough space for some seventy corpses. The dating of this catacomb is uncertain, though a date between 37 BCE and 70 CE seems likely.[5]

L.Y. Rahmani has published a lengthy article on Jewish rock-cut tombs in Jerusalem,[6] and from the details given in this article it is clear that many of even the simpler tombs were decorated and adorned. The ossuaries discovered in these tombs were also often decorated, most characteristically with rosettes. In chamber three of the Mahanayim Tomb, for example, which, on the basis of the pottery found, Rahmani

---

1.   Yadin (ed.), *Jerusalem Revealed*, p. 18; See plate six in Jeremias, *Heiligengräber*.
2.   Yadin, *Jerusalem Revealed*, p. 18.
3.   Yadin, *Jerusalem Revealed*, p. 18.
4.   Yadin, *Jerusalem Revealed*, p. 20.
5.   L.Y. Rahmani, 'Jewish Rock-Cut Tombs in Jerusalem', *Atiqot* 3 (1961), p. 96.
6.   Rahmani, 'Jewish Rock-Cut Tombs', pp. 93-120.

dates somewhere between 40 BCE and 70 CE,[1] one such ornate ossuary has been discovered. Rahmani describes the ossuary in some detail. It is white, being made from a block of limestone and decorated on the front with a

> multi-petalled geometric rosette in the centre, flanked by eight-petalled geometric rosettes encircled by a stylized olive- or palm-wreath. The whole ornament is enclosed in a frame of olive or palm leaves. [It has] 'Trees' of ivy leaves and roots between the rosettes.[2]

A second ossuary found in the same chamber of the tomb is similarly ornate, having two geometric six-petalled rosettes on the front with a stylized tree and 'roots' between them.[3]

In addition to these archaeological discoveries, there is the written evidence: 1 Macc. 13.27-29 describes the ornate tombstone and monument which Simon the Hasmonean erected over the grave of his father and brothers at Modi'in, and Josephus too gives a description of this edifice (*Ant.* 13.21). Josephus also records how Monobazus sent the body of Helena and the bones of his brother to Jerusalem with instructions that they should be buried at the 'Three Pyramids', a tomb to which he refers elsewhere (*War* 5.55, 119, 147). Furthermore, speaking of the sepulchres of the Patriarchs at Hebron in *War* 4.9, 7, Josephus says that 'their tombs are shown in this little town to this day, of really fine marble and of exquisite workmanship'.

There is also some evidence that the building of such tombs was not due entirely to architectural zeal alone, for, as Fischel has pointed out, by the first century CE there was widespread belief among the Jews that the tombs of prophets and martyrs were places where miracles could occur.[4] Prayers were offered at their tombs, and it was even believed that after their death these righteous individuals continued their intercession on behalf of Israel.[5] Little wonder, given these beliefs, that the tombs of martyrs and prophets were highly decorated.

It appears, therefore, that the practice of building large and elaborate tombs was widespread during the first few decades of the Christian era.[6]

---

1.   Rahmani, 'Jewish Rock-Cut Tombs', p. 107.
2.   Rahmani, 'Jewish Rock-Cut Tombs', p. 106.
3.   Rahmani, 'Jewish Rock-Cut Tombs', p. 106.
4.   H.A. Fischel, 'Martyr and Prophet (A Study in Jewish Literature)', *JQR* 37 (1946–47), p. 374.
5.   Fischel, 'Martyr and Prophet', p. 374.
6.   Garland, *Matthew 23*, p. 163 cites Jeremias *Heiligengräber*, pp. 118-21, in

This practice continued in later Judaism, and thus the saying 'you build the tombs of Prophets' cannot be said to be identifiably pre-70 CE. Yet once again it should be noted that the general understanding regarding the *Sitz im Leben* of Mt. 23.2-31 advanced in this study is not contradicted by this particular verse.

The practice of whitewashing tombs is perhaps similarly early. Already in the Mishnah there are several references to this custom: *m. Kat.* 1.2 reports that according to the Sages, during mid-festival a man may do all manner of public works such as repair roads, clean out waterways and 'mark graves'. Similarly, in *m. Shek.* 1.1 it is specifically stated that on the fifteenth day of Adar the *Megillah* should be read, roads repaired, pools cleaned out and graves marked. Details of how this marking of graves is to be effected are found in *m. Sheni* 5.1, which reads, 'A Fourth Year Vineyard must be marked by clods of earth, and trees of *Orlah*-fruit by potsherds, and a grave by whiting mingled with water poured over the grave'.[1] That the Jews of the first century took special care not to become defiled on the eve of the Passover is confirmed also by Jn 11.55 and 18.28.

An alternative suggestion is made by Samuel Tobias Lachs who thinks that the word 'τάφος' in Mt. 23.27-28 is best translated as 'ossuary' or 'sarcophagus'. As evidence, he points out that Sophocles uses the form 'ταφή' when speaking of the urn which contained the remains of Orestes.[2] Lachs further notes that in the Babylonian Talmud (*b. Ber.* 28a) a story is told in which 'whitened casks' containing dust are seen as fit symbols for individuals whose outward appearance masks inward corruption. Importantly, the main character in the story is Rabban Gamaliel II who lived around the time of the destruction of the temple. Lachs's argument lacks any solid evidence, however, for he is unable to cite any references where 'τάφος' is used of an ossuary; nevertheless it is an interesting possibility.

Thus the two references to tombs in Matthew 23 may well be

---

support of the view that there may even have been something of a 'tomb renaissance' around the beginning of the Christian era. This phenomenon, Garland notes, may have been due partly to the influence of Hellenistic culture and partly inspired by Herod himself. Whether such a renaissance actually occurred is of little consequence here, for, as has been shown above, the practice of building and adorning the tombs of holy men was certainly well established in Jewish tradition by the first century.

1.   Garland, *Matthew 23*, p. 150 notes also *b. Kat.* 1a; 5a.
2.   S.T. Lachs, 'On Matthew 23.27-28', *HTR* 68 (1975), pp. 385-88.

explicable in terms of pre-70 practice. It is certain that the tombs of prophets and wise men were adorned, and it is also probable that graves were marked with chalk to warn unwary passers-by. It may even be possible that the word 'τάφος' is used in this passage to refer to ossuaries or casks in which the ashes and bones of the dead were buried.

13. *The Pharisees*

Historians of Judaism have long disagreed on the question of who exactly the Pharisees were, and what role they played in pre-70 Jewish culture and the extent of this disagreement can be seen especially in the diametrically-opposed views of Jacob Neusner[1] and Ellis Rivkin.[2] More recent studies have done little to bring about a consensus; indeed if anything the poles of scholarship seem to be getting further apart.[3]

No attempt to solve this seeming intractable problem can be made

---

1.   J. Neusner, *The Rabbinic Traditions about the Pharisees before 70* (3 vols.; Leiden: Brill, 1971). According to Neusner the Pharisees formed an exclusivist purity sect. This is also the basic position of M. Simon (see *Jewish Sects at the Time of Jesus* [trans. J.H. Farley; Philadelphia: Fortress Press, 1967], pp. 27-43); L. Finkelstein (*The Pharisees: The Sociological Background of their Faith* [2 vols.; Philadelphia: Jewish Publication Society of America, 3rd edn, 1962]); and E. Schürer (*The History of the Jewish People in the Age of Jesus Christ* [3 vols.; trans. and rev. G. Vermes, F. Millar, M. Black and M. Goodman; Edinburgh: T. & T. Clark, 1973–87], II, pp. 381-403).

2.   E. Rivkin, *A Hidden Revolution* (Nashville: Abingdon, 1978); 'Scribes, Pharisees, Lawyers, Hypocrites: A Study in Synonymity', *HUCA* 49 (1978), pp. 135-42; 'Defining the Pharisees: The Tannaitic Sources', *HUCA* 40-41 (1969–70), pp. 205-49. Contrary to Neusner *et al.*, Rivkin argues that the Pharisees did indeed mix with the common Jews. According to him, they were a scholar class, concerned not so much with ritual purity as with the teaching of the law. Steve Mason, 'Pharisaic Dominance before 70 CE and the Gospels' Hypocrisy Charge (Matt 23.2-3)', *HTR* 83 (1990), pp. 363-81 also argues for the authority and influence of the Pharisees in the pre-70 CE period.

3.   See for example E.P. Sanders, *Jewish Law from Jesus to the Mishnah* (London: SPCK, 1990) and the stinging review by Neusner (J. Neusner, 'Mr Sanders' Pharisees and Mine', *SJT* 44 [1991], pp. 73-95). A.J. Saldarini, *Pharisees, Scribes and Sadducees in Palestinian Society: A Sociological Approach* (Edinburgh: T. & T. Clark, 1989); S.N. Manson, *Flavius Josephus on the Pharisees: A Composition-critical Study* (Leiden: Brill, 1991) and by the same author, 'Josephus on the Pharisees Reconsidered: A Critique of Smith/Neusner', *SR* 17 (1988), pp. 455-69. D. Goodblatt, 'The Place of the Pharisees in First Century Judaism: The State of the Debate', *JSJ* 20 (1989), pp. 12-30.

here. However, since the Pharisees (and with them the scribes) occupy a key position in Matthew 23, some brief account of the role of this group in pre-70 CE Judaism is clearly called for. Below, therefore, there follows a brief outline of the position adopted in this study together with references to some of the more useful secondary works.[1]

The evidence from Josephus concerning who the Pharisees were, and what role they played in Judaism, is fairly clear: for him, the Pharisees are a major force in Jewish society and this has long been the case. They have influence with 'the people' and with political leaders, and are the leading (or perhaps 'earliest') 'sect' of his day and were noted for their expertise in legal matters.[2] This statement does not stand alone, for Josephus frequently implies that the Pharisees were not only influential among the people (especially in legal matters), but also played an important role in political events.[3] In Josephus then, as in Matthew 23, the Pharisees are considered to be central figures in the religious life of popular Judaism. They are teachers of the law who occupy a position of considerable authority and influence.

Josephus' description of the Pharisees is not contradicted in the New Testament. Not surprisingly, the New Testament says very little on the political role of the Pharisees, but on matters of belief, authority and popular appeal it agrees with Josephus. Paul, for example, when describing his life as a Pharisee refers to his zeal for the traditions of the fathers (Gal. 1.14) and clearly implies that a particular (i.e. strict) attitude

1.   A fuller discussion is found in Newport, 'Sources and Sitz im Leben', pp. 267-95.

2.   War 2.162-63. On the possible meanings of 'πρῶτος' here see BAGD, p. 725 and G. Lampe, A Patristic Greek Lexicon (Oxford: Clarendon Press, 1961), p. 1201.

3.   Note e.g. Ant. 18.12-15 which states

> The Pharisees simplify their standard of living, making no concession to luxury. They follow the guidance of that which their doctrine has selected and transmitted as good, attaching the chief importance to the observance of those commandments which it has seen fit to dictate to them... They are, as a matter of fact, extremely influential among the townsfolk; and all prayers and sacred rites of divine worship are performed according to their exposition.

The passages in Antiquities were probably written in the early 90s CE and may on that account be discounted as solid evidence of the situation before 70 CE. What is to be noted, however, is their agreement with the statement in War 2.162-63 which antedates the Antiquities by almost two decades. See also Ant. 13.288-98; 399-415; Life 191.

to the Law was one of the defining characteristics of a Pharisaic party (Phil. 3.5b-6). It was, then, zeal for the law and traditions that marked Paul's Pharisaic life, not ritual purity and separation.

The Synoptic Gospels similarly bear witness to the fact that it was the Pharisees who were particularly concerned with legal matters. Whether the corn-field incident (Mk 2.23-27), the healing on the Sabbath episode (Mk 2.1-12), the debate about fasting (Mk 2.18-22), or the numerous debates between Jesus and the Pharisees on points of law and doctrine (Mk 7.1-22; 12.13-34), ever took place is, to some extent, immaterial. For these stories, even if untrue, witness to the conception of the Pharisees which their authors had. The Pharisees were thought of as just the sort of people who would challenge Jesus on legal points. Were they not the kind of people who would meet Jesus on the street and seek to trap him by using fine doctrinal and halakhic points? Again, there is no evidence that the Pharisees held themselves aloof from the people. They are portrayed rather as individuals who mixed with all the children of Israel, all that is except the unrepentant 'sinners', the *resha^{c}im*, who openly and wantonly flouted the will of God.[1]

The Gospel of John must also be taken into account (though the possible late date of this work perhaps limits the importance of its testimony). In Jn 3.1-2, for example, Nicodemus is described as 'a man of the Pharisees...a ruler of the Jews' and Jesus himself refers to Nicodemus as a 'teacher of Israel'. There is of course no suggestion here that the terms 'teacher of Israel', 'leader of the Jews' and 'Pharisee' were synonymous in the mind of John. However, it must at least be noted that (in John's day at least) a Pharisee might be a teacher of Israel and a leader of the Jews (as opposed to a separatist purity fanatic). The Pharisees in John, as in Josephus, Paul and the Synoptic Gospels, do not emerge as a separatist purity sect, but as a group which mixed with and were influential among the general populace. Indeed according to Jn 12.42-43 the Pharisees even controlled membership of the synagogue (see also Jn 7.45-52).

It would appear then that in both Josephus and the New Testament as a whole the Pharisees are portrayed as an influential group of legal experts whose concern it was to instruct the people.[2] Once again, then,

---

1. On the *resha^{c}im* see Sanders, *Jesus and Judaism*, ch. 6.
2. The extent to which this picture is carried over into the rabbinic literature is a matter of very great debate and cannot be entered into here. The question is, however, taken up in Newport, 'Sources and *Sitz im Leben*', pp. 279-90.

Mt. 23.2-31 is seen to be completely understandable within the historical context which suggested here. As we have seen, the pre-70 CE Pharisees were most probably a scholar class, skilled in the interpretation of the Torah, and ready to mix with the common Jews. They may indeed have sat 'upon the seat of Moses'; they were responsible for the teaching of the people, and may have been able, by virtue of the trust which the ᶜ*am ha-arets* had in them, to persuade them to shun the nascent Christian sect (Mt. 23.13).

14. *The Scribes*

As in the case regarding the Pharisees, there is much scholarly debate concerning who the 'scribes' were and what role they played in first-century Judaism. Jeremias, for example, argues strongly that the scribes are to be understood as a separate stratum of the Jewish upper classes, who were afforded great esteem and respect by the common people.[1] Some scribes were Pharisees,[2] and others were priests,[3] but all could be identified by their high learning. A similar view is put forward by Westerholm, who suggests that the scribes, by New Testament times at least, had won wide popular support.[4] The scribes were 'a recognizable group of practitioners who have made their knowledge of scripture a profession as "biblical teachers, lawyers, administrators, or scribes"'.[5] It is clear, then, that Jeremias and Westerholm agree on several fundamental points. The scribes were a scholar class who had made legal matters their profession; many scribes were Pharisees, though the two groups are not to be directly equated. This, basically, is the position also of the revised Schürer[6] and of G. Baumbach.[7]

This general picture of the scribes is supported in the New Testament: the scribes, who are frequently (but not always) mentioned in close

1.   J. Jeremias, *Jerusalem in the Time of Jesus* (trans. F.H. and C.H. Cave; London: SCM Press, 3rd edn, 1969), pp. 233-45; See also Jeremias's article 'γραμματεύς' in *TDNT*, I, pp. 740-42 for a summary of his views.
2.   Jeremias, *Jerusalem*, pp. 243-44.
3.   Jeremias, *Jerusalem*, p. 233.
4.   S. Westerholm, *Jesus and Scribal Authority* (Lund: Gleerup, 1978), pp. 26-27.
5.   Westerholm, *Jesus and Scribal Authority*, p. 26.
6.   Schürer, *History of the Jewish People*, II, pp. 322-36.
7.   H. Balz and G. Schneider (eds.), *Exegetisches Wörterbuch zum Neuen Testament* (3 vols.; Stuttgart: Kohlammer, 1980–83), I, cols. 624-27.

connection with the Pharisees, are legal experts. Like the Pharisees, they sit upon the seat of Moses (Mt. 23.2) and oppose Jesus on legal points (e.g. Mk 2.16; 7.5). Indeed, as Rivkin has shown (and his evidence need not be repeated here), in the New Testament there is very little distinction between the teachings and practices of the scribes and those of the Pharisees. Indeed, according to Rivkin, the similarity is so great that scribes and Pharisees constitute one single party.[1]

Rivkin's comments are important, and although his conclusions may not be as certain as he makes out, he has certainly argued a strong case. The New Testament writers present a picture of the scribes and Pharisees suggestive of a very significant overlap between the two groups.

It must be noted, however, that in several New Testament references there seems to be a distinction between the scribe and Pharisee. In Mk 7.5, for example, we read that the Pharisees *and* the scribes asked Jesus a question concerning fasting, and it is difficult to deny that some element of distinction is maintained in this verse. This apparent distinction is made also in Matthew 23, and similar texts could be quoted from the other gospels (e.g. Mt. 5.20; Lk. 5.21 [cf. Mk 2.6] and Jn 8.3). Rivkin deals with such texts by arguing that the καὶ in these verses does not mean 'and' but rather 'even' or 'that is'.[2] This translation is, of course, quite possible, though perhaps slightly unusual.[3]

Rivkin, then, may have overstated his case, but even if the scribes and Pharisees are not to be directly equated, it is clear that these two groups shared a great deal in common. They had the same teachings (Mk 12.18-28) and were called by the same names (Mt. 23.7); they may, therefore, have had the same critics.

It would seem, therefore, that the reference to the 'chair of Moses' and the sitting of the scribes and Pharisees upon it in Mt. 23.2 may be taken literally. Given the fact that the scribes were most widely known for their expertise in legal matters and their ability to read and write the holy words of God, it would be hardly surprising to find them occupying this seat during religious meetings. Jeremias's remark that 'It is disastrous that Matthew in particular (with the exception of 23.26) unites the two groups'[4] is difficult to accept; as noted above, the scribes and Pharisees had much in common, and it could well be that in the eyes of

1. Rivkin, *Revolution*, pp. 104-24; *idem*, 'Scribes, Pharisees', pp. 135-42.
2. Rivkin, 'Scribes, Pharisees', p. 141.
3. See BAGD, p. 393.
4. Jeremias, *Jerusalem*, p. 253.

their critics, the two groups shared common faults. Consequently, anyone who was attacking one group might pause to take a side-swipe at the other.

15. *Conclusion*

The historical situation presupposed in Mt. 23.2-31 cannot be said to be identifiably post-70 CE, for it appears that all of the religious practices mentioned are at home in the setting of pre-70 Judaism. The only possible exception to this is the use of the title 'Rabbi', but even here the evidence is not conclusive, and, as has been argued above, a pre-70 setting for the use of this title is quite plausible. It seems, then, that not one reference to a practice, custom or religious title found in Matthew 23 requires that the passage be set in a post-70 *Sitz im Leben*.

More positively, it appears that numerous individual sayings within ch. 23 (such as the reference to the temple and the altar) quite clearly presuppose a pre-70 CE *Sitz im Leben*, and many of them betray an accurate knowledge of the workings of Judaism. The reference to tithing marks the passage out as distinctly Palestinian, and the clear affirmation of the authority of the scribes and the Pharisees who sit upon the chair of Moses likewise strongly suggests a fundamentally Jewish setting. On the whole, therefore, it seems that this section of the Gospel is more likely to pre-date than to post-date the destruction of the temple, and to come from a fundamentally Jewish rather than Gentile milieu.

Chapter 4

EXEGESIS OF MATTHEW 23

In Chapter 1 of this study the most prominent compositional theories of
Matthew 23 were examined; it was suggested that none gave an
adequate or convincing explanation of the origin and sources of the
chapter. In Chapter 2 it was argued that Mt. 23.2-31 presupposes a
different *Sitz im Leben* from that of the Gospel as a whole. Indeed, for
several reasons 23.2-31 looks early (pre-70 CE) and, more importantly,
seems to have been written from within Judaism. Matthew and his
community had separated from the synagogue; the author of 23.2-31
had not. As shown in the previous chapter, this conclusion is not under-
mined when the various religious practices mentioned in Mt. 23.2-31 are
investigated, for it seems that all are at home in a pre-70 CE setting.

In the light of the evidence that has emerged from the preceding
chapters, a new source-critical theory seems necessary. Such a theory
has already been advanced sporadically above, though not all the
reasons for adopting it have been given as yet. In short, it is suggested
that Matthew 23 consists of two main sections: the first section extends
from 23.2 and extends to 23.31; the second section begins with 23.32
and ends with the lament over Jerusalem found in 23.37-39. The second
section, it is suggested, is later than the first, and in fact represents the
work of an eschatological redactor (almost certainly Matthew himself)
who has edited a non-eschatological source. The two sections betray
fundamentally different *Sitz im Leben*, and, as will be shown in Chapter
5 below, each has links with other sections within Matthew's Gospel.
The present chapter comprises a verse by verse study of Matthew 23. It
will put into practice the source-critical theory which has emerged in the
earlier chapters.

1. *Matthew 23.1-31*

Matthew 23.1

There can be little objection to the commonly held view that Mt. 23.1 is the evangelist's own creation;[1] the word τότε is one of the few words truly characteristic of the first evangelist,[2] and the reference to the crowds and the disciples appears also at 5.1, another verse probably created by Matthew to introduce a long section of traditional discourse material.[3]

The fact that the discourse is introduced here as being for the attention of the disciples and crowds has been seen by some as indicative of the fact that Matthew's purpose in ch. 23 is, in part at least, to warn the Christian Church against falling into the same errors which plague Pharisaic Judaism.[4] As argued above, however, this 'paradigmatic' understanding of the chapter hardly does full justice to the material it contains. Much of the chapter is hard polemical, and this polemic needs to be taken seriously. There is a severe attack upon the scribes and Pharisees in vv. 13-31, which, significantly, is followed by an attack upon all Jews in vv. 32-39. Matthew, then, most likely had polemical rather than homiletic purposes in including this chapter in his Gospel, though the two are not mutually exclusive.

---

1.   So Beare, *Matthew*, p. 448; Schweizer, *Matthew*, p. 437; Bonnard, *Matthieu*, p. 334; van Tilborg, *Jewish Leaders*, p. 163; and Garland, *Matthew 23*, p. 35; E. Lohmeyer, *Das Evangelium des Matthäus* (ed. W. Schmauch; MeyerK; Göttingen: Vandenhoeck & Ruprecht, 1967), p. 333; Garland, *Matthew 23*, p. 35 n. 3 gives several other references.

2.   Matthew, 90 occurrences; Mark, 6; Luke, 15; rest of the New Testament, 49.

3.   So Fenton, *Matthew*, p. 366. On the significance of the 'disciples' and 'crowds' in Matthew see U. Luz, 'The Disciples in the Gospel according to Matthew', in Stanton (ed.), *Interpretation of Matthew*, pp. 98-128; Garland, *Matthew 23*, pp. 36-41; P.S. Minear, 'The Disciples and the Crowds in the Gospel of Matthew', in M.H. Shepherd, Jr and E.C. Hobbs (eds.), *Gospel Studies in Honor of Sherman Elbridge Johnson* (ATR Sup, 3; 1974), pp. 28-44. In brief, Minear suggests that the 'disciples' in Matthew correspond to the Christian leaders in Matthew's community, the 'crowds', on the other hand, correspond to the laity. Luz too argued that behind the disciples in Matthew stands Matthew's own community. Garland agrees substantially with Minear, but argues that 'from 21.1 on, "the crowds" are no longer seen in a positive light but are shown to have sided with the authorities against Jesus' (p. 39). See also B.R. Doyle '"Crowds" in Matthew: Texts and Theology', *CTR* 6 (1984), pp. 28-33; Garland, *Matthew 23*, p. 35 nn. 5 and 6 gives further references.

4.   See especially Garland, *Matthew 23*, pp. 34-41, 120.

On a pre-Matthean level, too, the anti-Pharisaic discourse of vv. 2-31 is mainly polemic in its intent. It is true that vv. 8-12 pause to give advice to the community itself, but this does not detract from the main purpose of the passage which is to criticize the scribes and Pharisees. The pre-Matthean author may have been concerned to give direction to the community, but he was even more concerned to criticize his perceived opposition.

Matthew 23.2-3

As noted in the previous chapter, there is considerable disagreement among scholars concerning the origin and meaning of 23.2-3. Beare, for example, suggests that the verses are to be taken metaphorically, and does not think that they originate with Matthew himself.[1] In Beare's view the reference to 'Moses' chair' is 'hardly to be taken as a reference to a special chair in the synagogue for the chief elder'.[2] Grundmann too thinks that the 'Kathedra des Moses ist Bild für seine Autorität',[3] and such is the view also of several other scholars.[4]

Hill, on the other hand, states that the reference is 'not simply a metaphor. There was an actual stone seat in front of the synagogue, where the authoritative teacher (usually a Scribe) sat.'[5] Hill quotes E.L. Sukenik[6] in support of his view, and more recent studies likewise suggest that Hill's non-metaphorical understanding of the 'chair of Moses' may well be historically viable; this has been discussed in detail in the preceding chapter, and it is little wonder, given the historical evidence, that numerous scholars have seen in Mt. 23.2 a reference to an actual stone seat.

Several commentators have pointed to the rather unusual aorist ἐκάθισαν and have seen in the tense of this verb evidence that the verses were written from a later standpoint and indicate that their author was looking back to a previous era. Allen, for example, thinks that the verb implies that 'the editor writes from his own standpoint, and looks back at a time when the scribes and the Pharisees were in power'.[7]

---

1. Beare, *Matthew*, p. 448.
2. Beare, *Matthew*, p. 448.
3. Grundmann, *Matthäus*, p. 483
4. See above, p. 81 n. 1 for references.
5. Hill, *Matthew*, p. 310.
6. Hill, *Matthew*, p. 310.
7. Allen, *Matthew*, pp. 243-44.

McNeile, who quotes Allen, advances a similar view.[1]

But such an explanation is not the only one possible, for the aorist here may represent the sense of a semitic perfect, the sense of which would be similar to that of a Greek gnomic aorist.[2] Indeed, the fact that this verb is followed closely by two imperatives strongly suggests that it has present force.[3] The sense of the verse seems to be 'The scribes and Pharisees are now sitting on the seat of Moses, therefore do whatever they say', rather than 'The scribes and the Pharisees formerly sat on the seat of Moses, therefore obey them'. These Jewish leaders are accepted as authoritative teachers who should be obeyed.[4]

This interpretation is shunned by many scholars. Beare, for example, suggests that the words 'do whatever they tell you' are 'no more than a foil for the charge that they do not themselves practise what they preach'.[5] France also thinks that the words were perhaps spoken with 'an ironical, tongue-in-cheek tone', and that they function 'only as a foil' to what follows.[6] Similarly, Krister Stendahl finds it 'tempting' to say that the statement found in Mt. 23.2-3a is designed primarily to give maximum force to the denunciation which follows.[7] Garland goes even

1. McNeile, *Matthew*, p. 329. See Garland *Intention*, p. 47 n. 41.

2. See M. Black, *An Aramaic Approach to the Gospels and Acts* (Oxford: Oxford University Press, 2nd edn, 1967), p. 128.

3. Garland, *Matthew 23*, pp. 47-48. Garland discusses this point at some length, noting that Nigel Turner (Moulton, Howard and Turner, *Grammar*, IV, p. 33) argues that the Aorist here represents a Hebrew stative perfect. More recently S.W. Thompson (*The Apocalypse and Semitic Syntax* [Cambridge: Cambridge University Press, 1985], pp. 37-42) has given several examples of Greek aorists being used to translate Semitic perfect verbs in the LXX, Theodotion and the New Testament. W.W. Goodwin in his *A Greek Grammar* (London: Macmillan, 1916) § 1292 notes the use of the Gnomic aorist in Classical Greek, where the English requires a present, and A.T. Robertson, *A Grammar of the Greek New Testament in the Light of Historical Research* (New York: Hodder and Stoughton, 3rd edn, 1919), p. 866 similarly argues that the use of the aorist in this verse is Gnomic.

4. This position is adopted by Mason, 'Pharisaic Dominance'. He seeks to push the saying back to Jesus. In this study no such claim is made. However, Mason's point, that the words basically mean what they say, seems valid. The scribes and Pharisees (note that Mason thinks that the reference to the 'scribes' may have been added) do have real authority and must be obeyed.

5. Beare, *Matthew*, p. 448.

6. France, *Matthew*, p. 324.

7. Stendahl, *Matthew*, p. 792. This, basically, is the view taken also by R.J. Banks, *Jesus and the Law in the Synoptic Tradition* (SNTSMS, 28; Cambridge:

further; for him vv. 2-3 are an introduction not only to the charge 'they say but do not do' found in v. 3b, but for all of the charges found in the chapter. But it is difficult to see how the clear statement 'The scribes and Pharisees sit on Moses' seat; so practice and observe whatever they tell you' could ever be taken as an introduction to the rest of the chapter, which, according to Garland, deals 'largely with their failure to expound the Law correctly'.[1]

Other commentators, however, while allowing for the possibility that 23.2-3 means what it says, take it as obvious that Jesus (and/or Matthew) was here commanding obedience to the Torah (= God's gracious gift to Israel),[2] but not to the teaching of the scribes and the Pharisees themselves (= casuistry and cavil which obscures God's law).[3] Thus Gundry, who thinks that the verses are Matthew's own,[4] clearly states that the traditions of the scribes and Pharisees are not in view.[5] Similarly, Allen suggests that 'we must suppose that a limitation is to be inferred from "sit in Moses' seat". Do all things that they teach, in so far as is in harmony with the spirit of the Mosaic law.'[6] The suggestions of Gundry and Allen, however, lack any justification in the text.[7]

Cambridge University Press, 1975), pp. 176-77. See also M.J. Cook ('Interpreting "Pro-Jewish" Passages in Matthew', *HUCA* 54 [1983], pp. 135-46), who thinks that the apparent approval of the scribes and Pharisees is only 'theoretical' and that the material following this verse 'methodically dismantles any approval of the scribes and Pharisees in terms of their behaviour and pronouncements, so that whatever Matthew (not Jesus) ostensibly affirms in the passage is all but obliterated' (pp. 144-45).

1.   Garland, *Matthew 23*, p. 55. Garland further maintains that on a Matthean level vv. 2-3 can be understood only in the light of 23.4, which acts as a redactional modifier for the blanket traditional statement in 2-3a. But, as is shown below, there is no real contradiction between vv. 2-3 and 4, and all may have come from one hand.

2.   Albright-Mann, *Matthew*, p. 278.

3.   Albright-Mann, *Matthew*, p. 278.

4.   Gundry, *Matthew*, p. 454.

5.   Gundry, *Matthew*, p. 455.

6.   Allen, *Matthew*, p. 244.

7.   See further Garland, *Matthew 23*, p. 48 n. 49. The view that Mt. 23.2-3 mean what they say has recently been advocated by A.-J. Levine (*The Social and Ethnic Dimensions of Matthean Salvation History* [Lewiston, NY: Mellen Press, 1988], pp. 179-81). According to Levine, passages like Mt. 23.2-3; 5.17-20; 10.5 and 15.26 do not come from an anti-Gentile, pro-Jewish 'M' source, but are Matthew's own. Levine goes on to argue that such passages do not, however, conflict with Mt. 28.16-20, since it is Matthew's view that whereas the life of Jesus was the period of proclamation to the Jews, at the death of Jesus the disciples' missionary charge was

Hummel's suggestion differs from any of the above. For him, the verses are not so much 'theologische Aussage' as 'taktische Anweisung'.[1] As Garland notes, this hypothesis assumes that the dialogue with Judaism is *intra muros*,[2] and it is at this point that Hummel's suggestion fails, for, as is argued above, Matthew is working *extra muros*. If it were Matthew's intention to paper over the cracks between Judaism and Christianity and prevent further parting of the ways, he has done a very bad job of it. Matthew, it seems, is unconcerned with the Jewish people and does not have any qualms about portraying them in a bad light. As noted in Chapter 2 above, for Matthew the Jews are a wicked race who have received their just reward. Hummel is right to argue that Mt. 23.2-3 exhibits an *intra muros* stance, but he is almost certainly wrong to extend this to the Gospel as a whole. Consequently, it is quite possible that the verses are indeed 'theologische Aussage', though not that of the evangelist himself.

Neither is there any suggestion that the scribes and Pharisees lack divine commission (cf. Mt. 15.1-20; 16.11-12). Lenski's comments to the contrary[3] are merely a side-swipe at Pharisaism and have little to do with the text itself; the scribes and Pharisees properly sit on Moses' seat and are to be obeyed.

---

extended to include all the Gentiles as well. Furthermore, according to Levine, the words of Mt. 28.20 'teaching them to observe all that I have commanded you' are meant to include 23.2-3 (*Social Dimensions*, p. 181). Whether the evangelist Matthew thought of the scribes and Pharisees as authoritative leaders to be followed even by Gentile converts is, however, highly questionable. In Mt. 16.5, 12, for example, Matthew's Jesus specifically warns against the teachings of the Pharisees and in 15.13-14 says that this same group lacks divine commission and is in fact nothing but a group of 'blind guides leading the blind' who will inevitably fall into a pit. Levine makes almost no reference to this material.

1. R. Hummel, *Die Auseinandersetzung zwischen Kirche und Judentum im Matthäusevangelium*. (BEvT, 33; Munich: Kaiser Verlag, 1966), p. 31 as quoted in Garland, *Matthew 23*, pp. 53-54.

2. Garland, *Matthew 23*, p. 53.

3. R.C.H. Lenski, *The Interpretation of St Matthew's Gospel* (Ohio: Wartburg Press, 1943), pp. 893-94, states

> With ἐκάθισαν Jesus states merely the fact, which does not in any way admit the right of these men to Moses' seat. They were not called to this seat as Moses had been. He assumed the seat reluctantly, but these false followers of his assumed his seat of their own accord and were determined to have and to hold it. They were self-appointed usurpers and acted as though their dicta were as binding as the revelations God made to Moses, 15.3-9.

If such a literal understanding of 23.2 is adopted, it seems most probable that the verse originated within a firmly Jewish context. The scribes and the Pharisees, who sit upon the literal 'seat of Moses', are recognized as authoritative exponents of the Torah, and there is reference also to extra-biblical halakhah, since the advice is 'do *all* that they say'. This ties in well with v. 23, where the halakhic regulation concerning tithes, which in fact exceeds what is explicitly laid down in the books of Moses,[1] is likewise considered binding.

But while the words of the scribes and the Pharisees are to be heeded by the community, their practices are not to be copied. Though these leaders are respected for their high, God-given office, their lifestyle leaves a lot to be desired; they teach correctly the commandments of God, but, as 23.3b makes clear, they do not practise what they preach.

Such accusations are not without parallels; both Manson[2] and Bonnard[3] have drawn attention to several rabbinic passages concerned with the relationship between the study and practice of the Torah. McNeile's suggestion that 23.3b criticizes the motives of the Pharisees[4] seems completely wide of the mark. McNeile maintains that the Pharisees 'scrupulously observed their own rules' but 'their motive and manner deprived their actions of all value'.[5] This is a strange interpretation indeed of the words λέγουσιν γὰρ καὶ οὐ ποιοῦσιν.

McNeile is not the only commentator who adopts such an interpretation of Mt. 23.3b. Commenting on this verse, Filson states that 'though usually outwardly correct and formally obedient, they [the scribes and the Pharisees] lacked the personal dedication and unselfish integrity of good living'.[6] But, like McNeile, Filson seems to have missed the point; there is neither condemnation of motive nor of inward failing. The verse means exactly what it says, namely that while the rulings of the scribes and the Pharisees are binding, their actions are not to be followed. To use a common English expression, perhaps itself derived from this verse, they do not practice what they preach.

It should be fairly obvious that such a statement could hardly have been composed by Matthew himself, for the evangelist is working *extra*

---

1. Above, pp. 102-103.
2. Manson, *Sayings*, p. 229.
3. Bonnard, *Matthieu*, pp. 334-35.
4. McNeile, *Matthew*, p. 330.
5. McNeile, *Matthew*, p. 330.
6. Filson, *Matthew*, p. 243.

muros. As noted in Chapter 2 above, Matthew in fact thinks that Judaism is no longer the custodian of the covenant of God; the Jews as a whole are a wicked generation who have consciously rejected God's messengers and even his own Son; time and time again the Jewish leaders are portrayed by Matthew as a wicked group, and against this background the improbability of Matthew's having written Mt. 23.2-3 comes into sharp relief.

This understanding of the verses is, of course, not without precedent. Several commentators have attributed this saying to 'M', a special source used by Matthew in the compilation of this and other sections of his gospel.[1] Streeter, among others, suggests, that this 'M' source evinces a particularly 'Jewish' tone,[2] and it is hardly surprising therefore that we should find within it a saying which attributes to the scribes and Pharisees a high degree of authority. The present study, however, goes further than simply a restatement of the four-document hypothesis; Mt. 23.2-3 speak unequivocally of the validity of the Jewish religion; Mt. 23.23 does similarly; in Mt. 23.16-22, the altar is said to sanctify the gift and God is assumed to bless the temple with his presence. Could it not be that all these passages are linked, at least in that they seem to stem from an identical *Sitz im Leben*, and even in that they stem from one written source? In short, it may well be that the whole of Mt. 23.2-31 comes from one single source that Matthew has slotted into his gospel almost without change.

Matthew 23.4

There is widespread agreement concerning the meaning of Mt. 23.4. Schweizer, for example, thinks that the 'heavy burdens' are 'the multiplicity of individual commandments',[3] and Filson sees in the verse the suggestion that, though the scribes and Pharisees 'multiply duties, develop strict interpretations of the law, burden men with obligations... [they] leave them to carry the load unaided'.[4] Manson's statement that the Pharisees have multiplied 'the number of ways in which a man may offend God'[5] seems to have found approval, since it is quoted by

---

1. Streeter, *Four Gospels*, p. 257; Kilpatrick, *Origins*, pp. 35-36; Haenchen, 'Matthäus 23', p. 40; See Garland, *Matthew 23*, p. 52 n. 69 for other references.
2. Streeter, *Four Gospels*, pp. 254-59.
3. Schweizer, *Matthew*, p. 438.
4. Filson, *Matthew*, p. 243.
5. Manson, *Sayings*, p. 101.

Garland, who is in turn quoted by France. A. Plummer argues that 'it
was by their perverse interpretations of the details of the Law that they
"bound heavy burdens upon men's shoulders"', and he puts forward as
an example 'the rigour with which they prohibited exertion of any kind
on the Sabbath, so that the weekly day of rest, instead of being a
welcome blessing, became an intolerable burden'.[1]

Mt. 23.4 is seen by Hill as almost contradictory of 23.3,[2] and
Schweizer too attributes the verses to different hands.[3] Implicit in the
remarks of these commentators is the view that the author of 23.3, who
advised his readers to obey the scribes and the Pharisees, would not
have called their teachings φορτία βαρέα.[4]

There is, however, a fundamental similarity between vv. 2-3 and 4
which seems to have gone unnoticed by most commentators. The
parallelism between 'they say but they do not do' and 'they load...but
they do not lift a finger' is clear, and even if Hill and Schweizer are right,
and the two verses stem from different sources, they are seen to complement each other in such a way as to suggest redactional activity. But in
fact the kind of arguments advanced by Hill and Schweizer may not be
as strong as some have thought. Neither commentator mentions the use
of βαρύς in 23.23, where justice, mercy and faith are described as τὰ
βαρύτερα τοῦ νόμου, which most translators take to mean the
weightier i.e. 'the more important', matters of the law.[5] Why, then, should
the same word in 23.4 be taken so negatively? Is it not at the very least
possible, indeed probable, that φορτία βαρέα in 23.4 means 'important
loads'?[6]

It is of the utmost importance that the central criticism of 23.4 not be
allowed to slip from view. The scribes and the Pharisees load men's
backs with heavy (or 'important') loads, yet they do next to nothing

1. A. Plummer, *An Exegetical Commentary on the Gospel according to
S. Matthew* (London: Robert Scott, 1911), p. 314; see also Beare, *Matthew*, p. 449;
McNeile, *Matthew*, p. 330.

2. Hill, *Matthew*, p. 310.

3. Schweizer, *Matthew*, p. 438.

4. See also Garland, *Matthew 23*, pp. 52-55.

5. RSV 'weightier matters'; NIV 'more important matters'; NEB 'weightier
demands'.

6. 'Burden', the translation found in the RSV and most other English transla-
tions, surely carries a negative implication. However a φορτίον is simply a 'load' of
any kind as for example in Acts 27.10 where it is translated in the RSV as 'cargo'
(BAGD, p. 865).

when it comes to carrying out their own commandments; there is no explicit condemnation of the scribes and Pharisees for loading men's backs in the first place.[1] The yoke of the Torah[2] was not thought to be an intolerable burden, and many delighted to take it upon themselves. Nevertheless, few would have described the path they delighted to tread as an easy or soft option. The nickname given to the Pharisees by the Qumran sectarians, 'expounders of smooth things',[3] strongly suggests that this community did not think of their own religious system as smooth, but rather as a rough but blessed journey. One hardly needs to be reminded of the numerous Christian parallels found in the New Testament: 'If any man would come after me, let him deny himself and take up his cross and follow me' (Mk 8.34); Jesus' yoke, though easy, is still a yoke, his burden, though light, still a burden (Mt. 11.30).

It seems, therefore, that 23.3 and 4 may not be as dissimilar as some commentators claim. Not only are they in parallel, but their contents also complement and expand each other. The scribes and Pharisees are to be obeyed, and the loads they place upon men's backs are to be borne gladly. The practices of these teachers, however, are not to be imitated, for while they speak, they do not do, and while they load the backs of others, they themselves are not prepared to take up the loads or to bear them on their own shoulders. In short, they neglect fully the observance of the Torah which they themselves preach.

Gundry's understanding of this verse is quite different; he states that

> in Matthew the heavy burdens are not to be identified with scribal tradi-
> tions or interpretations of the law (as probably in Luke and Jesus' intent).
> Rather, they signify overbearing attempts to win adulation—to be noticed
> by men, gain the place of honour at banquets and the chief seats in the
> synagogues, receive greetings in the market place, and be called 'my Great
> One' (the meaning of 'Rabbi').[4]

---

1. Haenchen, 'Matthäus 23', p. 41, seems to have recognized this point clearly, for he states: 'Noch ist freilich das „Nein!'' dazu nicht grundsätzlich; es würde verstummen, wollten die Schriftgelehrten die gleiche Last selber tragen'. But Haenchen goes on to add: 'Aber sie wissen mit rabbinischem Scharfsinn die drückenden Gesetzesbestimmungen zu umgehen, mit denen sich die anderen abplagen müssen'. Bornkamm, *Tradition*, p. 24 makes a similar remark. Garland, *Matthew 23*, p. 51 n. 62 gives further references.

2. For the expression 'yoke of the Torah' see *Pirqe Aboth* 3.6 and *b. Ber.* 13a.

3. CD 1.18; 1QpHab 2.15; 4.2.

4. Gundry, *Matthew*, pp. 455-56.

This is so, Gundry maintains, since the verses which follow Mt. 23.4 'clearly define' what the heavy burdens are; and furthermore, Matthew's expansion of Mark at Mt. 11.28-30 confirms such a definition of the heavy burdens by contrasting the lightness of Jesus' yoke, which consists of meekness and humility. These qualities 'contrast sharply with the scribes' and Pharisees' overweening desire for recognition'.[1]

On this point Gundry is almost certainly wrong, for there is no indication that vv. 5-7 are meant as an explanation of the phrase 'they load heavy burdens upon men's backs'. Rather the verses begin a new section: the scribes and Pharisees load men's backs; they also love the best seats.

It seems, therefore, that a better explanation of 23.4 is that it refers to the practice of scribes and Pharisees in placing upon the people numerous halakhic formulations. There is nothing wrong with these formulations in themselves, nor in the fact that the scribes and the Pharisees are the ones who place them upon the shoulders of others. These leaders properly sit upon the seat of Moses and must be obeyed. That these leaders of the people do not themselves carry out their own precepts is, however, a matter of grave concern, and they are attacked ruthlessly for this failure. If such an explanation is accepted, it is apparent that once again the saying comes from within the heart of Judaism.

Matthew 23.5-7
The criticism of the scribes and the Pharisees continues in Mt. 23.5. Schweizer has noted that 'unlike verse 3, verse 5 implies that the Pharisees did what the law required', and he concludes that the verses must therefore be from different hands.[2] But Schweizer has perhaps pressed his point too far. It must be agreed that there is a seeming discrepancy between 'for they preach, but do not practise' and 'they do all their deeds to be seen by men', but it is not so great as to demand Schweizer's conclusion. The scribes and the Pharisees are under attack: they do not follow their own directives, but the criticism is not to be taken to its logical extreme. The author of Mt. 23.3 cannot mean that the scribes and the Pharisees do none of the law: his community knows of the reputation of these teachers and is accustomed to seeing them going about their various religious activities. If nothing else, they

---

1.   Gundry, *Matthew*, p. 456.
2.   Schweizer, *Matthew*, p. 438.

correctly tithe their garden produce, and are careful to strain out gnats (23.23-24).

Rather the author of the passage is stating his case in the strongest possible form: first, he says that the scribes and the Pharisees 'say but do not do', though as a Jew he knows that these individuals are not completely anomic in their lifestyle; secondly, he points out that even those works they do are done in order that they may be seen by men, and not to honour God. The scribes and the Pharisees are therefore attacked on two fronts: they do not do all the works they should, and even those they do are done from impure motives.

That the author of 23.2-31 has a first-hand knowledge of Judaism is suggested by 23.5b-7. This knowledge is not merely theoretical, but bears all the hallmarks of an intimate acquaintance with the practice of the religion. The description of the scribes and Pharisees in these verses is completely natural, and suggests that their author was accustomed to seeing such people on the streets where he himself walked. He knows that they make their phylacteries broad and their fringes long, because he himself has seen them. The author is aware also of the tendency of the scribes and the Pharisees to seek the best seats in the synagogue and places of honour at feasts. He knows this because he too is in the synagogue and at feasts, and frequently has to take a lower and less prestigious place than his rivals. He knows also that in the market place the scribes and the Pharisees are called 'Rabbi' by others. He knows this because he himself mingles among the crowds and traders and has heard these appellations first hand.

The criticisms of 23.5b-7 are not against the teaching of the scribes and Pharisees, but against their practices. There is nothing wrong with phylacteries *per se*, for indeed God himself commanded that they should be worn by his people. Thus Lagrange, who thinks that the word 'phylactery' refers to an 'amulet',[1] seems correct when he notes that 'Jésus ne reproche pas aux Pharisiens un usage superstitieux d'amulettes païennes qu'il serait impossible de prouver, mais de l'ostentation dans protestation extérieure de fidelité à la pensée de Dieu'.[2] Neither are tassels explicitly condemned, for these too are worn as a response to a commandment of God.[3] In the previous chapter the origin and

---

1. Lagrange, *Matthieu*, p. 439.
2. Lagrange, *Matthieu*, p. 439.
3. Plummer (*Matthew*, pp. 314-15) implied that the attack in vv. 5-7 is partly upon phylacteries and tassels themselves. Thus he writes: 'Scrupulosity about such

development of phylactery and tassel wearing was examined in some detail and it was concluded that both practices were widely known in the world of pre-70 CE Judaism. Similarly, the title 'Rabbi' may well have been in use prior to the destruction of the temple, though here the evidence is thinner.

Garland thinks that v. 5 provides an example of the scribes and the Pharisees saying but not doing,[1] but it is difficult to see why this should be the case. The criticism is not dependent upon what has been said in vv. 3-4, but rather stands on its own and is best understood at face value. The scribes and Pharisees make their phylacteries too broad and their fringes too long and in this they err, for it is no more than unnecessary ostentation. That phylacteries and tassels of the proper size and length should be worn is not, however, in question.

It must be noted also that it is with respect to the use of the title 'Rabbi' that the author of 23.2-31 for the first time speaks out against something other than the perceived 'hypocrisy' of the scribes and the Pharisees, for in Mt. 23.8 he warns the community leaders not to be called by this title of honour, indicating that in the mind of the author the use of such a title was wrong. Nevertheless, this is probably not an attack on their religious teaching, for it is unlikely that the scribes and Pharisees taught others to call them 'Rabbi' in the same way as they taught them to guard the Sabbath. This is not to say that the author of Mt. 23.2-31 thought that the teaching of the scribes and Pharisees was completely flawless, for they sometimes erred by being too lenient (e.g. vv. 16-22), but there is no attack on their teaching here. The attack in Mt. 23.5-7, as elsewhere in 23.2-31, is fundamentally upon the persons of the scribes and Pharisees: they are 'hypocrites', for they neglect the doing, though not the teaching, of the will of God and make an unnecessary show of their piety.

There seems no good reason why the author of these verses could not also have written 23.2, 3 and 4. There is no contradiction, but rather a clear progression of thought, and once again it is plain that the pericope evinces a fundamentally *intra muros* Jewish *Sitz im Leben*.

---

mere externals as 'phylacteries' and 'fringes'...is a good illustration of the formalism of Judaism. Such things were useful as reminders; they were fatal when they were regarded as charms'. But the verses in no way imply that phylacteries and fringes were regarded as 'mere externals'; they should be worn in obedience to the commands of God, but they should not be made excessively long.

1. Garland, *Matthew 23*, pp. 55-56.

Matthew 23.8-12[1]

It was noted above that several scholars have adopted a less than literal understanding of Mt. 23.2-3, and the same is true of Mt. 23.8-12. France seems to take the whole pericope in an almost metaphorical way: the emphasis is not upon individual titles, but rather upon the need for humility, and the real warning here is against adopting a 'status-seeking attitude'.[2] Clearly, France's views are not totally without merit: vv. 11-12 especially do indeed speak in no uncertain terms of the need for humility amongst the followers of Jesus. But what of vv. 8-10? Are they also to be understood simply as a plea for humility? Or is it not more likely that the verses mean what they say, namely that the use of particular titles is wrong?

Beare's understanding of the verse is also to be questioned. He suggests that the *Sitz im Leben* of Mt. 23.8-12 is that of the already established Christian church in which there was a growing tendency of Christian teachers and other leaders to assert authority over the rank and file of the members. Matthew is concerned about 'the danger of a distinction between clergy and laity' and is warning against it.[3] Hill has a similar understanding of these verses, and, commenting on Mt. 23.8, he writes:

> This verse introduces a passage addressed to the disciples only, continuing to verse 12. The section may represent the application of the preceding verses to the situation of the Matthean church, where a sort of Christian 'rabbinism' may have been developing.[4]

---

1.   See generally R. Hoet, *"Omnes Autem Vos Fratres Estis": Etude du Concept Ecclésiologique des "Frères" selon Mt. 23,8-12'*, *Analecta Gregoriana* (Rome: Università Gregoriana Editrice, 1982). According to Hoet, vv. 8-10 are probably redactional, though they may contain vestiges of original sayings of Jesus. Verses 11-12 are from a pre-Matthean source and most likely go back to Jesus himself. The verses now encapsulate Matthew's own ecclesiology, which centres upon the idea of an earthly fraternity under the headship of the Father in Heaven. Mt. 23.8-12 forms the focal point of the discourse as a whole, which continues until Mt. 25. In this pericope the evangelist sets his own ecclesiology in the context of Jesus' struggle with the religious leaders of the Jews. Hoet's work, like that of most commentators, is seriously weakened by his insistence that in Mt. 23 the scribes and Pharisees are criticized for their teaching, for, as is argued here, this is not the point of conflict. Neither is the authority of the scribes and Pharisees challenged.

2.   France, *Matthew*, p. 325.

3.   Beare, *Matthew*, p. 450.

4.   Hill, *Matthew*, p. 311.

Bonnard, too, holds open the possibility that these verses are directed at the members of the church to whom Matthew was addressing himself and may represent an attack upon 'une sorte de rabbinisme chrétien'.[1]

It is possible, however, that the verses are earlier than most commentators are prepared to allow. That the context is fundamentally Jewish is almost beyond doubt, for where, outside of Judaism, would there be a tendency on the part of the 'laity' to call its leaders 'Rabbi'? The words 'but you are not to be called rabbi', are a warning against the acceptance of such a title, which presumes that it must have been offered. The one who teaches is not to be called 'Rabbi'. The people may offer such titles of respect, but they are to be refused. Besides any theological objection on the part of the author, there may also have been a concern to distance himself and his community from his opponents.

Thus it seems that on a pre-Matthean level this passage is directed quite possibly not against an early form of 'Christian Rabbinism', but rather at a growing tendency within Judaism to afford particular titles to the leadership. The use of 'Rabbi' is wrong, and it detracts from the greatness of God. The use of 'Father' is also wrong, for there is in reality only one entitled to this name; the title Master is similarly not to be used, for the only Master is 'the Christ'.

The meaning of 23.9 is fairly plain; there is a strong warning against calling anyone upon earth 'father', for such appellation detracts from the fatherhood of God. 'Father' seems not to have been widely used as a title of honour, but Schweizer notes 2 Kgs 2.12; 6.21; 13; 14; Acts 7.2; 22.1,[2] and McNeile[3] cites Schürer and Dalman, who give further examples. Further remarks concerning the possible background to the title 'Father' have already been made in the preceding chapter.[4]

One further prohibition is contained in v. 10: the leaders of the community are not to be called 'Master', for there is only one who is

---

1. Bonnard, *Matthieu*, p. 336. So too McNeile, *Matthew*, p. 331 and Schweizer, *Matthew*, pp. 439-40; see also J.D.M. Derrett, 'Mt. 23,8-10 a Midrash on Is 54,13 and Jer 31,33-34', *Bib* 62 (1981), pp. 372-86. According to Derrett the verses are a warning to the disciples not to set themselves up in a position of authority even though they have had direct instruction from God, a favour which later generations of Christians have not enjoyed. The references to the titles 'Father' and 'Rabbi' are inserted by Matthew merely to contrast what is actually going on in the synagogues where religious leaders are claiming more for themselves than they ought.

2. Schweizer, *Matthew*, p. 439.

3. McNeile, *Matthew*, p. 331.

4. Above, pp. 95-96.

worthy of that name, and that is Christ himself. The word καθηγητής is unique in the New Testament, though Bauer gives examples from Hellenistic literature.[1] There is general agreement that the Greek word is equivalent here to the Hebrew מורה (from ירה), in which case it could be translated as 'expositor' or 'instructor'.[2] However, it cannot be denied that the word is somewhat unusual and may not mean simply 'teacher', but rather may have had a technical meaning.

It appears, therefore, that the author of Mt. 23.8-10 thought of the community as a brotherhood of equals; titles of honour are to be neither offered nor accepted. This is not to say, however, that he recognized no earthly authorities; the scribes and the Pharisees sit on Moses' seat and are therefore to be obeyed, but they are not to be copied or given titles which detract from the greatness of God or Christ. The community's own leaders are not to seek the esteem and honour of the 'laity', but are to recognize that they are all servants together under the leadership of Christ.

This exegesis is confirmed by vv. 11-12. It is of little consequence whether these verses were originally independent sayings of Jesus, for they fit together and complement each other so well that their inclusion at the very least betrays the hand of a careful redactor. They form an integral part of the pericope; and if vv. 8-10 are traditional to Matthew, so too, probably, are 11-12.

The sayings contained in Mt. 23.11-12 form a suitable conclusion to the pericope which began in 23.8. The one who is greatest will be the servant, whoever humbles himself will be exalted. No one should be called 'Rabbi', for no one is great but God; no one should be called 'Father', for there is only one true father; no one is to be called 'Master', for there is only one who is worthy of that name. The author of 23.2-31 may well have agreed with Paul that 'you are the body of Christ and individually members of it. And God has appointed in the church first apostles, second prophets and third teachers' (1 Cor. 12.27). The community of Mt. 23.2-31 is united under one head, and no one within the community is to seek station above a fellow member; all have their task to do, and all should be considered equal.

Verses 8-12 do not conflict with the earlier verses of this chapter. The scribes and Pharisees teach correctly, therefore they are to be followed in what they say. They should not, however, be afforded honorary titles.

1. BAGD, pp. 388-89.
2. BDB, pp. 434-35.

Neither should the members of the author's group accept such titles. They have one leader, the Christ, and all believers are brothers.

Matthew 23.13

Verse 13 contains the first of the seven woes. The criticism is that the scribes and the Pharisees lock up the Kingdom of Heaven; they do not enter themselves, neither do they allow others to go in. What precisely the scribes and the Pharisees did to effect this 'locking up' is much disputed: Garland thinks that Manson is right when he states that the scribes and the Pharisees were 'custodians of the revelation of the Old Testament', and as such were 'assigned the task of interpreting God's will to men, and had the power and authority to open up the way of the kingdom through the correct interpretation of the Law'.[1] But, according to Garland 'these masters of the Torah, who sat on Moses' seat, obstructed God's will and sidetracked his Law with their contravening traditions, precedents and pettifogging rules'; and 'their teaching fogged the simple and central truths of the Law with casuistry'.[2] Such is the interpretation basically given also by numerous other commentators such as Allen, Filson, Hill, Schlatter, Grundmann and Schweizer.[3]

This understanding is at best strange and difficult to accept. If the criticism in Mt. 23.13 has really to do with the law, it is surely not that the scribes and Pharisees are too strict or that the fence they have put around the law is too high. Rather, if we follow Garland's general suggestion that Mt. 23.13 is about law, the criticism is more likely to be that the scribes and Pharisees are too slack. They do not go far enough in their formulations: they correctly strain out gnats, but swallow camels; they correctly tithe mint, dill and cummin, but they neglect even more important aspects of the law. They correctly allow an oath taken by the gold of the Temple to have binding force, but do not afford the same status to an oath taken by the Temple itself.

On a Matthean redactional level an even more serious criticism of Garland (and others) may be made. Matthew the evangelist, it seems, thinks that the Jews, and therefore the scribes and Pharisees, are not even in possession of the kingdom and could therefore hardly be in a

---

1.   Garland, *Matthew 23*, pp. 126-27.

2.   Garland, *Matthew 23*, p. 127

3.   Allen, *Matthew*, p. 245; Filson, *Matthew*, pp. 244-45; Hill, *Matthew*, p. 311; Schlatter *Matthäus*, p. 672-73; Grundmann, *Matthäus*, p. 490; Schweizer, *Matthew*, p. 440. Garland, *Matthew 23*, p. 127 n. 14 gives numerous other references.

position to prevent access to it (note especially Mt. 8.11-12; 21.33-41). Garland's exegesis of this verse is very strained as he tries to fit it into the Matthean scheme.

A much more convincing interpretation of this verse is possible, however. The real criticism in the first woe probably has nothing to do with the interpretation of the law at all. Rather, it seems, the author of 23.13 is attacking the scribes and Pharisees for their failure to recognize Jesus for who he was, and, more specifically, for their policy of attempting to turn away would-be adherents to the Jewish sect which had grown up in allegiance to him. Jesus is the Christ, and entrance into God's kingdom is through him; only those who acknowledge Jesus, the Christ, as 'Master' will be admitted to the Kingdom. The scribes and Pharisees have failed to recognize this, and oppose his followers.

The fundamentally Jewish context of 23.13 is strongly suggested on two counts. First, the Jews are still regarded as custodians of the kingdom; though the scribes and Pharisees do not enter themselves, they at least have the opportunity of doing so; the fact that they can prevent implies that they could allow.[1] Secondly, the scribes and the Pharisees obviously have some command over the people and are, in the eyes of the author, able to prevent others from entering the kingdom. A Gentile convert would scarcely consult the scribes and Pharisees before making a commitment to the Christian faith. It is quite possible, however, that a Jew, hearing the preaching of early Christian missionaries in the synagogues, would take the time to consult the religious leaders of his day. The scribes and the Pharisees, disbelieving the claims of these same missionaries, warn the people to shun this new sect.[2]

It is unlikely, therefore, that these verses are the work of one concerned primarily with the Gentile mission (c.f. Mt. 28.19-20). Rather the passage most probably reflects the animosity felt by one who was within synagogal Judaism towards what he considered a complacent and hypocritical leadership.

---

1.   Saldarini, 'Delegitimation of Leaders', p. 673 correctly notes (but draws different conclusions from) the fact that for Matthew, it is Peter and not the Pharisees who stand at the gate of heaven allowing or obstructing entrance (Mt. 16.19). The logic of this passage seems non-Matthean.

2.   An interesting parallel is found in *Gos. Thom.* 102 which reads 'Jesus said, "Woe to the pharisees, for they are like a dog sleeping in the manger of oxen, for neither does he eat nor does he [let] the oxen eat"' (J.M. Robinson [ed.], *The Nag Hammadi Library in English* [San Francisco: Harper and Row, 3rd edn, 1988], p. 137).

Matthew 23.14

It has been widely recognized that Mt. 23.14 is not part of the original discourse, but rather represents the work of a later copyist who has taken the material directly from Mk 12.40.[1] The MSS evidence supports this judgment, for Mt. 23.14 is found in only a few later MSS.[2] It seems wise, therefore, to omit this verse from the text of Matthew 23.

Matthew 23.15

The second Matthean woe has no parallels. The language of the woe is strong, and this has led some to suggest that it could not have originated with Jesus.[3] The criticism is that the scribes and the Pharisees cross land and sea to make a convert whom they then turn into 'twice as much a child of hell' as they themselves. The verse is often seen as 'Matthean' on the grounds that it fits into Matthew's own *Sitz im Leben*. The attack, some argue, is upon the excessive zeal of the Pharisees in seeking to gain converts; Matthew's own community is in competition with these Jewish leaders, and hence friction arises. Green, for example, thinks that the bitterness of Mt. 23.15 is that of a competitor,[4] and Grundmann too suggests that the woe evinces a conflict between Jewish and Christian missionary activity. He writes:

> Die jüdische Mission hatte in der Zeit Jesu und der Apostel ihren
> Höhepunkt erreicht und kam durch das Wirken der Christenheit schon im
> ersten Jahrhundert zum Erliegen. Der Weheruf ist wahrscheinlich
> wesentlich mitbestimmt durch die Erfahrung der Urchristenheit, daß ihr in
> der Diaspora von Proselyten stärkerer Widerstand entgegengesetzt wurde
> als von Juden selbst.[5]

1. E.g. Hill, *Matthew*, p. 311; Lagrange, *Matthieu*, p. 442; Grundmann, *Matthäus*, p. 490 n. 33; Bonnard, *Matthieu*, p. 338; Green, *Matthew*, p. 191.
2. f^{13}; it; vg^{cl}; sy^c; bo^{pt}; the verse is also found in W, a few other uncial MSS and the Majority Text, but in these witnesses is placed after v. 12.
3. See for example H.J. Flowers, 'Matthew xxiii.15', *ExpTim* 73 (1961–62), pp. 67-69. According to Flowers, Jesus would not have said that the Pharisees were children of hell, though he may have made a 'playful' reference to them which was exaggerated by later editors. J. Hoad ('On Matthew xxiii.23: a Rejoinder', *ExpTim* 73 [1961–62], pp. 211-12) correctly notes that Jesus' language was on occasions strong indeed to the point where he called his chief disciple 'Satan'. Flowers, like many others, seems desperate to free Jesus from the charge of unfairness.
4. Green, *Matthew*, p. 191.
5. Grundmann, *Matthäus*, p. 490; and see Garland, *Matthew 23*, p. 129 n. 19 for other references.

Such an understanding of the background to Mt. 23.15 is possible, but
it is hardly convincing, for it seems that the criticism here is not so much
against proselytizing *per se*, but rather against the results of such
activity. Garland has already drawn attention to this possibility, and his
comments seem correct. On Mt. 23.15 he writes:

> It should not be overlooked...that the target of the woe is not proselytism
> *per se* but the final outcome of the proselytism of the scribes and the
> Pharisees. The proselyte, rather than becoming a son of the kingdom
> (8.12; 18.3), becomes a double son of Hell.[1]

And Garland is surely correct in seeing the focal point of the criticism
in the result rather than the activity of proselytism; it is right that the
scribes and the Pharisees go to great lengths to win a Gentile convert to
Judaism (or perhaps a Jewish convert to Pharisaism).[2] What is not right,
however, is the result of these proselytizing activities: the converts
become as hypocritical as their teachers by not practicing what they
know to be correct; they follow the bad example of the scribes and
Pharisees themselves and consequently become 'children of hell'.
Needless to say, the teachers do not point their pupils towards Jesus-
Messiah, and they even poison their minds against his followers. This is
true, whether the verse speaks of the proselytism of Gentiles to Judaism,
or the pharisaic proselytism of the Jews.

Similarly, the comments of many exegetes who suggest that it is the
teaching of the scribes and the Pharisees which is the cause of criticism,
seem unfounded. Mt. 23.15 does not speak of the Pharisees'
'dependence upon legal and ritual values for salvation',[3] and neither
does the verse criticize the Pharisees for their 'false interpretation of the
Law that...demands obedience to the ceremonial law for salvation'.[4]
Beare, whose comments are typical of many,[5] perhaps misses the point
altogether when he suggests that the converts become 'twice the sons of

---

1.   Garland, *Matthew 23*, p. 129. So also France, *Matthew*, p. 327; T.H. Robinson,
The Gospel of Matthew (London: Hodder and Stoughton, 1928), pp. 188-89; Simon,
Verus Israel, p. 283.

2.   See above pp. 98-100.

3.   Garland, *Matthew 23*, p. 129.

4.   Garland, *Matthew 23*, p. 131.

5.   E.g. France, *Matthew*, p. 327; Hill, *Matthew*, p. 312; Albright-Mann, *Matthew*,
p. 280; Green, *Matthew*, p. 191; Plummer, *Matthew*, p. 317; Schweizer, *Matthew*,
p. 440; Lagrange, *Matthieu*, p. 442; McNeile, *Matthew*, p. 333; Fenton, *Matthew*,
p. 370; Haenchen, 'Matthäus 23', p. 47.

hell' by their greater adherence to the beliefs and teachings of their converters.[1] The problem is not that these proselytes are stricter than the scribes and Pharisees themselves, like converted protestants trying to show themselves 'more Catholic than the Pope';[2] it is rather that like the Pharisees they are not strict enough. As Schlatter noted,[3] the Pharisee can give only what he himself has, and, in the mind of the author, the Pharisees have only a limited righteousness. The teachers 'say but do not do', and the converts too are neglectful of the law: they know what is right and they have correct teaching, yet they are not strict enough in matters of observance.

It would appear, then, that a suitable *Sitz im Leben* for Mt. 23.15 may be found within Judaism. The clash is between one Jewish sect which has particular beliefs about the law and about Jesus, and another group, the scribes and the Pharisees. While sharing a high regard for the law, these Jewish leaders are not, in the eyes of their critics, strict enough in carrying out its every command. If such an interpretation is adopted, it will be noticed that the thesis advanced in the previous chapters, that Mt. 23.2-31 is not a collection of disparate material, is plausible not only on a linguistic but also an exegetical level. Indeed, the passage looks less like a mosaic of individual and contradictory material which has been strung together by Matthew in a post-70 CE situation, than a unified discourse reflecting an intra-Jewish struggle and pre-dating the final redaction of the Gospel.

Matthew 23.16-22
The woe contained in vv. 16-22 is of a different type from the other six in the chapter: the opening is different, for here the scribes and Pharisees are not 'hypocrites' but 'blind guides', and the verses are concerned primarily with what is taught, and not with the teachers themselves. This is unique in the chapter, for, as we have seen, it is the persons of the scribes and the Pharisees, and in particular their lax attitude towards the doing of the law, that are generally the objects of criticism. It cannot, therefore, be denied that there is something of a contradiction between

1. Beare, *Matthew*, p. 454. So too B.C. Lategan, 'Die Botsing tussen Jesus en die Fariseërs volgens Matt. 23' (The Conflict between Jesus and the Pharisees according to Mt. 23), *Nederduits Gereformeerde Teologiese Tydskrif* 10 (1969), p. 220.
2. Lategan, 'Die Botsing', p. 220.
3. Schlatter, *Matthäus*, p. 676.

Mt. 23.2-3 and the present woe, but this apparent discrepancy is not as great as some commentators think.[1]

The setting of 23.16-22 is almost certainly pre-70 CE. Hill denies this, stating that

> The mention of these features of Jewish religion does not require us to presuppose a Jerusalem setting and a date before A.D. 70 for the composition of the Gospel; any literary work can contain evidence of a situation and practices which existed earlier than its composition.[2]

Hill's remarks carry some weight, but such an explanation is less than convincing in the case of the present pericope, especially since, for other reasons, it would seem that the whole of Mt. 23.2-31 is a pre-Matthean unit stemming from a pre-70 CE *Sitz im Leben*. The fact that we find here a halakhic debate over oath-forms further supports the view proposed here.

This observation remains valid despite the fact that examples of oaths 'by the temple' and 'by the temple service' are found in rabbinic literature.[3] If the verses were from Matthew's own hand, they would scarcely reflect a belief in the efficacy of the Jewish cult system. But, as in the rabbinic literature, such a belief is discernable. The question 'which is greater, the gift or the altar which sanctifies the gift?', betrays a belief that the altar does in fact sanctify. The statement 'he who swears by the temple swears by him who dwells in the temple' assumes that God does indeed bless the Jewish temple with his presence.[4] Matthew himself, who believes that the Jewish people as a nation have been rejected by God (Mt. 8.12), who has given the kingdom to 'others', can scarcely be the author of these verses. Thus, even though Hill's remark is valid, it appears that the logic of Mt. 23.16-22 marks out the passage as being of non-Matthean origin. It hardly needs to be pointed out that the author of Mt. 23.16-22 has a fundamentally different understanding of the Jewish cult from that of the author of Mt. 23.38, who can state quite definitively 'Behold, your house is forsaken and desolate'.

---

1. Cf. Garland, *Matthew 23*, p. 52 n. 68.
2. Hill, *Matthew*, p. 312.
3. *b. Ta'an.* 24a; *b. Kidd* 71a; these texts show that the comment made by Albright and Mann (*Matthew*, p. 280) that 'vs. 16 can only have come from a time before A.D. 70, when such oaths as are here described necessarily came to an end with the destruction of the temple' is a serious oversimplification.
4. Filson, *Matthew*, p. 246, makes a similar point though he does not dwell upon it.

The content of 23.16-22 therefore shares similarities with the previous verses. The dispute is over the formulation of oaths. The issues involved are in fact relatively minor, and this is just the kind of debate that fills the pages of the Mishnah. On the one side of the debate are the scribes and the Pharisees, who say that to swear by the temple, the altar, and perhaps the heavens, does not make the oath binding, though to swear by the gold of the temple, the gift upon the altar, and perhaps by the throne of God, does; and on the other side is the author of Mt. 23.16-22, who questions the sufficiency of such teaching. In the mind of their critic, the teaching of the scribes and Pharisees, while correct in substance, errs in being too slack. Whether one swears by the temple, the gold of the temple, the altar or the gift upon the altar, or by heaven, the oath is binding.

As was pointed out in greater detail in the preceding chapter, this disagreement over the form of oaths which were binding continued into later Judaism. Garland notes the discussion in *t. Ned.* 1.3, where 'Jerusalem', 'temple' and 'altar' are specifically excluded as terms which make an oath binding.[1] The concern in the rabbinic passage, as in Mt. 23.16-22, seems to be which words when used in an oath make the oath binding. The whole passage is best understood against the background of halakhic formulation. One can easily imagine a passage in the Mishnah reading as follows: 'Is it binding if a man swears by the temple?' Rabbi X says 'only if he swears by the gold of the temple', Rabbi Y says 'If he swears by the temple, it is enough', the sages say 'whether he swears by the temple or the gold of the temple, he is bound'. The debate reflected in Mt. 23.16-22 is about oath forms and the correct formulation of halakhah. In all probability it is not an attack by the Christian Matthew upon the scribes and Pharisees who try by their casuistry to avoid the consequences of oaths.[2]

The apparent contradiction between 23.16-22 and 23.2-3 is to be seen in this light. The author of ch. 23 is prepared to admit that the scribes and the Pharisees are authentic teachers, but on the question of oath forms they err in being too lenient. The passage suggests that its author took a very strict line indeed when it came to oaths; he knows that to swear by God makes an oath binding, and this view he shares with his opponents, but he goes further than they in considering oaths made by other objects as also binding. To swear by heaven is to swear by the

---

1.   Garland, *Matthew 23*, p. 134.
2.   Cf. Green, *Matthew*, p. 191; Schweizer, *Matthew*, pp. 440-41.

throne of God, which is to swear by God himself. Indeed, to swear by any of the cultic objects is to make oneself obligated. The author of 23.16-22 goes further than the scribal and Pharisaic rulings: he no doubt agrees with them that an oath taken 'by the gold of the temple' is binding; he agrees also that an oath taken on the gift upon the altar is valid; but whereas his opponents say that oaths made by other objects are not binding, the author of 23.2-31 disagrees, for in his view, any oath made is to be taken seriously.

The author of 23.16-22 does not reject the teaching of the scribes and Pharisees by allowing what they forbid; rather he forbids what they allow, and in so doing shows himself to be stricter than they. The author holds to be binding that which his opponents do not, and thus adds a prohibition: 'Do not casually swear by the altar etc.' Thus, while the scribes and Pharisees are right, they are, in the eyes of their antagonist, not right enough. In passing we should note also that the advice given in this passage does not run counter to that given in Mt. 5.33-37. To say 'all oaths are binding' does not contradict the statement 'do not swear'. This point is made more extensively in Chapter 5 below.

Matthew 23.23-24

Garland argues that Mt. 23.23-24 is primarily an attack not so much upon the persons of the scribes and the Pharisees, as upon their exposition of the law. The passage is designed by Matthew to show that the scribes and the Pharisees are false teachers.[1]

This interpretation of the passage is difficult to maintain, not least because of the unequivocal affirmation of scribal-Pharisaic halakhah in 23.23b. Garland's exegesis of this woe is possible only if 23.23b is ignored, which he is prepared to do on the grounds that the verse derives from 'an earlier tradition which cannot be pressed too far theologically'. He cites several other commentators who have made similar remarks.[2] One such commentator is Banks, who notes this verse and states that Matthew, 'rather than evidencing a nomistic tendency in this passage...highlighted the Pharisaic failure as against the law (v. 23b), through a concentration upon insignificant elements of their tradition (v. 24)'.[3] But Banks, like Garland, has failed to take seriously the injunction to obedience found in the second half of the verse. If, as

---

1. Garland, *Matthew 23*, p. 136.
2. Garland, *Matthew 23*, pp. 139-40 and especially n. 66.
3. Banks, *Jesus and the Law*, p. 180, as quoted in Garland, *Matthew 23*, p. 140.

Banks imagines, tithing of mint, dill and cummin is 'insignificant', why is there a clear command to keep doing these things?

Banks is by no means the only one to shy away from the most obvious meaning of the words 'these things you ought to have done without neglecting the former'. Hill, for example, states that 'provided there is no neglect of the great principles, the observance of the minutiae is not forbidden',[1] but 'not forbidden' hardly does justice to the phrase κἀκεῖνα μὴ ἀφιέναι. Manson too, who considers the form of Mt. 23.23 as it appears in Matthew to be a 'protest against meticulous fulfilment of legal trifles, and neglect of vital matters', sees 23.23b as an editorial attempt to protect Jesus from the general charge of anti-nomianism.[2] Such interpretations of 23.23-24 are far from fully convincing.

Neither is there any explicit condemnation of gnat-straining. The passage does not say 'you blind guides! you strain gnats, and in fact gnats do not matter', but rather 'you strain gnats and swallow camels'. Gnat-straining is good; it is camel-swallowing that is wrong. Neither is it the case that gnat-straining leads to camel swallowing, nor tithe-paying to neglect of justice, mercy and faith.[3] The argument is rather about which is greater, tithe paying on small garden produce or the practice of justice, mercy and faith. Quite obviously the latter is more important. Therefore, if you correctly tithe mint, dill and cummin, should you not *all the more* be scrupulous with respect to these greater matters of the law?[4]

Once again it appears that the material is best understood against a background of intra-Jewish controversy. What the scribes and the

1.   Hill, *Matthew*, p. 313.
2.   Manson, *Sayings*, p. 235.
3.   Cf. Hill, *Matthew*, p. 313 who states quite clearly that 'excessive zeal for minutiae led to neglect of more important things'.
4.   Cf. Garland, *Matthew 23*, p. 140 where he states that

> The fourth woe, rather than being an indirect affirmation of Pharisaic legalism, must be viewed as an attack upon the exegesis of the Torah by the scribes and Pharisees which has effectively obscured the intention of God's will by straining out gnats while swallowing camels. The scribes and Pharisees are false teachers.

Garland's exegesis, even on a Matthean level, is suspect. The woe does not castigate the scribes and Pharisees as false teachers, but as false doers. The woe more probably means what it says: the scribes and Pharisees, authentic teachers of the law, err in swallowing metaphorical camels, though they correctly strain literal gnats, which is good.

Pharisees say regarding tithing (and in fact they go further than what is required by the Torah) is correct. They should tithe dill, mint and cummin; they are correct also to strain gnats. The scribes and Pharisees, however, do not pay enough attention to the τὰ βαρύτερα τοῦ νόμου, such as mercy, justice and faith. They fall short: they are correct to tithe, but they spoil their good record by their failure in other, more important matters.

The accurate knowledge of the practices of Judaism evident in this pericope should not be overlooked; as shown in the preceding chapter, wine was indeed strained to ensure the removal of unclean insects, and the tithing of garden produce was a requirement observed by many.[1]

It appears, then, that Mt. 23.23-24 is primarily an attack upon the persons of the scribes and Pharisees rather than an attack upon their teaching. Like much of the other material found in ch. 23, there is a sharp note of hostility against the legal authorities. The teaching does not come under serious criticism, and there is nothing in these verses to suggest that the author rejected the halakhah of the scribes and the Pharisees. As stated above, these leaders are 'blind guides' and 'hypocrites' because they swallow camels, not because they strain gnats. Hill comments that the Pharisees are criticized 'for concentrating upon what is secondary and forgetting what is of first importance, and therefore for doing too little'.[2] He is right when he says that the Pharisees are criticized for doing too little; he is right also in saying that they are criticized for forgetting what is of first importance. He is wrong, however, to suggest that they come under attack for concentrating upon what is secondary. In the mind of the author, all aspects of the Torah/halakhah should be 'concentrated upon'.

Matthew 23.25-26

There has been much debate concerning the background to the material of vv. 25-26, and there is considerable agreement that in its original form the material once pertained to some kind of halakhic dispute on purity laws.[3] As the saying now appears in Matthew and Luke,

---

1.   Above, pp. 103-105.

2.   Hill, *Matthew*, p. 313.

3.   H. Maccoby ('The Cleansing of Cups'), however, denies this. For him, the saying (which goes back to Jesus) is a straightforward metaphor. The scribes and Pharisees, according to Mt. 23.25-26, are like cups which are clean on the outside and yet dirty within.

however, it is plainly metaphorical and is a condemnation of the scribes and Pharisees for being inwardly corrupt.[1]

Such an interpretation is clearly supported by the text itself. The scribes and Pharisees are criticized for inward failing. This is not unique in the chapter, for, as we have already seen, it is the view of the author of Mt. 23.2-31 that these authentic leaders fall short in many ways. Thus they swallow metaphorical camels by neglecting the important matters of the Torah, and they fail to do those things which they are so careful to instruct others to follow. They do their deeds in order to be seen by men, and are indeed inwardly corrupt, though they appear outwardly pure. That is not to say, however, that the scribes and Pharisees are rotten to the core, or that they are considered to lack authority as teachers. They properly sit upon the seat of Moses, and what they teach is basically correct, though they sometimes err in being too lenient.

Garland's position is different: he argues strongly that the purpose of the saying as found in Matthew is to condemn categorically the teaching of the scribes and Pharisees. This condemnation is not designed primarily to characterize these leaders as externally pious though inwardly corrupt, but rather to point out the 'failure of the religious leaders of Israel in their responsibility to profess the will of God to their charges'.[2]

Garland's exegesis depends upon an extremely literal interpretation of the saying, and for this he is heavily dependent upon the work of Neusner.[3] Garland suggests that the woe addresses itself directly to the scribes and Pharisees. These teachers of the law are known to cleanse the outside of cups and other vessels, and indeed, they have a 'meticulous concern' for such 'ceremonial matters'.[4] Nevertheless, these vessels, which are ritually pure, 'contain food and drink which were

1. E.g. Fenton, *Matthew*, p. 374; Schweizer, *Matthew*, p. 442; Beare, *Matthew*, p. 456; Garland, *Matthew 23*, p. 143 n. 75 gives several other references.

2. Garland, *Matthew 23*, p. 142.

3. Neusner, ' "First Cleanse the Inside" ', pp. 486-89. H. Maccoby issued a strong reply to Neusner in which he suggested that the saying in Mt. 23.25-26 is best understood as primarily metaphorical ('The Washing of Cups'). In so far as the verses relate to actual practice, Maccoby argues, they have to do only with hygiene and not ritual purity. Maccoby has perhaps overstated his case, for it certainly seems that the verses do in fact concern some aspect of ritual purity. He is probably right, however, to suggest that the context for the saying is far from clear. As is suggested here, the verses in Matthew are a rather untidy mixture of literal and metaphorical, and the precise halakhah behind it may be unrecoverable.

4. Garland, *Matthew 23*, p. 149.

morally impure because they were the harvest of greed and injustice'.[1] The scribes and Pharisees should first cleanse the inside of the cups (i.e. empty them of their ill-gained contents by giving up the 'inner disposition that leads to the plundering of neighbours'), before the 'external trappings of piety will have any significance before God'.[2]

From this exegetical foundation Garland goes on to argue that the woe specifically attacks the scribes and Pharisees according to their failure as teachers; they are blind guides who do not know τὰ βαρύτερα τοῦ νόμου.[3] The hypocrisy is not simply that they pretend to be pure but are actually corrupt, but rather that they have failed to make clear to the people the will of God. In Garland's words

> Their unrighteous loot condemns them; they have ignored the primary commandments and have taught as primary that which was secondary. They have focused on the outer/inner parts of utensils while the law really refers to people and moral character. Once again, the scribes and Pharisees have been shown up as failures in their assigned task of interpreting the law.[4]

Whether taken on the level of Matthew himself or a pre-Matthean source, Garland presses the text too far. There can be little doubt that the passage condemns the scribes and the Pharisees for a lack of moral rectitude, but the criticism does not spill over into a condemnation of their teaching. Neither is there any condemnation of the practice of cleansing the outside of the cup. The scribes and the Pharisees err, but in a general, moral sense, and not in their interpretation of the Torah.

Garland is also incorrect to press for a totally literal interpretation of the saying. His understanding of γέμουσιν ἐξ ἁρπαγῆς καὶ ἀκρασίας as full 'because of' greed and extortion[5] is possible,[6] and has in its favour the fact that it solves the difficulty noted by many commentators that cups and plates do not 'contain' robbery and indulgence.[7] But he has not solved all the problems. He admits himself that the saying has a metaphorical interpretation in Mt. 23.26 where 'first cleanse the inside' is really an injunction to the scribes and Pharisees to

1. Garland, *Matthew 23*, p. 149.
2. Garland, *Matthew 23*, p. 149.
3. Garland, *Matthew 23*, p. 149.
4. Garland, *Matthew 23*, p. 150.
5. Garland, *Matthew 23*, p. 148.
6. Turner, *Syntax*, p. 260.
7. E.g. Beare, *Matthew*, p. 456.

give up a certain disposition, to stop plundering neighbours and to practice mercy and justice.[1] Manson has pointed out that the fact that Mt. 23.27-28 clearly has a non-literal application, increases the likelihood that 23.25-26 may also have been meant figuratively.[2] Neither does Garland offer any evidence of how it was exactly that the scribes and the Pharisees 'plundered' their neighbours, or filled their cups through greed and injustice. Schweizer, too, fails to explain why the contents of the Pharisees' cups do not really belong to them, or how 'their abundant food and drink shortchanges others'.[3]

It is perhaps more plausible that the author of the saying contained in Mt. 23.25-26 was seeking to condemn what he considered to be the hypocrisy of the scribes and the Pharisees in neglecting important matters of the law even though they correctly paid full attention to smaller points. The scribes and Pharisees do not have a truly religious disposition. They need to examine themselves carefully and clean out this hypocrisy which is preventing their full observance of the commandments of God. It is not enough to tithe garden herbs, wash drinking vessels and strain gnats, though all these things are necessary. The one who wants to be truly righteous must exhibit a general God-like disposition, and observe all that he has commanded. In the mind of the author of Mt. 23.25-26, the scribes and the Pharisees have failed to do this, and they are therefore 'hypocrites'. The woe is a mixture of literal and metaphorical: the cups mentioned in v. 25 are no doubt real cups and the allusion is to an actual practice (as is the case with the gnat in 23.24), but the task of cleaning out the inside is metaphorical (as is the camel in 23.24).

Once again, the saying seems to fit better into a pre-Matthean context than a Matthean one. The woe is a sharp attack by one group of Jews upon another. There is a concern for inward as well as outward purity, though of course outward purity cannot be dispensed with.

Matthew 23.27-28

These verses reinforce the view that, whatever the original form of the saying found in Mt. 23.25-26, it was meant by the author of the pericope to be understood metaphorically. The verses contain the sixth of Matthew's seven woes, and clearly point a finger at the scribes and

1. Garland, *Matthew 23*, p. 149.
2. Manson, *Sayings*, p. 236.
3. Schweizer, *Matthew*, p. 442.

Pharisees, denouncing them as 'hypocrites'. The language is metaphorical; the scribes are 'whitewashed tombs',[1] clean on the outside, yet
full of uncleanness inwardly.

The opinion of the majority of commentators is that the verses speak
of the inward defilement of the scribes and Pharisees.[2] Schweizer, who
thinks that the verses are typical of Matthew himself, remarks that the
only important point of this saying is the contrast between 'outward
appearance' and 'inward filth', and further suggests that in its more
original form the polemic may have been even more bitter, perhaps
speaking of the scribes' and Pharisees' corrupting influence.[3] Garland
goes further; the attack, he suggests, is not simply upon the hypocrisy of
the scribes and Pharisees, but rather is critical also of their status as legal
exponents. The woe is a summary of the first five, and indicates that the
author of ch. 23 viewed the scribes and Pharisees as nothing but false
teachers who obscure the way to the kingdom through their concentration upon a 'legalistic ritualism' that distorts the intention of God.[4] The
failure of the scribes and Pharisees, Garland states, 'was not just an
ethical bankruptcy; it was a fatal distortion of the Law's intention and a
callous insensitivity to the message of the prophets'.[5] Again he goes too
far; the woe more probably speaks of the scribes' and Pharisees' failure
to measure up to the author's own high standards. These teachers
appear outwardly beautiful in that they can often be seen practicing the
law through their observance of tithes, washings, and other such good
acts. Their clothing too marks them out as being noble observants of the
Torah. The author of the passage knows of their public image (23.5b-7);
inwardly, however, they are unclean. Indeed, though they appear
righteous to men, they are in fact full of lawlessness. That is not to say
that what they teach is wrong; on the contrary, what they teach is right,
and this adds to the false impression that they give to onlookers, but,
since they fail to do even what they say (and they do not say enough)
they are far from righteous before God.

Hill's comment that the verses seek to underline the fact that the

---

1. Or perhaps 'Ossuaries', see above, p. 110.
2. So Schlatter, *Matthäus*, pp. 682-83; Hill *Matthew*, p. 313; Garland, *Matthew
23*, p. 151 n. 117. (But note that Garland's reference to Haenchen, 'Matthäus 23',
p. 20 should be p. 50.)
3. Schweizer, *Matthew*, p. 442.
4. Garland, *Matthew 23*, p. 159.
5. Garland, *Matthew 23*, pp. 159-60.

righteousness of the Pharisees is nothing but an external show, probably smudges their real intention.[1] The scribes and Pharisees are like whitewashed tombs in that, while they appear outwardly righteous, they are in fact full of iniquity. This does not mean that the author of this section thought that those elements which led to the Pharisees' seeming righteousness were nothing but an external show and could be dispensed with; the acts and words of the scribes and Pharisees made them 'look righteous', therefore what they did, e.g. tithe herbs, strain gnats, clean utensils and teach the halakhah, must have been thought by the author and his community to constitute a part of correct religious living. These things gave the appearance of righteousness. The emphasis is rather upon the lack of full righteousness. The scribes and Pharisees perhaps have a measure of righteousness, though they could do better, for inwardly they are full of hypocrisy and lawlessness (cf. Mt. 5.20). The sixth woe thus maintains the theme of the chapter generally. The scribes and Pharisees are hypocrites, since they do not practice fully what they preach. Neither do they pay attention to τὰ βαρύτερα τοῦ νόμου, which is also a serious failure on their part. It is unlikely, however, that the criticism extends beyond this general charge of hypocrisy. Attempts such as that of Garland to argue that the author of Mt. 23.27-28 saw the scribes and the Pharisees as an actual source of defilement through their incorrect teaching of the law, are not really supported by the text itself.[2]

Once again the verse seems to betray a practical knowledge of the workings of Judaism, for, as shown in the previous chapter, tombs were indeed whitewashed, especially before the Passover.

Matthew 23.29-31

The last of the seven woes is somewhat strange and its intention is not altogether clear. The scribes and Pharisees are said to build and adorn the tombs of prophets and saints, yet they are hypocrites since, by their own confession, they are the sons of those who murdered these holy men of God. Schweizer suggests that the attack may be upon a superficiality of devotion,[3] and Albright and Mann are inclined to agree

---

1.   Hill, *Matthew*, p. 313.

2.   Garland, *Matthew 23*, p. 157. So also Schweizer, *Matthew*, p. 442; J.S. Kloppenborg, *The Formation of Q: Trajectories in Ancient Wisdom Collections* (Studies in Antiquity and Christianity; Philadelphia: Fortress Press, 1987), p. 141.

3.   Schweizer, *Matthew*, p. 443.

with this interpretation.[1] Other commentators suggest that the hypocrisy stems from the continuing persecution of 'prophets' and 'holy men' (in the form of the Christian church) at the hands of those who build and adorn the burial places of former great figures of Israel's religious history.[2] Several commentators further suggest that there may be a play on the double meaning of 'son' in the Semitic languages.[3] The scribes and Pharisees are not only literal descendants of prophet-killers, but by their present actions, they show themselves to be of basically the same ilk as their murderous fathers. Derrett takes the argument further: he suggests that there is a pun on the Semitic root בון, which forms the basis of the words 'builders', 'sons', 'scholars' and 'understanders'.[4]

None of the above interpretations is an altogether satisfactory interpretation of the woe, for there is nothing to suggest that the scribes and Pharisees were in any way superficial in their honour of the great heroes of Israel's past. Neither is there any evidence in the woe itself for the continuing persecution of the author's own community at the hands of the scribes and Pharisees, though as is argued below, this is the interpretation given to the woe by the final editor of Matthew 23. The woe more probably indicates that, in the author's mind, the Jewish people as a whole bear the guilt of the killing of prophets in former times. Not only the scribes and Pharisees, but all the descendants of Abraham, himself included, must admit to their misdemeanors, but the scribes and Pharisees fail to do just this. They too are responsible for the murders committed by their ancestors. Disclaimers such as 'if we had been there we would not have participated in the blood of the prophets' are not sufficient to free them from guilt. An acknowledgment of past sins and a new disposition towards those who claim divine commission are needed on the part of all Jews.[5] The practice of adorning the graves of holy men is not condemned. It is right for the members of present Israel to do all things possible to right a past wrong, but wrongs should not be forgotten; rather they should remain in the mind as a reminder of the need for openness towards those who claim divine commission.

1.   Albright-Mann, *Matthew*, p. 281.
2.   E.g. Garland, *Matthew 23*, p. 165.
3.   Garland, *Matthew 23*, p. 165 n. 17 gives several references. To which we might add Fenton, *Matthew*, p. 376; Manson, *Sayings*, p. 238.
4.   Derrett, '"You Build the Tombs of the Prophets"', pp. 187-93.
5.   So Garland, *Matthew 23*, p. 165.

Garland has noted that the present woe has no clear ending,[1] and in this he seems correct, for unlike the previous six, the seventh woe has no obvious application. After v. 31 we might expect a statement such as 'You fools! which is more important, to accept the prophets God has sent to you in the present, or to build the tombs of those that have been slain in the past?' But no such conclusion is found. Rather, the woe seems to have been cut short, and the ending replaced with a charge to 'fill up' the guilt of the prophet-slayers of old. The importance of this observation is brought more clearly into focus in the following pages, for it is here it seems that the evangelist has picked up his pen and begun his own work. With 23.31 the source ends and redaction begins.

2. *Matthew 23.32-39*

The beginning and end of Matthew 23 display remarkable dissimilarity. In vv. 2-3 we read: 'The scribes and the Pharisees sit on Moses' seat; so practice and do whatever they tell you'. The author of this statement was plainly of the opinion that the scribes and the Pharisees were indeed authentic and authoritative representatives of the will of God, and is standing well within Judaism. In vv. 37-39, however, the picture is altogether different, for here we read that the temple is left desolate, and there is a clear implication that the Jewish nation as a whole has been rejected by God.

It seems, therefore, that a dramatic change has taken place somewhere between these two points, and that the extent of this discrepancy is even greater than we have so far indicated. It should be noted, for example, that, while the woes of Mt. 23.13-31 are addressed to the Pharisees and the scribes alone, it is 'Jerusalem' herself that is addressed in the lament. So too in 23.36 the warning is not that the blood of the righteous will come upon the scribes and the Pharisees only, but rather upon 'this generation'.[2] The material of 23.2-31 is primarily polemical and deals with halakhic and 'ecclesiological' matters. The material found in 23.33-39, on the other hand, is pronouncement, and has distinctly eschatological concerns.

The question must be asked, therefore, at what point this switch takes place. While it is not absolutely necessary that we identify clearly the

---

1.   Garland, *Matthew 23*, pp. 164-66.
2.   The Greek γενεά here almost certainly means 'race' and refers to the whole of Israel.

exact point at which the redactor picked up his pen (or possibly his scissors and paste), we ought at least to be able to narrow the choices to within a few verses. And this task does seem possible, for, in the light of what has been said immediately above, it seems highly probable that the switch does not come before v. 31, since all of this material adheres well together and moves in the same general direction. From v. 32 on, however, the discourse changes direction.

It appears, therefore, that v. 32 is the most probable point at which the change is effected, for it is here that the theme of persecution first appears. As is clear not only from Mt. 23.34 itself, but also from other sections of the gospel, this persecution is *extra muros* and takes place in 'their synagogues'. With this working hypothesis in mind, we turn to the remainder of Matthew 23.

Matthew 23.32

Several commentators have seen Mt. 23.32 as an editorial addition made by the evangelist himself to source material.[1] This is indeed a distinct possibility, for there can be little doubt that the nature of the material undergoes a distinct shift between the seventh woe and the saying contained in 23.33. As we have seen, 23.2-31 contains polemical material and reflects a pre-70 CE *Sitz im Leben*; the passage beginning with 23.33, however, is distinctly eschatological, and seems to have more in common with the material which follows it (i.e. the eschatological discourse of Mt. 24) than with that which comes before.[2]

Given this apparent switch from polemical to eschatological material,

---

1.   Garland, *Matthew 23*, p. 166. Manson, *Sayings*, p. 238; Haenchen, 'Matthäus 23', p. 52; Strecker, *Weg der Gerechtigkeit*, p. 159 n. 1; Hare, *Jewish Persecution*, pp. 86, 88; all of whom agree that Mt. 23.32 is Matthean. See also Brooks, *Matthew's Community*, p. 116. It is possible that the substance of Mt. 23.32-36 has been drawn from some pre-Matthean source known also to Paul, for in 1 Thess. 2.15-16 a similar idea is found and several key words are present. See Garland, *Matthew 23*, pp. 169-70. Even if a source has been used, it is plain that the thrust of vv. 32-39 is different from that of Mt. 23.2-31 and thus a layer of editorial activity is evident.

2.   See further S. Brown, 'The Matthean Apocalypse', *JSNT* 4 (1979), pp. 2-27. Brown suggests that Matthew's apocalypse begins not in Mt. 24.1, but rather in 23.32. According to Brown the Matthean apocalypse, which extends from Mt. 23.32-25.46, may be divided into five sections: (1) Mt. 23.32-39; (2) Mt. 24.1-3; (3) Mt. 24.4-31; (4) 24.32-25.30; (5) Mt. 25.31-46. Brown's outline shows that Mt. 23.32-39 does indeed function as a transitory passage, but, as argued here at length, it also serves as a conclusion to Mt. 23.2-31.

it is possible, indeed perhaps probable, that Mt. 23.32 is an editorial attempt to facilitate the transition. The editor has picked up on the theme of the guilt of Israel for the slaying of the prophets, and extends its application to include current and future Jewish persecution of his own community, and thus broadens out the whole controversy.

The verb πληρώσατε should certainly be taken in this imperative form rather than the aorist indicative found in D and H, or the future indicative in B e and Sy^s, for, as Garland has noted, these other readings may easily be explained in terms of a softening of the original imperative. The imperative may have predictative force, being used in the same way as a Hebrew imperative of assurance.[1] If so the sense would be 'and you will indeed fill up the measure of your fathers'. But whether the verb is taken as a straightforward imperative or predictative imperative, the meaning is much the same, and it is plain that the editor is keen to condemn the present practices of not only the scribes and Pharisees, but ultimately the whole of 'this generation'.

The *Sitz im Leben* of this verse is manifestly not that of the preceding woes. The verse is clearly connected to vv. 34-39, which themselves betray an *extra muros* stance. Unlike the author of 23.2-31, who seems to be urging a reformation from within, the author of vv. 32-39 sees no hope at all for the Jewish nation. The Jews will reject God's messengers and will in turn be rejected.

Matthew 23.33

Verse 33 may also be taken as an editorial addition. Its function is to introduce in a very definite way the material which is to follow. The theme of judgment appears for the first time in the chapter, introduced with words reminiscent of those spoken by the Baptist to the scribes and Pharisees in Mt. 3.7 and by Jesus in Mt. 12.34. There is no criticism of any individual act, but rather a blanket dismissal of the opponents as a 'generation of vipers'. Thus, taking the seventh woe as the starting point, the redactor has successfully made the transition from controversy to eschatological material.[2]

---

1. GKC, p. 324.
2. Stanton, 'Matthew and Judaism', pp. 270-71 presents a similar hypothesis. Stanton thinks that much of Mt. 23 is based on Q material, but suggests that Matthew himself has heightened the level of anti-Jewish polemic. Stanton states that in Mt. 23, as in many other passages in the gospel, Matthew 'conflates his sources and sharpens and extends considerably their polemic' (p. 271). He sees the seventh woe as a good

Matthew 23.34-36

The pericope found in these verses takes its cue from the seventh woe. The Jews as a nation are guilty of slaying the prophets, but whereas in the last woe there is no mention of the continuing persecution of the community at the hands of the Jews, in the present passage there is a clear indication that Jewish persecution was either known or expected by its author. The Jewish people will not receive those messengers whom God has sent, but rather they will treat them as enemies, killing some, stoning others, and pursuing others from city to city. Eventually their deeds will be complete and they will have 'filled up' the measure of their fathers' wickedness.

The saying 'you are the sons of prophet-killers' is taken up and used as the basis for eschatological speculation. The seventh woe is itself basically non-eschatological, as indeed is Mt. 23.2-31 as a whole. As pointed out in the following chapter, this apparent tendency to use non-eschatological material to make an eschatological point is a phenomenon found elsewhere in Matthew (e.g. 22.11-14).

It should be noted carefully that, unlike Mt. 23.2-31, the present pericope evinces an *extra muros* stance on the part of its author. The beatings take place not in *the* synagogues (cf. Mt. 23.6), but *their* synagogues. Similarly, the use of the word 'scribe' is altogether different.

The extent of this dissimilarity, and consequently the possibility that vv. 33-36 are in fact redactional and not original to their present context, has been obscured by the fact that the verses appear in roughly the same context in Luke and are therefore assumed to have been found in this setting already in Q. However, as several scholars point out, it is quite plausible that Luke has used Matthew in the compilation of his gospel, an argument that has had it supporters in the past and now has a new champion in Goulder.[1] Even Gundry, usually thought to be a fairly hard line two-documentarian, is prepared to allow for this possibility.[2] It may be, therefore, that the section extending from Mt. 23.33-36 is redactional material probably stemming from the hand of Matthew

example of this tendency. Naturally, since he is working on the basis of the Q hypothesis, the extent of this redaction is limited, but the similarities between his suggestions and those presented here are plain. Hare, *Jewish Persecution*, p. 92 (to whom Stanton refers), puts forward a similar suggestion.

1.   M.D. Goulder, *Luke: A New Paradigm* (Sheffield: JSOT Press, repr. 1995 [1989]).

2.   Gundry, *Matthew*, p. 5.

himself, and that its occurrence in Luke is an example of Luke's use of Matthew.

There are obvious connections between this pericope and other sections of the gospel. These are examined in detail in the following chapter, and we may simply note in passing that in Matthew the theme of persecution frequently accompanies a reference to eschatological events (e.g. Mt. 10.34-36; 24.9ff.). These passages too are most likely the work of a redactor (probably Matthew himself), and if this conclusion is accepted, it becomes even more probable that vv. 33-36 are the work of an editor and are not original to their present context.

Matthew 23.37-39

This passage is designed as a conclusion to the discourse begun in 23.2, though it also aids in the transition to the material which follows in ch. 24. This is not to say that the whole of Matthew 23 is the work of one hand, but rather that the 'eschatological redactor' who has added the eschatological appendix intends by his placing of the saying found in 23.37-39 to colour the way in which the whole of the chapter is understood. The next chapter begins with a short narrative describing how Jesus left the temple area and then began to speak once again to his followers. This being so, it may be assumed that 24.2 begins a separate discourse, and that consequently 23.37-39 is the conclusion of the discourse which began in 23.2 and, on a Matthean level, a conclusion to the whole of the controversy section which began in 21.1. This is important, for the saying of 23.37-39 suggests that its author believed that the Jewish people as a nation had been rejected.

The pericope fits well into its context, for it continues the expansion of the seventh woe; Jerusalem (and not simply the scribes and the Pharisees) has stoned and killed the messengers sent to her, and consequently she herself will be rejected. There is a reference to the destruction of the temple with the words 'behold your house has been made desolate'. Finally, there is a prediction of the future coming of Jesus in glory, at which time Jerusalem will confess 'blessed is he who comes in the name of the Lord'. These last words might suggest that the author of the passage felt that the ones to whom the words were addressed ('Jerusalem') would one day accept the messiahship of Jesus and some commentators have naturally taken this view. However, given Matthew's hostility towards the Jewish nation elsewhere and his apparent conviction that the kingdom had been taken from them and given to others (21.33–22.14) such exegesis seems unlikely.[1]

It is at this point that the material found in Matthew 23 draws closest to its Lucan counterpart, for the wording of vv. 37-39 is virtually identical to that of Lk. 13.34-35. This is hardly surprising, however, since the saying almost certainly once had a separate existence, and may have been available separately to Matthew and Luke. The fact that the saying is found in an entirely different context in Luke has, in fact, persuaded several commentators that such is indeed the case.[2] If so, it seems entirely possible that Matthew has selected this logion not because it contained the words 'until you say, blessed is he who comes in the name of the Lord', words which seem generally out of tune with the rest of the Matthean material, but rather because it spoke of Israel's rejection of her messiah (a common enough theme in Matthew) and contained also the words 'your house is forsaken and desolate'.

The addition of the lament over Jerusalem may, then, be an example of one way in which Matthew's and Luke's traditions have developed separately. Alternatively, if it is assumed that Luke used Matthew, who was himself responsible for the whole of the eschatological appendix extending from Mt. 23.33-39, it seems that Luke chose to transpose this particular element of the tradition to another place in his Gospel. Such an understanding is not without its problems, but the fact that several scholars have been able to explain why Luke has broken up not only the discourse of Mt. 23.2-39, but all the sayings material, suggests that they

1.   See e.g. Bonnard (*Matthieu*, p. 344), who thinks that this verse indicates Matthew's probable belief that the Jews would eventually come to repentance. To be noted also is the suggestion made by D.C. Allison in his article 'Matt 23.39 = Luke 13.35b as a Conditional Prophecy', *JSNT* 18 (1983), pp. 75-84. According to Allison, Mt. 23.39 is to be understood as a conditional prophecy; Jesus will not return until (= 'unless') the Jews confess him as Lord. Indeed, 'the date of the redemption is contingent upon Israel's acceptance of the person and work of Jesus' (p. 77). This exegesis may be valid on a pre-Matthean level, and we may speculate that the verse contains an original saying of Jesus, who, seeing the unbelief of his fellow Jews, warned them that he had done all he could and that the onus was upon them. When the Jews say 'blessed is he who comes in the name of the Lord' Jesus would again take up his role of prophet to Israel. On a Matthean level, however, Allison's suggestion is perhaps found wanting, for as has been suggested in Chapter Two above, for Matthew the Jews were most probably a lost cause. See also H. van der Kwaak, 'Die Klage über Jerusalem (Matth. xxiii 37-39)', *NovT* 8 (1966), pp. 156-70 according to whom ἕως ἄν εἴπητε is conditional.

2.   Garland, *Matthew 23*, p. 187.

are not unsolvable.[1] It should be noted also that several commentators believe that Mt. 23.33-39 preserves the order of Q, while Luke has disrupted the flow of Q by moving the lament over Jerusalem to another place.[2] These scholars too must explain why Luke chose to treat his material in this way.

3. Conclusion

The above discussion has shown that Matthew 23 stems largely from an *intra muros Sitz im Leben*. Much of the material is polemic and betrays a close association with Judaism. The chapter ends, however, on a distinctly eschatological note, and to that extent the whole chapter can be seen as a unity. This eschatological conclusion may be seen as the point towards which the material has been moving. Thus Garland may be right in suggesting that the overall purpose of Matthew 23 is to 'elucidate the problem of the rejection of Jesus by the Jews and God's rejection of Israel'.[3] The editor may also have had it in mind to warn of the impending crisis and the coming of the Son of Man. Yet this purpose is that of the final redactor of the chapter. Within ch. 23 there is division: vv. 2-31 form a controversy dialogue which has little to do with eschatological matters and is inner-Jewish, being made up of an attack upon just one group, whereas in vv. 32-39, on the other hand, the attack is upon all Jews.

In this context the general assertion of Stanton that Matthew has intensified the level of anti-Jewish polemic found in his sources is seen to be basically correct.[4] As is argued at length in this study, the source behind Mt. 23.2-31 is not Q, but in other respects the suggestions made here overlap with those made by Stanton. Matthew has intensified the level of polemic in two ways: first, the place the evangelist has given the discourse in the overall plan of the Gospel colours the way in which it is read; and secondly, Matthew himself has added an appendix to the chapter in the form of an expansion of the seventh woe, and in so doing

---

1. The number of scholars who are arguing for Luke's dependence on Matthew is growing. Note for example the recent work of E.P. Sanders and M. Davies, *Studying the Synoptics Gospels* (London: SCM Press, 1989), p. 117 and, most impressively, Goulder, *Midrash*, pp. 452-71; *idem, Luke: A New Paradigm*.
2. See Garland, *Matthew 23*, p. 188 n. 82 for references.
3. Garland, *Matthew 23*, p. 215.
4. Stanton, 'Matthew and Judaism', pp. 270-71.

has caused the attack to mushroom out to a general criticism against 'this generation' (the Jews in general) and not simply the scribes and Pharisees. In the formation of this appendix, two other units of pre-Matthean tradition may have been used: Mt. 23.32-36 may be based upon a tradition known also to Paul,[1] and 23.37-39 may also once have stood alone. If so the editor has carefully combined these units into a coherent whole. Most probably, however, Matthew has created these verses himself. The word statistics presented in Chapter 1 above support this hypothesis.

We should also note carefully is that in Mt. 23.2-31 an intimate acquaintance with Jewish life is presupposed. The description of various aspects of Jewish life such as the chair of Moses, phylacteries, tassels and the practices of gnat-straining and cup-washing seem entirely natural, and, as shown in the preceding chapter, are quite explicable in terms of pre-70 CE Judaism.

The position of the author of vv. 2-31 likewise seems to be *intra muros*. Unlike Matthew's Gospel as a whole, the pericope of 23.2-31 does not betray a belief that the Jewish nation has lost its divine inheritance; God still dwells in the temple and the altar still sanctifies. Neither are the scribes and Pharisees rejected out of hand as nothing but perverters of God's purpose; they are attacked bitterly, but it is for their failure to be as thorough as they ought regarding the keeping of the law. They are not condemned for being too strict.

1.   Above p. 150 n. 1.

Chapter 5

LINKS BETWEEN MATTHEW 23 AND OTHER MATERIAL
IN THE GOSPEL

In Chapter 2 above the *Sitz im Leben* of Matthew's Gospel as a whole
was briefly examined and compared with that of parts of Matthew 23.
The conclusion was fairly clear: the final edition of Matthew's Gospel
was written by an individual who stood outside of Judaism; Mt. 23.2-31,
on the other hand, seems to contain an unusual concentration of material
which has its origin within Judaism. We have seen also that there is a
sharp division within Matthew 23. The apparent unity of the entire
chapter, it seems, has been imposed upon it from above and is the work
of a redactor, not the result of the material's having welled up from a
common source. It has already been argued at some length that the
discourse of 23.2-31 is best understood as one unit of tradition, and not,
as many commentators have suggested, a compilation of disunified and
even contradictory individual pericopae. This particular section evinces
an *intra muros* stance; to this discourse an eschatological appendix has
been added, and it seems that the editor was writing *extra muros*. In this
respect Matthew 23 is not unique in the Gospel, for, as pointed out in
the appendix to this chapter, such use of non-eschatological material to
support eschatological conclusions is a process observable elsewhere in
Matthew's Gospel.

It is the purpose of the present chapter to set the sources and redaction of Matthew 23 within the context of that of the Gospel as a whole.
If, as is suggested here, the chapter may be divided into two parts, the
first comprised of vv. 2-31, and the second consisting of vv. 32-39, is it
possible that these two sections have significant ties with material elsewhere in the Gospel? Can any stratification of source/redactional
material be found?

Clearly, the material discussed in the present chapter and that offered
in Chapter 1 complement each other, for we have already seen that

there is a considerable overlap in the vocabulary of the Sermon on the Mount and Mt. 23.2-31. This chapter explores the link in greater detail, arguing that the *Sitz im Leben* of the Sermon on the Mount is remarkably similar, if not identical, to that of Mt. 23.2-31. In fact, almost all of the material in Mt. 23.2-31 has close links with the Sermon on the Mount. The material found in vv. 32-39, on the other hand, does not tie in closely with the Sermon on the Mount, but has links with other, different sections in the Gospel. It is noted also in passing, but not explored fully, that 23.2-31 also has certain links with parts of ch. 18.

1. *The* Sitz im Leben *of the Sermon on the Mount[1] and Matthew 23:* *General Remarks*

The Gospel of Matthew is, as a whole, distinctly pro-Gentile. So much so, in fact, that some (probably wrongly) have attributed the Gospel to a Gentile hand. In the Sermon on the Mount, however, several equally distinctive anti-Gentile references are found. In Mt. 5.47 the question is asked, 'If you salute only your brethren, what more are you doing than others? Do not even the Gentiles (οἱ ἐθνικοὶ) do the same?' Similarly in Mt. 6.7 the advice is 'And in praying do not heap up empty phrases as the Gentiles (οἱ ἐθνικοὶ) do; for they think that they will be heard for their many words'. The saying, 'Do not give dogs what is holy; and do not throw your pearls before swine' (Mt. 7.6), may well indicate that the author was totally opposed to a mission to the Gentiles, a position which

---

1.   We might note here in particular the work of H.D. Betz (discussed in Newport, 'Sources and *Sitz im Leben*', pp. 53-55, 200-206). Betz suggests that the Sermon is an 'epitome' of the teachings of Jesus collected together and edited at some time prior to that of the final redaction of the Gospel by someone other than the evangelist himself. Betz then seeks to identify the original *Sitz im Leben* of this pre-Matthean material and in so doing engages in an exercise not dissimilar from the purposes of the present study. Criticisms of Betz are possible. In particular it would seem that he has not given nearly enough weight to the element of anti-Pharisaism in the Sermon and emphasized too much the extent to which the material is critical of Gentile (in particular Pauline) Christianity. However, Betz's basic starting point, that the Sermon almost as it now stands, is pre-Matthean, seems to be an avenue well worth exploring. See further the several essays on the Sermon now available in convenient form in H.D. Betz, *The Sermon on the Mount* (Philadelphia: Fortress Press, 1985) and 'The Sermon on the Mount and Q: Some Aspects of the Problem' in J.E. Goehring *et al.*, *Gospel Origins & Christian Beginnings* (Sonoma, CA: Polebridge Press, 1990).

seems to be redactionally 'corrected' in 15.28.[1] It seems, then, that Matthew's Gospel as a whole differs from the Sermon on the Mount in particular, in that whereas the former evinces a generally pro-Gentile attitude on the part of its author, the latter seems not to favour the non-Israelite nations. The Sermon on the Mount, or at least these sections of it, stems from a different *Sitz im Leben* from that of the Gospel as a whole. Its hard-line Jewish tone, however, links it closely to 23.2-31.

In Mt. 23.2-3 the Jewish leaders are seen as authoritative; the same seems true for the Sermon on the Mount. In 5.22, for example, it is clearly stated that the one who insults his brother by calling him 'Raka', should be brought before the Sanhedrin. It is also possible that the 'κρίσις' of the same verse refers to the '*Beth-din*'.[2]

Also to be noted is the warning 'Thus when you give alms, sound no trumpet before you as the hypocrites do in the synagogues and in the streets'; the originator of this saying quite clearly had a working knowledge of Judaism, a knowledge that was not merely theoretical, but also practical. He was acquainted with the practices of the scribes and the Pharisees and, like the author of 23.5-7, probably attended the synagogues himself where he witnessed their actions first hand. Any one could have criticized the Pharisees for ostentatious prayer on street corners, but the use of the phrase 'hypocrites in the synagogues' seems to suggest a sub-group working within Judaism. Matthew, who was himself probably a converted Jew, no doubt had a sufficient knowledge of the practices of his former co-religionists to enable him to have created this saying himself in an *extra muros* situation, but the *Sitz im Leben* of the saying, unlike that of the Gospel as a whole, seems to be found within the heart of Judaism. The passage is most explicable in

1. Cf. Mt. 18.17 where again 'Gentile' seems to be a term of abuse and is placed in paralled with 'tax collector'.

2. The word 'κρίσις' here is difficult to explain. Hill (*Matthew*, p. 120) suggests that it refers to the *beth-din,* that is a council which exercised a certain degree of legal authority even in pre-70 CE Judaism, and in this he may be right, though the evidence is far from conclusive. Certainly there were councils of various types in existence in pre-70 CE Judaism, but the names by which they were called and their composition are a matter of some debate (see further E. Rivkin, 'Beth Din, Boulé, Sanhedrin: A Tragedy of Errors', *HUCA* 46 [1975], pp. 181-99). Even if 'κρίσις' here refers not to an actual 'house of judgment' but the act of judging itself (as maintained for example by McNeile, *Matthew*, p. 61, and Gundry, *Matthew*, p. 84), the unambiguous reference to the Sanhedrin in Mt. 5.22, sets this whole pericope within a firmly Jewish context.

terms of an *intra muros* debate between one body of Jews and another whom they consider 'hypocrites'.

It was noted above that in Mt. 23.6 the phrase 'They love the best seats in *the* synagogues' is found. This contrasts with the frequent use of 'their' or 'your' synagogues elsewhere in Matthew. The importance of this observation is increased greatly when it is noted that there are only two other places where the phrase 'the synagogue' occurs and that both of these are in the Sermon on the Mount (6.2, 5). Thus the *Sitz im Leben* of parts of the Sermon and that of 23.2-31 seems to be the same, and this *Sitz im Leben* seems not to be that of the final redactor of the Gospel. Further evidence is found in Mt. 5.23-24, which states, 'So if you are offering your gift at the altar, and there remember that your brother has something against you, leave your gift there before the altar and go; first be reconciled with your brother, and then come and offer your gift'. Bultmann thinks that at this point the Matthean material is earlier than the Marcan (Mk 11.25). He suggests that the saying 'presupposes the existence of the sacrificial system in Jerusalem'.[1] Bultmann seems correct; the temple is still standing and the followers of Jesus are in the habit of offering gifts in it. In Mt. 23.16-22, too, the temple is still in existence and the cult system is still thought of as efficacious.

It seems, then, that there are several good reasons for thinking that Mt. 23.2-31 and the Sermon on the Mount may be linked: there is the significant verbal overlap pointed out in Chapter One, and there is evidence also that they stem from a similar if not identical *Sitz im Leben*, a *Sitz im Leben* that seems notably different from that of the gospel as a whole. This hypothesis will now be explored further on a verse by verse basis.

2. *Links between Matthew 23 and Other Sections of the Gospel: Specific Notes*

Matthew 23.2-31

Matthew 23.2-3a. Nowhere else in Matthew's Gospel, nor indeed in the whole of the New Testament, is there a direct command to obedience to the scribes and Pharisees; in fact in Mt. 16.5-12 the very opposite advice is given. Views related to those expressed in Mt. 23.2-3a, however, appear elsewhere in the Gospel. Clearly 23.2-3a expresses concern for

---

1.   Bultmann, *The History of the Synoptic Tradition*, p. 132.

strict observance of the law. Not only Torah, but also halakhah should be obeyed, and a similar intense concern is found in the Sermon on the Mount. In both these sections the concern is not so much for a general 'bearing of fruit' (cf. Mt. 3.8; 22.41) on the part of the believer, but rather that the convert should seek to obey the letter as well as the spirit of the law, and seek to avoid breaking even the smallest commandment.

This theme is clearly brought out in Mt. 5.17-19. Jesus has come not to destroy the law, but rather to fulfil it (5.17). Not even one jot will pass away from the law, but rather it shall remain until the end of the age (5.18). The one who infringes the least of its commandments will in turn be called the least in the kingdom of heaven, but the one who keeps the law and teaches others to do likewise will be given a place of great honour (5.19).

The six antitheses which follow Mt. 5.17-19 are probably an attempt to guard against transgression by being stricter than the law requires. It is not enough to avoid killing one's fellow human beings. Even anger for one's brother constitutes a serious offence and, if committed, should be brought to the attention of the κρίσις (5.21), probably the *beth-din* or some other legal authority.[1] Similarly, anyone who refers to a brother as 'Raka' should be brought before the Sanhedrin (5.22). Anyone who calls his neighbor a fool risks hell-fire (5.22). Adultery should, of course, be avoided; and this extends even to the adulterous thoughts of the mind (5.27-30). Divorce, except in the case of adultery, is forbidden absolutely (5.31-32). Oaths should not be taken lest they be broken (5.33-37), and revenge should not be sought even though it is the aggrieved's legal right (5.38-42).[2] Love should not be restricted to one's neighbour but should be extended to all humanity (5.43-48). In all things the believers are to seek a greater righteousness than that of the scribes and Pharisees, who are hypocrites and have their reward already.

In 23.2-3a the scribes and the Pharisees are thought of as authoritative figures. They 'sit upon the seat of Moses', and therefore ought to be obeyed. In the Sermon on the Mount Jewish authorities are also regarded as legitimate, for possibly the *beth-din*, and certainly the Sanhedrin, are considered to be authoritative in legal matters. In the remainder of the Gospel, however, the Jewish authorities in general, and often the Pharisees in particular, are portrayed as powers fundamentally

---

1. Above, p. 159 n. 2.
2. Hill, *Matthew*, p. 127 gives examples of similar statements found in the Dead Sea Scrolls (1QS 10.18; CD viii. 5-6).

opposed to the person and message of Jesus. They are not authoritative legal experts or competent judges.[1]

Matthew 23.3b-4. The bitter attack upon the scribes and the Pharisees is one of the characteristic features of Matthew 23. This attack is not upon the teaching of the scribes and the Pharisees, nor upon the scribal office or Pharisaic party *per se*, but rather upon what the author considers to be the failure of these individuals to practice fully what they themselves preach. The condemnation, expressed succinctly in 23.3, is that they 'λέγουσιν...καὶ οὐ ποιοῦσιν'.

Once again links with the Sermon on the Mount are evident, for a very similar sentiment is found in Mt. 5.20, which reads 'I tell you, unless your righteousness exceeds that of the scribes and the Pharisees, you will never enter the kingdom of heaven'. The scribes and the Pharisees, who, according to Josephus at least, were held to be accurate (ἀκριβῶς) in matters of Torah and halakhah observance,[2] in fact have only a limited measure of righteousness, and that which they have will not effect their entrance into the kingdom. Unless the believer's own righteousness surpasses that of the scribes and Pharisees, he too will be excluded. The community to which the Sermon on the Mount is addressed, like that of Mt. 23.2-31, must seek to outdo the scribes and the Pharisees in righteousness. Indeed, according to Mt. 5.48, individuals should seek to be 'perfect'.

3. *Matthew 23.5-7.* This passage clearly condemns ostentation, and this is the theme also of 6.1-18. In 23.5-7 it is the deeds of the scribes and Pharisees which come under attack: they make a show of their religious clothing, and always seek the best seats at the feasts and in the synagogues. In 6.1-18 the 'hypocrites' are singled out for condemnation. The author of 6.1-18 encourages his community to do their acts of righteousness in secret. Alms should be given without any of the show which so often accompanies the good deeds of the 'hypocrites'. Prayer should not be done to attract the praise of men. 'The hypocrites' love to stand on street corners so that they may be seen performing their good works, but this practice is not to be imitated. Prayer should be a private

1.   See especially Van Tilborg, *Jewish Leaders*, p. 1 *et passim*; and Kingsbury, *Matthew as Story*, pp. 17-23.

2.   *War* 2.162. Acts 22.3; 26.5. See further A.I. Baumgarten, 'The Name of the Pharisees', *JBL* 102 (1983), pp. 411-28.

matter. Fasting too must be carried out in secret, and every effort made to conceal this good deed from one's fellows should be made. 'The hypocrites', on the other hand, often look unsightly, putting on a gloomy face, so as to make their deeds known by all, just as those in Mt. 23.5 'do all their deeds to be seen by men'.

There is, therefore, quite a clear overlap between Mt. 23.5-7 and 6.1-18. In both passages it is, in all probability, the same group that comes under attack: elsewhere in ch. 23 'hypocrites' is synonymous with 'scribes and Pharisees', and in 6.1-18 it is the 'hypocrites' who are condemned. The condemnation in both passages is the same and in identical wording; they do their deeds πρὸς το θεαθῆναι by men (6.1; 23.5).

In addition to this similarity, however, there is apparent contradiction, for Mt. 5.16 contains the injunction, 'Let your light so shine before men, that they may see your good works and give glory to your Father who is in heaven'. This passage is in tension not only with 23.5-7, but also with 6.1-18; yet the element of discrepancy should not be overestimated. Probably the sense of this verse is not 'make your tassels long, your phylacteries broad and stand around on street corners making sure you are seen by others', but rather, 'be perfect, and as a consequence people will see your good works and praise God'. The truly righteous person will be recognized as such wherever he goes; he need not seek recognition, for his piety will be apparent to all.

Matthew 23.8-10. The prohibition against the use of honorific titles is not found elsewhere in Matthew. However, there is a link between the command 'do not call anyone on earth your father' and the Sermon on the Mount. The Lord's Prayer begins with the words 'Our Father who is in heaven', and elsewhere in the Sermon on the Mount God is frequently referred to as 'your heavenly Father' (5.16, 45, 48; 6.1, 4, 6 [bis], 8, 14, 15, 18, 26, 32; 7.11). Despite Hawkins's view[1], this is not a characteristic of the Gospel as a whole, for elsewhere God is referred to as 'your Father' only twice (10.20, 29) and 'their Father' once (13.43).

Thus once again a link between ch. 23 and the Sermon on the Mount is evident: the author of 23.8-10 forbade the use of the title 'Father' in addressing earthly authorities on the grounds that 'there is only one Father, your Father in heaven'; the community behind the Sermon on

---

1. Hawkins, *Horae Synopticae*, p. 31. See further above, p. 23.

the Mount opened their prayer with 'Our Father in heaven', and else-where in the Sermon there is evidence to suggest that 'Father in heaven' was commonly used as a circumlocution for 'God' in the community to which it was addressed.

Matthew 23.11-12. Both the sayings contained in Mt. 23.11-12 have near parallels elsewhere in the gospel: 23.11 is almost identical with 20.28, and 23.12 has clear links with 18.4, which states that 'whoever humbles himself like this child, he is the greatest in the kingdom of heaven' (compare 23.12 'whoever humbles himself will be exalted').

As other commentators acknowledge,[1] the two sayings were probably once independent of the contexts in which they now stand, and many parallels are found in Jewish literature; *b. 'Erub.* 13b, for example, states that

> him who humbles himself the Holy One, blessed be He, raises up, and him who exalts himself the Holy One, blessed be He, humbles: from him who seeks greatness, greatness flees, but him who flees from greatness, greatness follows.[2]

It is quite probable, therefore, that sayings such as those contained in Mt. 23.11-12 were known in the ancient world independent of any context. This being the case, it is reasonable to assume that 23.11-12 may have been inserted into the chapter by a redactor. While most com-mentators would argue that this redactor was Matthew himself, there seems no good reason why this process should not have occurred on a pre-Matthean level.

Matthew 23.13. It is argued above that 23.13 attacks the scribes and the Pharisees for attempting to turn aside those who are on the verge of joining the nascent Christian sect which stands behind the pericope.[3] If this exegesis is correct, a partial parallel is that found in Mt. 18.6. Here the attack is upon a group of individuals who cause those who believe in Jesus to stumble (whether this means cause them to commit a sin or cause them to give up their belief in Jesus is not clear, but the latter is at least a possibility).[4]

---

1. E.g. Beare, *Matthew*, p. 451; Schweizer, *Matthew*, p. 432.
2. See also *m. Ab.* 6.5; *b. Ber.* 7b, 47b.
3. Above, pp. 133-34.
4. BAGD, pp. 752-53.

We must take careful note of the fact that Mt. 18.6 is itself closely tied to the Sermon on the Mount. 18.7 repeats in different words the thought of 18.6, stating, 'Woe to the world for temptations to sin [τὰ σκάνδαλα possibly 'stumbling blocks']! For it is necessary for temptations [or stumbling blocks] to come, but woe to the man by whom the temptation [or stumbling blocks] comes!' Immediately following come two fairly long verses which bear substantial similarity to Mt. 5.29-30. The verses read as follows:

> And if your hand or your foot causes you to sin, cut it off and throw it from you; it is better for you to enter life maimed or lame than with two hands or two feet to be thrown into the eternal fire. And if your eye causes you to sin, pluck it out and throw it from you; it is better for you to enter life with one eye than with two eyes to be thrown into the hell [Gehenna] of fire.

We may compare Mt. 5.29-30:

> If your right eye causes you to sin, pluck it out and throw it away; it is better that you lose one of your members than that your whole body be thrown into hell [Gehenna]. And if your right hand causes you to sin, cut it off and throw it away; it is better for you to lose one of your members than that your whole body go into hell [Gehenna].

Furthermore, the pericope in which 18.6 now stands has other links with ch. 23, for 23.12 is linked with 18.4, and it is perhaps unsafe to dismiss as pure coincidence the fact that 18.7 uses the word οὐαὶ twice. In short, Mt. 23.13 has links with 18.6 (cf. 5.19), and this verse itself stands in a pericope which displays other similarities with ch. 23, and is also tied closely to the Sermon on the Mount.

Matthew 23.15. There is no substantial overlap between 23.15 and any other material in the Gospel. We might note, however, that the use of 'hypocrites' here, as in the other woes, almost certainly refers to the same group as the one addressed in Mt. 6.2, 5, 16; 7.5.

Matthew 23.16-22. The third woe is without parallel in the other Gospels. Within Matthew, however, there is one other pericope which is concerned with oaths, namely the fourth antithesis of 5.33-37. Beare seems to imply that there is something of a contradiction between these two passages, stating that

> This third Woe is again without parallel in the other Gospels. It is related
> to injunction against swearing which is the theme of the fourth Antithesis
> (5.33-37)…These verses [Mt. 23.21-22] do not deal with further
> distinctions of detail, but seem to express the thought that whatever form
> of words is used, the one who swears is really swearing by God, and his
> oath is equally binding whatever the form. In the Antithesis on the other
> hand, we have a flat prohibition of swearing.[1]

But the dissimilarity should not be overestimated. In 23.16-22 it is the
opposition who are addressed. The author seizes upon what he considers
to be fallacious reasoning on the part of the scribes and the Pharisees,
and uses it to win points against them.[2] How can they say that to swear
by the altar is nothing, yet allow validity to an oath taken by the gift
upon it? In Mt. 5.33-37, on the other hand, it is the members of the
author's own community who are being addressed. Since all oaths are
binding, it is better not to take oaths lest they be broken, causing sin.
The statement 'if you take an oath—keep it, but best of all do not take
an oath in the first place' is not a self-contradictory one. Oaths provide
the opportunity for sin where none existed and they are, to this extent,
of the Devil (Mt. 5.37).

Not only is there nothing in 23.16-22 to contradict the material in
5.33-37, but there is an obvious, strong link between the pericopae. The
criticism of 23.16-22 is that the scribes and Pharisees are wrong in
allowing some oaths binding force while denying it to others.[3] All oaths
ultimately are binding. To swear by the temple is to swear by him who
dwells in it; to swear by heaven is to swear by the throne of God, which
is to swear by God himself. In Mt. 5.33-37, similar reasoning is evident.
One should not swear by heaven since it is God's throne, nor by the
earth since it is his footstool, nor yet by Jerusalem since it is the city of
the great king. It is even unsafe to swear by the hair of one's own head,
since this oath too is binding. It is clear, therefore, that the author of
Mt. 5.33-37, like the author of 23.16-22, took oaths with the utmost
seriousness, and both for similar reasons.

Matthew 23.23-24. Mt. 7.1-5 contains something of a parallel to
23.23-24. Both passages are concerned to point out to certain individuals
the inconsistency of paying attention to small matters, while neglecting

1.   Beare, *Matthew*, p. 454.
2.   So Garland, *Matthew 23*, p. 133.
3.   Above, pp. 137-40.

larger ones. In 23.23-24 it is the scribes and the Pharisees who come under attack. They are 'hypocrites', for they neglect important aspects of the law, though they correctly pay attention to such matters as the tithing of garden produce. In 7.1-5 too the author advises the 'hypocrite' first to take the log from his own eye, so that he may see clearly the splinter in his brother's. In 23.24 the scribes and the Pharisees strain a gnat, yet swallow a camel. In 7.3-5 the hypocrite pays attention to a splinter while leaving a log untouched.

Both 23.34 and 7.1-5 clearly contain an element of hyperbole. Goulder maintains that hyperbole is a characteristic of Matthew's Gospel,[1] but, as has been shown, he has counted as hyperbolic those sayings which are not really such.[2] The only genuine examples of hyperbole in Matthew are the faith–mountain sayings (17.20; 21.21), the log of 7.3-5, and the camel of 23.24. Thus a clear link between ch. 23 and the Sermon on the Mount is evident.

Matthew 23.25-26. The most obvious pericope with which to compare 23.25-26 is 15.1-20. Both passages are addressed to the scribes and Pharisees, and in both these individuals are called 'hypocrites'. In 15.14, as in 23.16, the opponents are referred to as 'blind guides'. Both passages have also to do with the general distinction between inner and outer cleanliness (washing hands/washing the outside of the cup while remaining dirty inside).

Practically the whole of Mt. 15.1-20 is paralleled in Mk 7.1-23, and it is therefore most common to explain the existence of Mt. 15.1-20 as an example of Matthew's use of Mark. Mark's passage has the same criticism of the scribes and Pharisees, whom he also calls 'hypocrites' (Mk 7.6) but not 'blind guides'. Mark also has the quotation from Isaiah which is used to accuse the scribes and Pharisees of paying only lip service to God, while being in fact far from him (Mk 7.6-7). Mark, like Matthew, has the statement, 'You have a fine way of rejecting the commandment of God, in order to keep your tradition!' (Mk 7.9). Thus if Marcan priority is correct, it would seem that Matthew has taken over the Marcan pericope and redacted it using a certain amount of material from the source upon which he is dependent for Matthew 23 and the Sermon on the Mount. The use of 'blind guides' at 15.14 may be dependent upon Matthew's knowledge of the phrase in the source he

1. Goulder, *Midrash*, p. 397.
2. Above, pp. 33-34.

used for 23.16. Hawkins and others have suggested that Matthew may have picked up single sayings from his sources and repeated them elsewhere in the Gospel,[1] and in this they may well be correct.

But the tradition history of Mt. 15.1-20 may not be quite so simple, for on closer examination it appears that the whole pericope may be a combination of diverse material. 15.1-2 clearly introduces what might be expected to be the theme of the whole pericope, namely whether eating with unwashed hands defiles a man. Yet vv. 3-9 diverge from this theme and speak of other matters (the Korban issue), and it is not until v. 10 that the defilement issue is taken up in detail. It is possible, therefore, that 15.3-9 consists of redactional material which has been added to an earlier controversy source either on a pre-Marcan or pre-Matthean level. This possibility is increased when it is noted that 15.1 introduces the opposition as the 'scribes and the Pharisees', yet in 15.12 it is the Pharisees alone who are 'shocked' at the words of Jesus. They therefore come under condemnation in 15.13-14, where they are described as 'blind guides' who, according to the author, lack any divine commission for their work as teachers. It may be that the controversy source spoke originally of a conflict over hand-washing between Jesus and the Pharisees, and that the editor responsible for the inclusion of vss 2-9 changed the introduction to include the scribes also. It may be that he failed to change v. 12, which he should have done in order to retain the integrity of the pericope as a whole.

Verses 10-20 of ch. 15 go on to attack the Pharisees, who, it seems (naturally enough in the light of the Old Testament food laws), teach that what goes into a man may defile him. The author of this section disagrees: it is not what goes into an individual, but what comes out of him which causes him to become defiled. Since they are working on the basis of the two-document hypothesis, most commentators do not consider the material found in Mt. 15.1-20 to be of Matthean origin, and indeed it is highly unlikely that Matthew the Jew created this discourse himself. Such commentators do not think therefore that this pericope stems from the same hand as the bulk of the material in ch. 23; rather, it comes from Mark and shows a few characteristically Matthean changes (e.g. the omission of 'thus he declared all foods clean', which Matthew found offensive). Mt. 23.2-31, on the other hand, come from a variety of sources. Only a small fraction comes from Mark, which was Matthew's main source for 15.1-20. But even if no source-critical hypothesis is

1.   Hawkins, *Horae Synopticae*, pp. 168-69; Luz, *Matthew 1–7*, p. 73.

assumed, the internal evidence alone is enough to make common authorship of Mt. 23.2-31 and 15.1-20 virtually impossible. In 15.10-20 there is an implied, if not outright attack upon the law, for even though Matthew lacks the statement 'thus he [Jesus] declared all foods clean' found in Mk 7.19, Mt. 15.11 unequivocally states that it is not what goes into the mouth that defiles a man, but that which comes out. As is argued here at length, the author of 23.2-31 is a conservative and strict observer of Torah, and for him this statement would have been impossible. Authors may contradict themselves from time to time, but it is surely highly unlikely that the same person who created the saying 'it is not what goes into a man that defiles him' also wrote 'the scribes and Pharisees sit upon the seat of Moses, so practice and observe whatever they tell you'.

It appears, therefore, that although there is some overlap between Mt. 23.25-26 (and indeed ch. 23 generally) and Mt. 15.1-20, these similarities are limited to the occurrences of individual words and phrases such as 'hypocrite' and 'blind guide'. The general outlook of the two pericopae *vis-à-vis* the law is such as to suggest divergent authorship.

There can be little doubt that in 15.2-9 there is severe criticism of the Pharisees and also of the scribes. These verses, which may be an interpolation into a source which had originally to do only with the washing-of-hands issue, contain an attack on these respected members of Jewish society who are accused of 'hypocrisy' and are said to use their tradition to overturn the commandment of God. Their reverence for the Divine is worthless, for their hearts are far from him, though they pay him lip service. The lessons they teach are nothing but human commandments. Unless Marcan priority is assumed, this passage too may be Matthew's own. Here he makes an outright attack upon the halakhah of the scribes and Pharisees. The main criticism comes in the form of a quotation taken from Isa. 29.13 (LXX). With this, as with all quotations, careful attention must be paid to the question of what concepts or words were the ones which made the author pick out this particular verse from Scripture. To this question there is no clear answer. It may be that the author of Mt. 15.2-9 wanted to underline the lack of divine sanction possessed by the teaching of the scribes and Pharisees and that he thus chose a verse which spoke of 'their teachings' as 'human commandments'. It is equally possible that the real interest that the author of the pericope had in Isa. 29.13 was that it brought clearly into focus the discrepancy between the state of the people's hearts and the confession they made with their lips. In either case, Mt. 15.6 makes it clear that the author of this passage rejected as 'the teachings of men' the various halakhic formulations held in such high regard by the Pharisees and scribes themselves (cf. Mt. 23.2-3, 23)

It appears, therefore, that Mt. 23.25-26 bears some resemblance to 15.1-20. This similarity may be explained in terms of the evangelist's use of certain words and phrases picked up by him from the source he was using for Mt. 23.2-31 and the Sermon on the Mount, and repeating them in a pericope which he understood to be concerned with similar matters. The fundamentally different outlook towards the law and the halakhah found in these two passages makes common authorship unlikely.

Matthew 23.27-28. The sixth woe follows on naturally from the fifth; the scribes and Pharisees are like whitewashed tombs, beautiful on the outside, while being full of uncleanness inwardly. The comparison is therefore between outer appearance and inward reality. Mt. 6.1-18 gives a similar warning against an outward show of righteousness. The links with this section should not be overstressed, since in 6.1-18 there is no condemnation of impurity, but only of superficiality and unnecessary ostentation.

Matthew 23.29-31. There is little overlap between the seventh woe and any other part of the Gospel. Verse 32 does indeed have some links with Mt. 5.11-12 (which several scholars think is redactional) and 10.16, 17, 23, but, as argued above, v. 32 was not originally part of the seventh woe.[1]

Goulder points out that the pairing of 'prophets and saints' is found also at 10.41 and 13.17,[2] and this fact does perhaps suggests that 23.29 may contain a certain Matthean element. This is not to propose that the whole pericope stems from the evangelist's own hand, but simply that he may have done a certain (but very slight) amount of touching-up of his source material.[3]

---

1. Above pp. 150-51.
2. Goulder, *Midrash,* p. 427.
3. As possibly with the phrase 'Kingdom of heaven', above, pp. 25-26.

Matthew 23.32-39

It has been argued above that the material of Matthew 23 undergoes a distinct shift at the end of the seventh woe. The attack is no longer upon the scribes and Pharisees only, but upon all Jews of 'this generation'. The chapter will end with the lament over Jerusalem, where there is a solemn prediction of the temple's destruction.

This latter part of the discourse has some significant parallels with other parts of Matthew, though, as we shall see, these parallels are found in different sections from those of vv. 2-31. Before discussing these Matthean parallels, however, attention must be given to 1 Thess. 2.15-16, for this passage too overlaps with Mt. 23.32-39. Garland has already discussed this overlap in some detail, and there is no need to repeat his work. He points out that, despite several dissimilarities in certain verbal forms, the parallels between Mt. 23.32-39 and 1 Thess. 2.15-16 are striking. The two passages share several key words such as προφήτας, φονεύω, διώκω and ἀποκτείνω. Similarly, the central thought behind the two passages is the same: the Jews persecute the Church and in so doing 'fill up' the measure of their fathers. God's wrath has, therefore, come upon them.

As Garland notes, these similarities are too great to be coincidental, and it is of little surprise that several commentators have argued that Paul (assuming he was the author) knew a tradition which was known also to Matthew.[1] In forming Mt. 23.32-39, then, it is possible that Matthew may have drawn upon another source. There is, however, such divergence between Mt. 23.32-39 and 1 Thess. 2.15-16 that it is clear that the tradition has undergone either some significant expansion by Matthew (or a pre-Matthean editor), or some drastic cutting by Paul. In all likelihood it is the former that has happened, and the presence of several Matthean words and phrases in Mt. 23.32-39 supports this conclusion.[2]

Matthew 23.32-33. It has been argued in detail above that Matthew 23.32 may be a redactional verse added to facilitate the switch from controversy to eschatological material.[3] The theme of present persecution being a continuation of earlier Jewish wickedness is found also at

---

1.   Garland *Matthew 23*, p. 169 n. 26 gives several references.
2.   See above, pp. 28-29.
3.   Above, pp. 150-51.

Mt. 5.12, but, as several commentators have noted,[1] this verse too may be the work of a redactor, for there are several differences between this verse and the other beatitudes. Mt. 5.12 has even closer links with 23.34-36, and for this reason detailed discussion of the redactional nature of 5.12 is left for the discussion of 23.34-36 below.

Mt. 23.33 bears very great similarity also to Mt. 3.7, the major difference being that whereas in 23.33 the 'generation of vipers' is asked 'How will you escape the judgment of Gehenna?', in 3.7 it is asked 'Who warned you to flee from the coming wrath?' It is perhaps also important to note that 3.7 immediately precedes a pericope which has specifically to do with the worthlessness of Abrahamic descent. God is able to raise children of Abraham from the stones. Already the axe has been laid at the root of the tree, and all those who do not bear fruit will be thrown into the fire. Mt. 23.33-39 too has as one of its main themes the author's belief that Israel as a nation has been rejected. Salvation does not depend upon membership of Israel. Indeed, it may even be hampered by it, for the Jews, on account of the hardness of their hearts, and since they have rejected God's messengers, have themselves been rejected by God. The other occurrence of the phrase 'brood of vipers' is in 12.34. This verse too is followed by a reference to the day of judgment and is probably from the same hand as Mt. 3.7; 23.33.

Matthew 23.34 has clear links with the material found in Mt. 10.16, 17, 23. The following parallel shows the extent of this similarity.

Mt. 23.34	Mt. 10.16, 17, 23
Διὰ τοῦτο ἰδοὺ ἐγὼ ἀποστέλλω πρὸς ὑμᾶς προφήτας καὶ σοφοὺς καὶ γραμματεῖς· ἐξ αὐτῶν ἀποκτενεῖτε καὶ σταυρώσετε καὶ ἐξ αὐτῶν μαστιγώσετε ἐν ταῖς συναγωγαῖς ὑμῶν καὶ διώξετε ἀπὸ πόλεως εἰς πόλιν·	Ἰδοὺ ἐγὼ ἀποστέλλω ὑμᾶς ὡς πρόβατα...προσέχετε δὲ ἀπὸ τῶν ἀνθρώπων· παραδώσουσιν γὰρ ὑμᾶς εἰς συνέδρια καὶ ἐν ταῖς συναγωγαῖς αὐτῶν μαστιγώσουσιν ὑμᾶς...ὅταν δὲ διώκωσιν ὑμᾶς ἐν τῇ πόλει, ταύτῃ φεύγετε εἰς τὴν ἑτέραν·

The theme of mission is evident in both passages. Both passages also mention beatings in 'their [your] synagogues', and similarly both speak of persecution from city to city. The *Sitz im Leben* seems identical and the passages may well be the work of one author, an author who knew or expected persecution at Jewish hands.

1. See below, p. 173 n. 1 for references.

There are four other occurrences of the verb διώκω in Matthew's gospel, all of them in the Sermon on the Mount. Three of these examples are found in close proximity in vv. 5.10, 11 and 12, which read:

> μακάριοι οἱ δεδιωγμένοι ἕνεκεν δικαιοσύνης, ὅτι αὐτῶν ἐστιν ἡ βασιλεία τῶν οὐρανῶν. μακάριοι ἐστε ὅταν ὀνειδίσουσιν ὑμᾶς καὶ διώξωσιν καὶ εἴπωσιν πᾶν πονηρὸν καθ' ὑμῶν ψευδόμενοι ἕνεκεν ἐμοῦ. χαίρετε καὶ ἀγαλλιᾶσθε, ὅτι ὁ μισθὸς ὑμῶν πολύς ἐν τοῖς οὐρανοῖς· οὕτως γὰρ ἐδίωξαν τοὺς προφήτας τοὺς πρὸ ὑμῶν.

For several reasons many commentators ascribe vv. 11 and 12 to the hand of a redactor,[1] and in this judgment they seem correct. Not only is there an obvious shift between the general macarisms of vv. 3-10, to the much more specific 'blessed are you' in v. 11, but there seems also to be a shift in subject matter. Verses 3-9 speak of such inward religious virtues as 'meekness', 'cleanness of heart' and 'hungering and thirsting after righteousness'; vv. 11-12, on the other hand, take up the theme of persecution, giving encouragement to a troubled community. Commentators note that since these verses occur also in Luke (6.22-23), this redaction will have taken place on a pre-Q level. Alternatively Luke may have been dependent directly upon Matthew at this point and Mt. 5.11-12, like 23.32-39, may be the work of Matthew himself.

Verse 10 may also be editorial. There is a shift between the perfect participle δεδιωγμένοι and the present participles of vv. 4, 6, and 7. The verse is absent from Luke, and Manson thinks that it is from M, which indicates his own suspicion of the verse's originality to the context in which it is now found.[2] Bultmann, however, thinks that Mt. 5.10 is from the evangelist's own hand, referring to it as a 'Matthean formulation'.[3]

The verse is clearly connected to the material which it follows, more so than to that which it precedes. Two explanations of this are possible; either Mt. 5.11-12 is an expansion of 5.10, possibly in the same way that Mt. 23.32-36 is an expansion of 23.29-31, or 5.10-12 came to Matthew (assuming he was the redactor) as a separate unit which he then pasted into a source which originally contained only seven beatitudes.

---

1. See for example Beare, *Matthew*, pp. 135-36; Green, *Matthew*, pp. 78-79; McNeile, *Matthew*, pp. 53-54; Bultmann, *History of the Synoptic Tradition*, p. 110. Luz, *Matthew 1–7*, pp. 228-29, 241-43; Allison-Davies, *Matthew*, pp. 459-66.

2. Manson, *Sayings*, p. 48.

3. Bultmann, *History of the Synoptic Tradition*, p. 110.

In either case, the redactional verses show distinct similarities with Mt. 10.16, 17, 23 and 23.32-39. The verses reflect the work of one who knew persecution at first hand (or at the very least expected it) and was seeking to encourage his community at a time of crisis. Other possible references to persecution are found at 5.44; 7.6; 13.21; 22.6; 24.9 and 25.34, though these are scant and do not lend themselves to detailed comparison with other passages.[1]

Matthew 23.35. This verse gives a clear indication that its author thought the Jewish people responsible for the slaying of the prophets. The author believes that as a result of their wickedness the Jews will face a terrible judgment when they will be held responsible for the blood which they have spilt.

It has already been noted that Mt. 5.12 contains an allusion to the guilt of the Jewish people. The author of 5.12 is seeking to encourage a suffering community; tribulation will come surely, but there is a great reward awaiting those who are presently called upon to suffer. The Jews are known prophet-killers, for they 'persecuted the prophets before you'.

This belief that the Jewish people are guilty of the blood of prophets is heavily underscored in ch. 27. Condemning Jesus to death at, we are told, the instigation of a screaming mob, Pilate washes his hands declaring, 'I am innocent of this man's blood' (27.24). 'The people', on the other hand, acknowledge what they are doing and bring down a curse upon themselves with the words 'His blood be on us and on our children'.[2] Commentators have long recognized that this is a redactional overlay to a more original form of the trial narrative.[3] Thus it seems that there is evidence in Matthew for the hand of a redactor who was specifically interested in laying the guilt for Jesus' death on the doorstep of the Jews. The same individual who is responsible for the accretions to ch. 27 may well be responsible both for 23.32-39 (where the theme of Jewish guilt is likewise emphasized) as well as 5.10-12.

Matthew 23.36. Persecution and increased eschatological expectation often go hand in hand. The community behind 23.32-39 either knew or expected persecution, and as a result there is vivid speculation

---

1.   See Hare, *The Theme of Jewish Persecution*, pp. 121ff.

2.   See further above, pp. 74-75.

3.   E.G. Green, *Matthew*, p. 221; Beare, *Matthew*, p. 531; Gundry, *Matthew*, p. 565.

concerning end-time events. In v. 33 the question has already been asked, 'How will you escape from the judgment of Gehenna?', introducing the theme of a final reckoning. Verse 36 goes one step further and predicts that all these things will come upon the present generation.

There exist several near parallels to 23.36. The most obvious of these is Mt. 24.34: ἀμὴν λέγω ὑμῖν ὅτι οὐ μὴ παρέλθῃ ἡ γενεά. This verse is set within the firmly eschatological context of Mt. 24. The phrase 'this generation' appears also at 12.41, where the context is again one of final judgment. Mt. 23.36, therefore, can be seen to belong to the eschatological layer of tradition in Matthew's Gospel, and this is probably true of the pericope 23.32-39 as a whole.

Matthew 23.37-39. Several commentators have recognized that the saying preserved in Mt. 23.37-39 was once an independent logion, though most would argue that the saying was joined together with 23.33-36 already in Q.[1] The pericope fits its context very well. The theme of Jewish guilt for the murder of God's messengers was introduced in the seventh woe, and this theme has been expanded in vv. 32-36. Eschatological expectation is also apparent in the verses which immediately precede the present pericope and 23.37-39 combines these two themes. Jerusalem is deemed guilty of the slaying of those whom God has sent to her; the inhabitants of the city have rejected God's offer, and God has in turn rejected them. The temple has been left desolate, and they will no longer see Jesus, God's final messenger, until his return in glory, at which time they will say 'blessed is he who comes in the name of the Lord'.

Once again several parallels are to be noted. The parable of the wedding feast speaks of Israel's rejection of God's messengers, and in Mt. 22.3 we read that the king sent his servants to call those who had been invited, but they would not come (οὐκ ἤθελον ἐλθεῖν, cf. 23.37 οὐκ ἠθελήσατε). The destruction of the temple is alluded to in Mt. 22.7, and the parable of the wicked tenants is also designed to underline the guilt of the Jews for rejecting God's messengers.[2]

The phrase, 'Blessed is he who comes in the name of the Lord', is

---

1. E.g. Bultmann, *History of the Synoptic Tradition*, p. 115; Schweizer, *Matthew*, p. 436. Garland, *Matthew 23,* pp. 187-97 has a detailed discussion of this point and gives numerous other references. .

2. Above, pp. 74-75.

found also at 21.9, though here it refers to Jesus' entry into Jerusalem. In 23.39 it clearly refers to an end-time event. The Jews will recognize Jesus as one who 'comes in the name of the Lord' at the end of the age. ἄρτι is found also at 26.29 and 26.64, both of which verses have clearly eschatological settings. Bonnard[1] and Benoit[2] keep open the possibility that it is Matthew's view that at the end of the age the Jewish people will recognize Jesus as king and thus attain salvation, but this seems improbable given the context of this saying. More likely it expresses the conviction that the Jews will one day recognize Jesus for who he is. That day will be the day of Judgment, when Jesus will return as the eschatological Son of Man to judge the earth. At this time the season for repentance will have passed, and the gateway to heaven closed. The Jews, who in the present age reject God's call, will then go into the outer darkness to weep and gnash their teeth. Mt. 23.37-39, then, like other material in the pericope of Mt. 23.32ff., has distinct ties with other eschatological material in the Gospel.

3. *Conclusion*

Much of the material found in Matthew 23 is paralleled elsewhere in the Gospel. The first part of the chapter, namely the criticisms of the scribes and the Pharisees and the woes against them, has several close links with the Sermon on the Mount. A few parallels to this section are also seen in Matthew 18, especially vv. 1-9, and ch. 18 itself has links with the Sermon on the Mount. Ties may be seen between these sections on several levels. The linguistic similarities should not be overlooked, and the similar *Sitz im Leben* also deserves close attention.

The latter part of ch. 23 is paralleled primarily in the eschatological sections of the Gospel; this, of course, would be expected, since 23.32-39 has several explicitly eschatological verses. But the extent of this overlap exceeds that which might be expected if the only points of contact were similar subject matter. Several points of linguistic similarity are evident, and the reference to persecution at the hands of the Jews is a major theme. The community behind these pericope knew, or at least expected, persecution at first hand. Its members had obviously split from the main body of Judaism, and no longer thought of 'their synagogues' as the place of true worship. The community behind Mt. 5.21-26,

---

1.   Bonnard, *Matthieu*, p. 344.
2.   Benoit, *Matthieu*, p. 144.

however, thought that serious breaches of the law should be brought before the Sanhedrin, just as that behind Mt. 23.2-3 respected the scribes and Pharisees who sat upon 'Moses' seat'.

The parallels to Mt. 23.2-31 and 23.32-39, then, are found in different sections of the Gospel, and this supports the view that there is such a division within ch. 23. The two sections of the discourse belong to differing layers of the Synoptic tradition.

It must of course be pointed out clearly that the kind of layering of the Matthean material suggested above does not run along generally assumed source-critical fault lines. Thus for example Mt. 23.37-39, usually thought to be Q material, is identified here as belonging to a layer of tradition probably stemming from Matthew himself. Conversely, Mt. 5.17-20 is probably not the result of Matthew's own expansion of Q (cf. Lk. 16.17), but is from the same source as 23.2-3 (usually thought to be M material). The Lord's Prayer (generally assumed to be based upon Q material [Lk. 11.2-4]), which begins in Mt. 6.9 with the word 'Father' may reflect a particular use of this title, a sensitivity towards which is found also in Mt. 23.9 (often thought to be Matthean). This kind of layering of material is not explained by the two-document hypothesis, unless, that is, one is prepared seriously to qualify that hypothesis by allowing for an M-Q overlap or the possibility of Luke's knowledge of Matthew's redactional activity.

Appendix

Evidence of an Eschatological Redactor in Matthew's Gospel.

It has been suggested that Mt. 23.32-39 forms an eschatological appendix to a basically non-eschatological discourse. If this suggestion is accepted, the apparently different *Sitz im Leben* of this passage compared with that of vv. 2-31 can easily be explained, as can the differences in language. The present appendix explores this possibility further by examining other pericopae in Matthew which seem similarly to have gone through the hands of an eschatologically-orientated redactor.

1. *The Parable of the Tares*

The Parable of the Tares, together with its interpretation, provides evidence for the presence of an eschatological redactor's influence in Matthew's Gospel. This is true since, it seems, the Parable and its interpretation are not from the same hand. The interpretation is distinctly eschatologically orientated, though the parable itself is chiefly concerned with ecclesiological matters.

Bultmann argues that the interpretation is a later accretion,[1] and there is significant evidence to support his case. The very fact that Mt. 13.36-43 contains an interpretation suggests that it is secondary to the parable itself. Streeter also argues that the interpretation is secondary to the parable, suggesting that it is the work of Matthew himself.[2] Beare agrees that the interpretation is the evangelist's own work.[3] We might note also that although the Parable of the Tares has a parallel in the *Gospel of Thomas* (logion 57), the interpretation found in Mt. 13.36b-43 does not.

Even a cursory reading of the parable and its interpretation reveals a distinct shift in the emphases of the two passages. The parable speaks of a man who goes out to sow in his field. While the sower is sleeping, an enemy comes and throws bad seed into the ground, which grows up into weeds. The servants, seeing the weeds, ask if they should pull them up, for they are plainly not the result of the master's own sowing. The master, however, advises patience; the weeds should not be uprooted lest some of the good crop also be damaged. At harvest time the weeds will be sorted out and thrown into the fire. The master's wheat, on the other hand, will be stored in the barn.

There is, of course, some degree of eschatological concern evident in the parable, but its main thrust seems to be ecclesiological. The parable probably relates to the *corpus mixtum* state of the religious community in which it originated. It is clear that there are good and bad people in the church, but what should be done? Are the bad to be rooted out, or left until the final judgment? The high point of the parable probably comes in the command of the master, 'Let both grow together until the harvest', and the prediction of future destruction is perhaps important only in so far as it explains the community's present attitude towards the 'weeds' found in its midst.[4]

The interpretation of the parable is markedly different in its emphasis. The figure of the Son of Man is introduced, and it is announced that he will send his angels at the end of the age to gather up all those who have done lawlessness, and throw them into the fire. The whole of the interpretation centres upon the awesome spectacle of final judgment, when the sorting out of good and bad will take place. There seems an almost complete lack of interest in any present application that the parable may have. The only way in which the parable, as interpreted by the redactor, relates to the present is that it encourages good behaviour. The threat of future judgment is used as an incentive to orthopraxy, but nevertheless it is future judgment and not present practice which dominates the interpretation.

---

1.   Bultmann, *History of the Synoptic Tradition*, p. 187; so also Schweizer, *Matthew*, pp. 308-309.

2.   Streeter, *Four Gospels*, p. 522.

3.   Beare, *Matthew*, p. 303.

4.   So Bultmann, *History of the Synoptic Tradition*, p. 187; J.D. Kingsbury, *The Parables of Jesus in Matthew 13* (London: SPCK, 1969), p. 66. D.R. Catchpole 'John the Baptist, Jesus, and The Parable of the Tares', *SJT* 31 (1978), p. 561 n. 2 gives several further references. Catchpole's own discussion of the layers of tradition and redaction found in the Parable and its interpretation is interesting indeed. Like most, Catchpole thinks that the interpretation is secondary, but he also sees a further layer within the parable itself. According to him, the parable was originally concerned only to issue a warning that the day was coming when God would separate the good from the bad. Into this parable a secondary motif has been inserted, namely an explanation of the origin of the bad weeds.

If this division between the Parable of the Tares and its interpretation is accepted, and, as seems likely, the two pericopae stem from different hands, then the passages contain evidence for the presence of an eschatologically concerned redactor. A parable which, though it has eschatological implications, seems primarily ecclesiological in purpose, has been understood and interpreted in a fundamentally eschatological way. It might be said that the author of Mt. 13.36-43 simply misunderstood the parable, and that as a result he was bound in his interpretation to use eschatological language and display a concern for future events. This suggestion is itself supportive of the view advanced here, for it seems that the interpreter has read the parable through eschatologically tinted spectacles. The fact that other parables in Matthew have been treated in the same way as that of the Tares adds further evidence to the case.

2. *The Parable of the Dragnet*

Beare has noted the distinct similarity that exists between the parable of the Tares and that of the Dragnet. He writes

> There is an obvious kinship between this parable [the dragnet] and that of the Tares…The interpretation does not entirely fit the picture in the Parable…The interpretation is obviously secondary, not only to the parable of the dragnet, but also to the Matthean allegorical interpretation of the Tares. Matthew must have composed it himself, though he does not give any list of correspondents…Indeed the parable does not lend itself to full-blown allegorization.[1]

Bultmann is only slightly less confident than Beare in stating the opposite case. There is, he argues, 'no need to entertain doubts' about the originality of the interpretation of the parable of the Dragnet to the parable itself.[2] Kilpatrick agrees more with Beare than with Bultmann, though, unlike Beare, he does not put the interpretation down to Matthew's own hand.[3]

Quite clearly, Mt. 13.47-50 may be divided into two parts: vv. 47-48 contain the parable, and vv. 49-50, which begin with the words 'so it shall be', contain the interpretation or application.[4] Kilpatrick notes that whereas the parable gives as its theme the kingdom of heaven, the explanation treats the parable as one of judgment.[5] This is a point not to be missed, for the parable, like that of the Tares, was perhaps originally concerned with the state of the church.[6]

Manson goes even further: for him, the original form of the Parable is contained in v. 47 only,[7] 48-50 being secondary. This suggestion should not be dismissed too quickly, for the saying 'The Kingdom of Heaven is like a net thrown into the sea

---

1.   Beare, *Matthew*, p. 315.
2.   Bultmann, *History of the Synoptic Tradition*, p. 173.
3.   Kilpatrick, *Origins*, pp. 34-35.
4.   So Catchpole, 'Parable of the Tares', pp. 558-59.
5.   Kilpatrick, *Origins*, p. 34.
6.   See further C.W.F. Smith, 'The Mixed State of the Church in Matthew's Gospel', *JBL* 82 (1963), pp. 153-54.
7.   Manson, *Sayings*, p. 197; so too Schweizer, *Matthew*, p. 313.

which gathered fish of all kinds' does indeed seem somewhat self-contained, and it has the short, snappy style of the two parables which precede it (Hidden Treasure, Pearl of Great Price). The eschatological interpretation of the parable is introduced in v. 48 with the reference to the sorting out of the good and bad fish, and to this extent the verse (like Mt. 23.32-33) may be seen as transitional material designed to effect the switch from non-eschatological to eschatological material. Verses 49-50 are quite definitely eschatological, containing references to angels who will sort out the evil from the righteous, and referring also to the burning of those rejected. These things will happen in the 'summing up of the age'. It seems, then, that Manson may be right.

Such an understanding is further supported by the appearance of a parable somewhat similar to the Matthean Dragnet in the *Gospel of Thomas* (logion 8). Jeremias does not include the parable of the Great Fish as among those parables found in the *Gospel of Thomas* which have Synoptic parallels,[1] but W.G. Morrice has argued that the similarities between the two are such as to suggest that they are independent recensions of a more original parable, which perhaps originated with Jesus himself.[2] As it appears in the *Gospel of Thomas*, the parable has no real eschatological implications, but speaks rather of the joy which a fisherman has in discovering a large fish; in fact, as Jeremias notes, the primary point of the Parable of the Great Fish in the *Gospel of Thomas* is the same as that of the parables of the Pearl and Hidden Treasure in Matthew,[3] and these three parables could quite easily have once formed an independent unit.

It appears, therefore, that at one time the Matthean Parable of the Dragnet may have been a rather simpler parable which spoke of a fisherman who cast his net and caught several fish. The parable in the *Gospel of Thomas* concentrates on the size of one of the fish and the joy which the fisherman had in finding it; the parable in Matthew, on the other hand, has a different point to make, for here the emphasis is upon the mixture of fish, some of which were good and others bad. Most noticeably, the Matthean version is concerned with the sorting out of the fish, and with their ultimate fate.

If it is accepted that v. 47 does indeed contain the original form of the parable, then it is clear that it has undergone extensive redaction at the hand of one who was concerned to make an eschatological point. The whole pericope of Mt. 13.47-50, then, may contain a basically non-eschatological source to which an eschatological appendix has been added. The author of vv. 48-50 has a strongly eschatological intention.

3. *The Parable of the Great Feast*

Mt. 22.1-10 has many parallels with Luke. Mt. 22.11-14, however, is unparalleled, and this has led some commentators to see Mt. 22.1-14 as a conflation of two parables, one of which was in Q, and the other of which was known to Matthew via

1.   See J. Jeremias, *Parables of Jesus* (London: SCM Press, 1954), p. 24.
2.   W.G. Morrice, 'The Parable of the Dragnet and the Gospel of Thomas', *ExpTim* 95 (1983–84), pp. 269-73.
3.   Jeremias, *Parables of Jesus*, pp. 200-201.

another source.[1] This view of the sources of Mt. 22.1-14 is not without foundation, for, as many commentators have noted, vv. 11-14 are not really appropriate to 1-10. Allen points out that people who have been invited from the streets could hardly be expected to be properly dressed for the occasion of a king's wedding feast.[2] It seems that the parable contained in 22.1-10 is concerned primarily with the rejection of one group of invitees and their replacement by others. Unlike 22.11-14, it is not concerned with the preparation and readiness of those who eventually attend.

There are also certain linguistic differences between the passages. In 22.1-10 we hear of the δοῦλοι of the king who are sent out to call the people. In 22.11-14, on the other hand, the king's servants are διάκονοι. It would seem, then, that Mt. 22.1-14 may be the work of more than one author. Two explanations are possible: either the pericope contains material from two sources, brought together by an editor,[3] or, alternatively, Mt. 22.11-14 is an appended note which has been added by a redactor concerned to slant the whole pericope in a certain way.[4]

Whichever of these two options is adopted, the basic conclusion will be the same. If an editor has added a second parable from another source to the parable contained in 22.1-10, he has probably done so with the clear understanding that such juxtaposition will seriously affect the central theme of the whole passage. The material of Mt. 22.11-14 has the effect of ending the passage on an eschatological note. The 'wedding feast' is understood eschatologically and as being symbolic of a future event. If 22.11-14 is omitted, the passage looks far more like a parable designed to give dominical justification to the Gentile mission. The appending of vv. 11-14, therefore, may be further evidence for the input of a redactor concerned with eschatological matters.

Conclusion

The parables of the Tares, Dragnet and Wedding Feast clearly reveal the hand of an editor whose primary concern was with eschatological matters. In this light, the suggestion made here that Mt. 23.2-31 is source material to which an eschatological ending (Mt. 23.32-39) has been added, is seen to be quite plausible.

1. E.g. Beare, *Matthew*, p. 436; Manson, *Sayings*, pp. 224-226; Bultmann, *History of the Synoptic Tradition*, p. 203; See also Lagrange, *Matthieu*, p. 424.

2. Allen, *Matthew*, p. 235.

3. Smith ('Mixed State', pp. 156-57) notes that Mt. 22.11-14 have a near parallel in a parable attributed to Johanan ben Zakkai which perhaps lends further support to the two-parable theory.

4. So Beare, *Matthew*, p. 436.

Chapter 6

CONCLUSION

In his commentary Beare makes the following observations on Matthew 23:

> This entire chapter consists of a number of sayings which have no internal unity and are linked only by the atmosphere of hostility towards the religious leaders of Judaism. They can scarcely be taken to reflect the mind of Jesus. There is a sustained note of fierceness which betrays rather the bitterness engendered by persecution and by the continuing controversy between the Jewish-Christian churches of the late first century and the scribal-Pharisaic leadership which was rebuilding Judaism on intolerant lines after the fall of Jerusalem in AD 70.[1]

These comments are interesting in that they illustrate how, despite Beare's remark to the contrary, it is extremely difficult to explain Matthew 23 in terms of a mosaic of disparate units of tradition. Beare is thinking of the chapter as a Matthean redaction of M, Q and Marcan material, and has been blinded by this source-critical theory. This results in the plainly contradictory statements that the chapter has 'no internal unity' and yet shows a 'sustained note of fierceness'.

In this study we have challenged Beare's view at several points. Throughout it has been the contention that Matthew 23 is made up largely of a unified and coherent source. This source material, which extends from 23.2 to 23.31, predates the fall of the temple and stems from an *intra muros* debate between various factions within Judaism. As such, the material has close links with the Sermon on the Mount, which similarly exhibits an *intra muros* stance. The source has been lightly edited by a later redactor (almost certainly Matthew himself), and (like Mt. 13.47-48; 22.1-10) has had an 'eschatological appendix' added to it. But the evangelist has by no means completely covered his tracks; consequently Mt. 23.2-31 stands out in fairly sharp relief against the background of the Gospel as a whole.

1. Beare, *Matthew*, p. 447.

This understanding of the possible sources of Matthew 23 has been hinted at before, though even Brown, whose source theory perhaps comes closest to the one presented here, differs in major ways on several key points.[1] In particular Brown still finds room for a Q document, albeit one which is available in radically different recensions to Matthew and Luke. Less direct though still clear overlaps also exist between the source-critical proposal put forward here and the work of scholars such as Knox, Wenham and Green.[2]

It is hoped that sufficient evidence has been presented above to suggest that the fissures of tradition and redaction in Matthew 23 do not run along the most commonly accepted lines. At the very least, then, the present study has assisted in raising once again the perennial question of Synoptic sources. But hopefully its contribution does not stop there, for it has been the intention throughout not only to raise questions, but also to suggest answers. The Synoptic problem as a whole will most likely remain unsolved, but with respect to Matthew 23 at least it is suggested that the study presented here gives a completely reasonable account of the probable sources used by the evangelist. Obviously some attempt could have been made to trace the tradition even further back; vv. 11-12, for example, may have once had independent existence, and it may even be that vv. 8-12 in their entirety were added by a pre-Matthean editor to an even earlier source. Likewise, vv. 23.16-22 may have once stood as a separate unit; the other six woes, however, were most probably written at the same time, and perhaps a pre-Matthean redactor has taken the saying about oaths found in Mt. 23.16-22 and turned it into another woe; this would at least explain the somewhat different style of this particular criticism. Such speculation, while justifiable, is, however, hardly going to lead to anything like solid a conclusion. What seems more definite is that Mt. 23.2-31 as it now stands does not stem from the hand of the evangelist. Goulder's arguments to the contrary, as impressive and scholarly as they are, seem invalid.

The proof of the source-critical theory is, of course, in the exegesis, and it is suggested that the exegesis offered in Chapter 4 above bears out the earlier source-critical remarks. Indeed, the coherence of source-critical theory and exegesis may be one of the strongest arguments in favour of the hypothesis presented here. Thus, in Chapter 4 it was shown that Mt. 23.2-31 may indeed be explained on the supposition that

1.   Brown, 'The Form of Q'.
2.   See Newport, 'Sources and *Sitz im Leben*', pp. 36-38, 49-53, 55-56.

it consists of pre-70 CE source material to which a later appendix has been added. The purely historical work done in Chapter 3 does not in any way undermine this basic conclusion; nothing found in Mt. 23.2-31 definitely requires a post-70 CE date and much of the material seems to assume it.

The source-critical theory suggested here, then, allows for reasonable exegesis: we have not been left 'puzzled' by 'strange' or confusing verses;[1] we have not had to resort to the rather implausible suggestion that Mt. 23.2-3 is a 'tongue-in-cheek' remark;[2] neither do we need to see it as merely 'taktische Anweisung'.[3] In the same way, the prohibition of certain titles in vv. 8-10 has been explained realistically. The leaders of the community, who, it seems, are likely to be called by such 'Jewish' titles as 'Rabbi' and 'father' are to reject these appellations. The source theory has also allowed for the full implication of v. 13: the scribes and Pharisees really do have the power to turn others from the kingdom of heaven, and thus, presumably, have the power to let them enter it. Mt. 23.16-22 can easily be explained on the basis of the theory presented here: God dwells in the temple of Jerusalem, the altar sanctifies, and all oaths taken by cultic objects are binding. And since it is suggested that the saying found in Mt. 23.23 stems from within Judaism, we do not have to view it as a vague attempt to guard Jesus against the general charge of anti-nomianism.[4] The verse means what it says: tithing of mint, dill and cummin are required. Mt. 23.2-31 has, then, been explained realistically, and we have given an account of the reasons for the fierce bitterness against, and yet the apparent acceptance of, the scribes and Pharisees. The source-critical theory and resultant exegesis go hand-in-hand and complement each other fully.

On a Matthean level, too, a explanation of the material which allows for its full (if unpleasant) force has been given. As we have seen, exegetes seek to explain the origin of the violent discourse in a number of different ways. Some, such as Schweizer and Legasse,[5] suggest that the discourse is in fact aimed primarily against Matthew's own community. The scribes and Pharisees are held up merely as examples of what the Christian is not to be. According to this interpretation the

1. Cf. the remarks of Beare quoted, p. 11 above.
2. Cf. the remarks of France quoted, p. 120 above.
3. Cf. the remarks of Hummel quoted, p. 122 above.
4. Cf. the remarks of Manson quoted, p. 141 above.
5. Above, p. 69.

whole chapter becomes a kind of satirical cartoon. In the strange and distorted picture painted of the Jewish leaders one is supposed to see oneself potentially mirrored. But such interpretations have not treated the passage with due historical seriousness; Matthew 23 is a scathing attack on the perceived opposition, and Christian commentators who seek to wriggle out of the embarrassing implications of this chapter by viewing it as a paradigm cannot really be said to have taken the level of animosity found in the passage seriously.

One other potentially important observation has also been made: the remarks of many commentators on Matthew 23 often seem to have been influenced by a negative attitude towards the religion of Judaism. We noted, for example, that it was often assumed that the φορτία βαρέα mentioned in 23.4 were legalistic trivia which the Pharisees and scribes loaded onto the backs of others.[1] These requirements were burdensome regulations and 'pettifogging rules'. But, as noted above, this interpretation is not really supported by the text itself.

This is not the place to enter into a full discussion of the extent to which Christian anti-Judaism has led to faulty exegesis of Matthew 23, however, it is at least worth noting in passing that some element of such anti-Judaism has played a role in the understanding of ch. 23 which some commentators have. For the most part this anti-Judaism is second hand and evinces merely the acceptance of widely held, if erroneous, views; thus, since it is widely 'known' that the Pharisees were interested only in minute legal details and depended upon strict observance of their traditions for salvation, it is hardly surprising to find many commentators reading these criticisms into Matthew 23. But in fact, as has been shown here, the real conflict in the chapter is quite different.

The implications of the findings presented above are potentially far reaching, for if Matthew 23 consists largely of an already redacted pre-Matthean source, what of other sections of the Gospel? Is it perhaps possible that other passages have similarly come to Matthew in coherent and already redacted units? It has already been shown in Chapter 5 that ch. 23 shares many similarities with other sections of the Gospel, and, it seems, it is quite possible that there are layers of tradition which are quite different from those previously imagined. There is certainly some evidence for an 'eschatological redactor', and it is by no means certain that the hand responsible for the redaction of Mt. 23.2-31 (and probably the Sermon on the Mount) has not left its mark in one or two other

1.   Above, pp. 124-27.

sections of the Gospel. This possibility has not been explored in any real depth, but it has at least been noted in passing that Matthew 18 has one or two points of contact with chs. 5–7 and 23.

The domino effect continues, for if Matthew is dependent upon material which has been already redacted, this will have very serious implications for the results of redaction criticism, and some of the findings of the numerous redactional critical studies done of Matthean pericopae already undertaken may need to be revised.

Thus several of the apparent anomalies mentioned in the introduction to this study have been explained. This has been done primarily through a re-evaluation of the sources used for Matthew 23, for it has been shown that the chapter contains an extensive source which is a coherent unit and which fits well into a pre-70 CE *Sitz im Leben*. Indeed, this is the key to the problem, and it is perhaps only the dominance of the two-document hypothesis that has prevented it from being found before.

BIBLIOGRAPHY

Abrahams, I., *Studies in Pharisaism and the Gospels* (Cambridge: Cambridge University Press, 2nd series, 1924).

Aland, K. (ed.), *Synopsis Quattuor Evangeliorum* (Stuttgart: Württembergische Bibelanstalt, 2nd edn, 1967).

Albright, W.F., and C.S Mann, *Matthew* (AB; Garden City, NY: Doubleday, 1971).

Allegro, J.M., *The Dead Sea Scrolls* (Harmondsworth: Penguin Books, 1956).

Allen, W.C., *A Critical and Exegetical Commentary on the Gospel according to S. Matthew* (ICC; Edinburgh: T. & T. Clark, 3rd edn, 1912).

Allison, D.C., 'Jesus and Moses', *ExpTim* 98 (1987), pp. 203-205.

—*The New Moses* (Edinburgh: T. & T. Clark, 1993).

—'Matt 23:39 = Luke 13:35b as a Conditional Prophecy', *JSNT* 18 (1983), pp. 75-84.

Bacher, W., 'Le Siège de Moïse', *Revue des Etudes Juives* 34 (1897), pp. 299-301.

Bacon, B.W., *Studies in Matthew* (New York: Henry Holt, 1930).

—'The "Five Books" of Matthew against the Jews', *Expositor* 15 (1918), pp. 56-66.

Balz, H., and G. Schneider (eds.), *Exegetisches Wörterbuch zum Neuen Testament* (3 vols.; Stuttgart: Kohlammer, 1980–83).

Bamberger, B.J., *Proselytism in the Talmudic Period* (Cincinnati: Hebrew Union College Press, 1939).

Banks, R.J., *Jesus and the Law in the Synoptic Tradition* (SNTSMS, 28; Cambridge: Cambridge University Press, 1975).

Baumgarten, A.I., 'The Name of the Pharisees', *JBL* 102 (1983), pp. 411-28.

Beare, F.W., *The Gospel according to Matthew* (Oxford: Basil Blackwell, 1981).

Benoit, P., and M.E. Boismard, *Synopse des Quatre Evangiles en Français* (2 vols.; Paris: Cerf, 1972).

—*L'Evangile selon Matthieu* (Paris: Cerf, 1961).

Betz, H.D., *Essays on the Sermon on the Mount* (Philadelphia: Fortress Press, 1985).

—'The Sermon on the Mount and Q: Some Aspects of the Problem', in J.E. Goehring *et al.* (eds.), *Gospel Origins & Christian Beginnings* (Sonoma; CA: Polebridge Press, 1990).

Black, M., *An Aramaic Approach to the Gospels and Acts* (Oxford: Clarendon Press, 3rd edn,1967).

Bonnard, P., *L'Evangile selon Saint Matthieu* (Commentaire du Nouveau Testament; Neuchâtel: Delachaux & Niestlé, 2nd edn, 1970).

Bornkamm, G., G. Barth and H.J. Held, *Tradition and Interpretation in Matthew* (trans. P. Scott; Philadelphia: Westminster Press, 1963).

Bowman, J., 'Phylacteries', *SE*, I, pp. 523-38.

Braude, W.G., and I.J. Kapstein (trans. and ed.), *Pĕsikta dĕ-Rab Kahăna* (Philadelphia: Jewish Publication Society of America, 1975).

Brooks, S.H., *Matthew's Community: The Evidence of his Special Sayings Material* (JSNTSup, 16; Sheffield: JSOT Press, 1987).

Brown, S., 'The Matthean Apocalypse', *JSNT* 4 (1979), pp. 2-27.

Brown, J.P., 'The Form of "Q" known to Matthew', *NTS* 8 (1961–62), pp. 27-42.

Brown, R.E., *The Gospel according to John* (2 vols.; AB; New York: Doubleday, 1966–70).

Buck, E., 'Anti-Judaic Sentiments in the Passion Narrative according to Matthew', in P. Richardson (ed.), *Anti-Judaism in Early Christianity* (2 vols.; Ontario: Wilfred Laurier University Press, 1986), I, pp. 165-80.

Bultmann, R., *The History of the Synoptic Tradition* (trans. J. Marsh; Oxford: Basil Blackwell, rev. edn, 1972).

Burnett, F.W., Review of *The Intention of Matthew 23*, by David E. Garland, *Christian Scholar's Review* 11 (1982), pp. 267-68.

Butler, B.C., *The Originality Of St Matthew: A Critique of the Two-Document Hypothesis* (Cambridge: Cambridge University Press, 1951).

Catchpole, D., Review of *Midrash and Lection in Matthew*, by M.D. Goulder, *EvQ* 47 (1975), pp. 239-40.

—'John the Baptist, Jesus and the Parable of the Tares', *SJT* 31 (1978), pp. 557-70.

Charlesworth, J.H. (ed.), *The Old Testament Pseudepigrapha* (2 vols.; New York: Doubleday, 1983–85).

Clark, K.W., 'The Gentile Bias in Matthew', *JBL* 66 (1947), pp. 165–72.

—'Worship in the Jerusalem Temple after A.D. 70', *NTS* 6 (1960), pp. 269-80.

Cook, M.J., 'Interpreting "Pro-Jewish" Passages in Matthew', *HUCA* 54 (1983), pp. 135-46.

Cope, O.L., *Matthew: A Scribe Trained for the Kingdom of Heaven* (Washington, DC: Catholic Biblical Association, 1976).

Crossan, J.D., 'From Moses to Jesus: Parallel Themes', *Bible Review* 2 (1986), pp. 18-27.

Dalman, G., *The Words of Jesus: Considered in Light of Post Biblical Jewish Writings and the Aramaic Language* (trans. D.M. Kay; Edinburgh: T. & T. Clark, 1909).

Danby, H. (trans.), *The Mishnah* (London: Oxford University Press, 1933).

Davies, W.D., *The Setting of the Sermon on the Mount* (Cambridge: Cambridge University Press, 1964).

Derrett, J.D.M., ' "You Build the Tombs of the Prophets" (Lk 11, 47-51, Mt 23, 29–31)', *SE*, IV, pp. 187-93.

Didier, M. (ed.), *L'Evangile selon Matthieu: Rédaction et Theologie* (Gembloux: Duculot, 1971).

Donaldson, J., 'The Title Rabbi in the Gospels–Some Reflections on the Evidence of the Synoptics', *JQR* 63 (1973) pp. 287-91.

Doyle, B.R., ' "Crowds" in Matthew: Texts and Theology', *Catholic Theological Review* 6 (1984), pp. 28-33.

Epstein, I. (ed.), *The Babylonian Talmud* (35 vols.; London: Soncino Press, 1948).

Farmer, W.R., 'A Reply to Michael Goulder', in C.M Tuckett, (ed.), *Synoptic Studies. The Ampleforth Conferences of 1982 and 1983* (Sheffield: JSOT Press, 1984), pp. 105-109.

—'Certain Results Reached by Sir John C. Hawkins and C.F. Burney Which Make More Sense if Luke Knew Matthew, and Mark Knew Matthew and Luke', in Tuckett (ed.), *Synoptic Studies*, pp. 75-98.

Farrar, A., 'On Dispensing with Q', in D.E. Nineham (ed.), *Studies in the Gospels* (Oxford: Basil Blackwell, 1955), pp. 55-88.

Fenton, J.C., *The Gospel according to Matthew* (Pelican Gospel Commentary; Harmondsworth: Penguin Books, 1963).

—'Inclusio and Chiasmus in Matthew', *SE*, I, pp. 174-79.

Figuras, P., *Decorated Jewish Ossuaries* (Documenta et Monumenta Orentis Antiqui; Leiden: Brill, 1983).

Filson, F.V., *The Gospel according to Matthew* (BNTC; London: A. & C. Black, 2nd edn, 1971).

Finkelstein, L., *The Pharisees: The Sociological Background of their Faith* (2 vols.; Philadelphia: Jewish Publication Society of America, 3rd edn, 1962).

Fischel, H.A., 'Martyr and Prophet (A Study in Jewish Literature)', *JQR* 37 (1946–1947), pp. 265-80, pp. 363-86.

Flowers, H.J., 'Matthew xxiii.15', *ExpTim* 73 (1961–62), pp. 67-9.

Fox, G., 'The Matthean Misrepresentation of Tephillin', *JNES* 1 (1942), pp. 373-75.

France, R.T., *The Gospel according to Matthew* (TNTC; Leicester: Inter-Varsity Press, 1985).

Freedman, H., and M. Simon (trans. and eds.), *Midrash Rabbah* (10 vols.; London: Soncino Press, 2nd edn,.1951).

Frey, P.J.-B., *Corpus Inscriptionum Judaicarum: Recueil des Inscriptions Juives qui Vont du IIIᵉ Siècle avant Jésus-Christ au VIIᵉ Siècle de notre Ere* (2 vols.; Rome: Pontificio Instituto di Archeologia Cristiana, 1935–1936).

Freyne, S., 'Vilifying the Other and Defining the Self: Matthew's and John's Anti-Jewish Polemic in Focus', in J. Neusner and E.S. Frerichs, (eds.), *'To See Ourselves as Others See Us': Christians, Jews, 'Others' in Late Antiquity* (Chico, CA: Scholars Press, 1985).

Garland, D.E., *The Intention of Matthew 23* (NovTSup, 52; Leiden: Brill, 1979).

Gaston, L., 'The Messiah of Israel as Teacher of the Gentiles', *Int* 29 (1975), pp. 24-40.

Gill, T.A., 'The Woes to the Scribes and the Pharisees in Matthew 23' (MLitt thesis, University of Oxford, 1983. Bodleian MS M.Litt, c. 680).

Ginsburger, M., 'La "Chaire de Moïse"', *Revue des Etudes Juives* 90 (1931), pp. 161-65.

Gnilka, J., *Das Matthäusevangelium* (2 vols.; Freiburg, Basel, Wein: Herder, 1986–1988).

Goodblatt, D., 'The Place of the Pharisees in First-Century Judaism: The State of the Debate', *JSJ* 20 (1989), pp. 12-30.

Goodman, M., 'Jewish Proselytizing in the First Century', in J. Lieu, J. North and T. Rajak (eds.), *The Jews among Pagans and Christians* (London: Routledge, 1992), pp. 53-78.

Goulder, M.D., *Luke: A New Paradigm* (Sheffield: JSOT Press, repr. 1995 [1989]).

—*Midrash and Lection in Matthew* (London: SPCK, 1974).

—'Some Observations on Professor Farmer's "Certain Results"' and W.R. Farmer, 'Reply to Michael Goulder', in Tuckett (ed.), *Synoptic Studies*, pp. 99-104.

—'A House Built on Sand', in A.E. Harvey (ed.), *Alternative Approaches to New Testament Study* (London: SPCK, 1985), pp. 1-24.

Green, F.W., *St Matthew* (Oxford: Clarendon Press, 1936).

Green, H.B., *The Gospel according to Matthew* (New Clarendon Bible; London: Oxford University Press, 1975).

Grundmann, W., *Das Evangelium nach Matthäus* (THNT, 1; Berlin: Evangelische Verlagsanstalt, 4th edn, 1975).

Gundry, R.H., *The Use of the Old Testament in St Matthew's Gospel with Special Reference to the Messianic Hope* (NovTSup, 18; Leiden: Brill, 1967).

—*Matthew: A Commentary on his Literary and Theological Art* (Grand Rapids: Eerdmans, 1982).

Haenchen, E., 'Matthäus 23', *ZTK* 48 (1951), pp. 38-63.

Hare, D.R.A., Review of *The Intention of Matthew 23*, by David E. Garland, *CBQ* 44 (1982), pp. 323-25.

—*The Theme of Jewish Persecution of Christians in the Gospel according to St Matthew* (SNTSMS, 6; Cambridge: University Press, 1967).

Harvey, A.E., Review of *Midrash and Lection in Matthew*, by M.D. Goulder, *JTS* 27 (1976), pp. 188-95.

Hatch, E., and H.A. Redpath, *A Concordance to the Septuagint* (2 vols.; Oxford: Clarendon Press, 1897).

Hawkins, J.C., *Horae Synopticae: Contributions to the Study of the Synoptic Problem.* (Oxford: Clarendon Press, 2nd edn,1909).

Hill, D., *The Gospel of Matthew* (NCB; London: Marshall, Morgan & Scott, 1972).

Hoad, J., 'On Matthew xxiii.15: A Rejoinder', *ExpTim* 73 (1961–62), pp. 211-12.

Hoet, R., *'Omnes Autem Vos Fratres Estis': Etude du Concept Ecclésiologique des "Frères" selon Mt 23,8-12. Analecta Gregoriana* (vol. 232; Rome: Università Gregoriana Editrice, 1982).

Hummel, R., *Die Auseinandersetzung zwischen Kirche und Judentum im Matthäusevangelium* (BEvT, 33; Munich: Chr. Kaiser Verlag, 1966).

Jastrow, M., *A Dictionary of the Targumim, the Talmud Babli and Yerushalmi, and the Midrashic Literature* (2 vols.; New York: Judaica Press, 1975).

Jeremias, J., *The Parables of Jesus* (rev. and trans. S.H. Hooke; New York: Charles Scribner's Sons, 1963).

—'Die Muttersprache des Evangelisten Matthäus', *ZNW* 50 (1959), pp. 270-74.

—*Jerusalem in the Time of Jesus* (trans. F.H. and C.H. Cave; London: SCM Press, 3rd edn, 1969).

—*Heiligengräber in Jesu Umwelt (Mt 23,29; Lk 11,47): Eine Untersuchung zur Volksreligion der Zeit Jesu* (Göttingen: Vandenhoeck & Ruprecht, 1958).

Johnston, L.T., 'The New Testament's Anti-Jewish Slander and the Conventions of Ancient Polemic', *JBL* 108 (1989), pp. 419-41.

Juvenal, *The Sixteen Satires* (trans. P. Green; Harmondsworth: Penguin Books, 1967).

Kelly, M., 'The Woes against the Scribes and Pharisees in Matthew 23: What did they mean for the Author and What do they Mean in the Gospel Today?' (MA thesis, University of Bristol, 1972).

Kilpatrick, G.D., *The Origins of the Gospel according to St Matthew* (Oxford: Clarendon Press, 1946).

Kimelman, R., '*Birkat-ha-Minim* and the Lack of Evidence for an Anti-Christian Jewish Prayer in Late Antiquity', in E.P. Sanders (ed.), *Jewish and Christian Self Definition* (3 vols.; London: SCM Press, 1980–82), II, pp. 226-44.

Kingsbury, J.D., *Matthew as Story* (Philadelphia: Fortress Press, 1986).

—*The Parables of Jesus in Matthew 13* (London: SPCK, 1969).

—*Matthew: Structure, Christology, Kingdom* (London: SPCK, 1975).

Kloppenborg, J.S., *The Formation of Q: Trajectories in Ancient Wisdom Collections*. (Studies in Antiquity and Christianity; Philadelphia: Fortress Press, 1987).

Knox, W.L., *The Sources of the Synoptic Gospels* (2 vols.; Cambridge: University Press, 1953–1957).

Kohler, K., 'Abba, Father. Title of Spiritual Leader and Saint', *JQR* 13 (1900–1901), pp. 567–80.

Kuhn, K.G., *Phylakterien aus Höhle 4 von Qumran* (Heidleberg: Abhandlungen der Heidelberger Akademie der Wissenschaften, 1957).

Kümmel, W.G., *Introduction to the New Testament* (trans. H.C. Kee; London: SCM Press, rev. edn, 1975).

Lachs, S T., 'On Matthew 23.27-28', *HTR* 68 (1975), pp. 385-88.

Lagrange, M.-J., *Evangile selon Saint Matthieu* (Paris: Gabalda, 5th edn, 1941).

Lampe, G., *A Patristic Greek Lexicon* (Oxford: Clarendon Press, 1961).

Lategan, B.C., 'Die Botsing tussen Jesus en die Fariseërs volgens Matt. 23', *Nederduits Gereformeerde Teologiese Tydskrif* 10 (1969), pp. 217-30.

Legasse, S., 'L'antijudaïsme dans L'Évangile selon Matthieu', in M. Didier (ed.), *L'Évangile selon Matthieu: Rédaction et Theologie* (Gembloux: Duculot, 1971), pp. 417-28.

Levine, A.-J., *The Social and Ethnic Dimensions of Matthean Salvation History* (Lewiston, NY: Edwin Mellen Press, 1988).

Lieberman, S., *Greek in Jewish Palestine: Studies in the Life and Manners of Jewish Palestine in the ii-iv Centuries C.E.* (New York: Jewish Theological Seminary of America, 1942).

Limbeck, M., 'Die nichts bewegen wollen! Zum Gesetzes-verständnis des Evangelisten Matthäus', *TQ* 168 (1988), pp. 299-320.

Lindars, B., *The Gospel of John* (NCB; London: Marshall Morgan & Scott, 1972).

Lohmeyer, E., 'Das Evangelium des Matthäus', in W. Schmauch (ed.), *Kritisch-exegetischer Kommentar Über das Neue Testament* (Göttingen: Vandenhoeck & Ruprecht, 4th edn,1967).

Luz, U., 'The Disciples in the Gospel according to Matthew', in G.N. Stanton (ed.), *The Interpretation of Matthew* (trans. R. Morgan; London: SPCK, 1983), pp. 98-128.

—Review of *The Intention of Matthew 23* by David E. Garland, *TLZ* 107 (1982), pp. 348-49.

—*Matthew 1-7: A Commentary* (trans. W.C. Linss; Edinburgh: T. & T. Clark, 1989).

Maccoby, H., 'The Washing of Cups', *JSNT* 14 (1982), pp. 3-15.

Manson, S.N., 'Josephus on the Pharisees Reconsidered: A Critique of Smith/Neusner', *SR* 17 (1988), pp. 455-69.

—*Flavius Josephus on the Pharisees: A Composition-critical Study* (Leiden: Brill, 1991).

Manson, T.W., *The Sayings of Jesus* (London: SCM Press, repr. edn, 1971).

Mason, S., 'Pharisaic Dominance before 70 CE and the Gospels', Hypocrisy Charge (Matt 23:2-3)', *HTR* 83 (1990), pp 363-81.

Matera, F.J., 'The Plot of Matthew's Gospel', *CBQ* 49 (1987), pp 233-53.

Mazur, B., *Studies in Jewry in Greece* (Athens, 1925).

McKnight, S., *A Light among the Gentiles: Jewish Missionary Activity in the Second Temple Period* (Minneapolis, MN: Fortress Press, 1991).

McNeile, A.H., *The Gospel According to St. Matthew* (London: Macmillan, 1915).

Michaels, J.R., Review of *The Intention of Matthew 23* by David E. Garland, *JBL* 100 (1981),pp. 302-304.

Minear, P.S., 'The Disciples and the Crowds in the Gospel of Matthew', in M.H. Shepherd, Jr and E.C. Hobbs (eds.), *Gospel Studies in Honor of Sherman Elbridge Johnson* (ATR Sup, 3; 1974), pp. 28-44.

Mitton, C.L., Review of *Midrash and Lection in Matthew*, by M.D. Goulder, *ExpTim* 86 (1975), pp. 97-99.

Montefiore, C.G., *The Synoptic Gospels: Edited with an Introduction and Commentary* (2 vols.; London: Macmillan, 1927).

Morrice, W.G., 'The Parable of the Dragnet and the Gospel of Thomas', *ExpTim.* 95 (1983–84), pp. 269-73.

Moule, C.F.D., Review of *The Intention of Matthew 23*, by David E. Garland, *JTS* 32 (1981), pp. 227-29.

Moulton, J.H., W.F. Howard, and N. Turner, *A Grammar of New Testament Greek* (4 vols.; Edinburgh: T. & T. Clark, 3rd edn, 1976).

Munck, J., *Paul and the Salvation of Mankind* (Richmond, VA: John Knox Press, 1959).

Nepper-Christensen, P., *Das Matthäus Evangelium—ein judenchristliches Evangelium?* (Aarhus: Universitetsforlaget, 1958).

Neusner, J., *The Rabbinic Traditions about the Pharisees before 70* (3 vols.; Leiden: E.J. Brill, 1971).

—' "First Cleanse the Inside", the "Halakhic" Background to a Controversy Saying'. *NTS* 22 (1976), pp. 485-95.

Newport, K.G.C., 'The Sources and *Sitz im Leben* of Matthew 23' (DPhil thesis, Oxford University, 1988).

Renov, I., 'The Seat of Moses', *IEJ* 5 (1955) pp. 262-67.

Obermann, H.A., *The Roots of Anti-Semitism in the Age of Renaissance and Reformation* (trans. J.I. Porter; Philadelphia: Fortress Press, 1983).

Ory, J., 'An Inscription Newly Found in the Synagogue of Kerazeh', *PEFQS* (1927), pp. 51-52.

Pelikan, J. and T.H. Lehmann (eds.), *Luther's Works* (55 vols.; Philadelphia: Fortress Press, 1958–1986).

Plummer, A., *An Exegetical Commentary on the Gospel according to S. Matthew* (London: Robert Scott, 1911).

Poliakov, L., *The History of Anti-Semitism* (4 vols.; London: Routledge & Kegan Paul, 1966–1984).

Pollak, M., *Mandarins, Jews, and Missionaries: The Jewish Experience in the Chinese Empire* (Philadelphia: Jewish Publication Society of America, 1980).

Przybylski, B., 'The Setting of Matthean Anti-Judaism', in P. Richardson (ed.), *Anti-Judaism in Early Christianity* (2 vols.; Ontario: Wilfred Laurier University Press, 1986), I, pp. 181-200.

Rahmani, L.Y., 'Jewish Rock-Cut Tombs in Jerusalem', *Atiqot* 3 (1961), pp. 93-120.

Rajak, T., *Josephus: The Historian and His Society* (London: Duckworth, 1983).

Rengstorf, K H., (ed.), *A Complete Concordance to Flavius Josephus.* (4 vols.; Leiden: E.J. Brill, 1973-1983).

Rivkin, E., *A Hidden Revolution* (Nashville: Abingdon, 1978).

—'Scribes, Pharisees, Lawyers, Hypocrites: A Study in Synonymity', *HUCA* 49 (1978), pp. 135-42.

—'Defining the Pharisees: The Tannaitic Sources', *HUCA* 40-41 (1969-1970), pp. 205-49.

—'Beth Din, Boulé, Sanhedrin: A Tragedy of Errors', *HUCA* 46 (1975), pp. 181-99

Robert, A., and A. Feuillet (eds.), *Introduction to the New Testament* (trans. P.W. Skehan *et al.*; Paris: Desclée, 1965).

Robinson, A.T., *A Grammar of the Greek New Testament in the Light of Historical Research* (New York: Hodder and Stoughton, 3rd edn, 1919).

Robinson, J.A.T., 'The Parable of the Wicked Husbandmen: A Test of Synoptic Relationships', *NTS* 21 (1974–75), pp. 443-61.

—*Redating the New Testament* (London: SCM Press , 1976).

—*The Priority of John* (London: SCM Press, 1985).

Robinson, T.H., *The Gospel of Matthew* (London: Hodder and Stoughton, 1928).

Robinson, J.R. (ed.), *The Nag Hammadi Library in English* (San Francisco: Harper and Row, 3rd edn, 1988).

Roth, C., 'The Chair of Moses and its Survivals', *PEQ* 81 (1949), pp. 100-11.

Rothfuchs, W., *Die Erfüllungszitate des Matthäus-evangeliums* (Stuttgart: Kohlhammer, 1969).

Russell, E.A., ' "Antisemitism", in the Gospel of St Matthew', *IBS* 8 (1986), pp. 183-96.

Safrai, S., and M. Stern (eds.), *The Jewish People in the First Century: Historical Geography, Political History, Social Culture and Religious Life and Institutions* (2 vols.; Amsterdam: van Gorcum, 1974–76).

Saldarini, A.J., 'Delegitimation of Leaders in Matthew 23', *CBQ* 54 (1992), pp. 659-80.

—*Pharisees, Scribes and Sadducees in Palestinian Society: A Sociological Approach* (Edinburgh: T. & T. Clark, 1989).

Sanders, E.P., *Jesus and Judaism* (London: SCM Press, 1985).

—and M. Davies, *Studying the Synoptic Gospels* (London: SCM Press, 1989).

—*Jewish Law from Jesus to the Mishnah* (London: SCM Press, 1990).

—*The Tendencies of the Synoptic Tradition* (SNTSMS, 9; Cambridge: Cambridge University Press, 1969).

—*Paul and Palestinian Judaism* (London: SCM Press, 1977).

Schaff, P. (ed.), *The Nicene and Post-Nicene Fathers* (first series, 14 vols.; Grand Rapids: Eerdmans, repr. edn, 1969).

Schlatter, A., *Der Evangelist Matthäus* (Stuttgart: Calwer Verlag, 6th edn, 1963).

Schmid, J., *Das Evangelium nach Matthäus* (RNT; Regensburg: Verlag Friedrich Pustet, 1965).

Schniewind, J., *Das Evangelium nach Matthäus* (NTD; Göttingen: Vandenhoeck & Ruprecht, 12th edn, 1968).

Schulz, S., *Q: Die Spruchquelle der Evangelisten* (Zurich: Theologischer Verlag, 1972).

Schürer, E., *The History of the Jewish People in the Age of Jesus Christ* (3 vols.; trans. and rev. by G. Vermes, F. Millar, M. Black, and M. Goodman; Edinburgh: T. & T. Clark, 1973–87).

Schweizer, E., *The Good News according to Matthew* (trans. D.E. Green; Atlanta: John Knox Press, 1975).

— 'Matthew's Church', in Stanton (ed.), *Interpretation of Matthew*, pp. 129-55

Seager, A.R., 'Ancient Synagogue Architecture: An Overview', in J. Gutmann (ed.),

Ancient Synagogues: The State of Research (BJS, 22; Chico, CA: Scholars Press, 1981) pp. 39-43.

Shanks, H., 'Origins of the Title "Rabbi"', *JQR* 59 (1969), pp. 152-57.

—'Is the Title "Rabbi", Anachronistic in the Gospels?', *JQR* 53 (1963), pp. 337-45.

Simon, M., *Verus Israel: A Study of the Relations between Christians and Jews in the Roman Empire (135–425)* (trans. H. McKeating; Oxford: Oxford University Press, 1986).

— *Jewish Sects at the Time of Jesus* (trans. J.H. Farley; Philadelphia: Fortress Press, 1967).

Smith, C.W.F., 'The Mixed State of the Church in Matthew's Gospel', *JBL* 82 (1963), pp. 149-68.

Soares Prabhu, G.M., *The Formula Quotations in the Infancy Narrative of Matthew* (Rome: Pontifical Biblical Institute, 1976).

Spicq, C., 'Une Allusion au Docteur de Justice dans Matthieu, xxiii, 10?', *RB* 66 (1959), pp. 387-96.

Stanton, G.N., *A Gospel for a New People* (Edinburgh: T. & T. Clark, 1992).

—'The Gospel of Matthew and Judaism', *BJRL* 66 (1984), pp. 264-84.

—'The Origin and Purpose of Matthew's Gospel: Matthean Scholarship from 1945 to the Present Day', *ANRW* II.25.3.

—'5 Ezra and Matthean Christianity in the Second Century', *JTS* 28 (1977), pp. 67-83.

Stendahl, K., *The School of St Matthew and its Use of the Old Testament* (Philadelphia: Fortress Press, 2nd edn, 1968).

Strecker, G., *Der Weg der Gerechtigkeit. Untersuchung zur Theologie des Matthäus* (FRLANT, 82; Göttingen: Vandenhoeck & Ruprecht, 3rd edn, 1971).

Streeter, B H., 'St Mark's Knowledge and use of Q', in W. Sanday (ed.), *Studies in the Synoptic Problem* (Oxford: Clarendon Press, 1911), pp. 165-83.

—*The Four Gospels: A Study in Origins* (London: MacMillan, 1926).

Sukenik, E.L., *Ancient Synagogues in Palestine and Greece* (The Schweich Lectures of the British Academy; London: Oxford University Press, 1934)

Sulzberger, M., 'Encore le Siège de Moïse', *REJ* 35 (1897), pp. 110-11.

Tevis, D.G., *An Analysis of Words and Phrases Characteristic of the Gospel of Matthew* (PhD thesis, Southern Methodist University, 1983).

Thackeray, H.St.J., R. Marcus, A. Wikgren, and L.H. Feldman (eds. and trans.), *Josephus* (9 vols.; LCL; Cambridge, MA: Harvard University Press, 1926–65).

Thompson, W.G., *Matthew's Advice to a Divided Community: Matthew 17,22–18,35* (Rome: Pontifical Biblical Institute, 1970).

Thompson, S.W., *The Apocalypse and Semitic Syntax* (SNTSMS, 52; Cambridge: Cambridge University Press, 1985).

Tigay, J.H., 'On the Term Phylacteries (Matt 23:5)', *HTR* 72 (1979), pp. 45-53.

Torrance, D.W., and F.T. Torrance (eds.), *Calvin's Commentaries* (12 vols.; Edinburgh: Saint Andrew's Press, 1972.)

Townsend, J.T., 'Matthew xxiii.9', *JTS* 12 (1961), pp. 56-59.

Trilling, W., *Das Wahre Israel. Studien zur Theologie des Matthäus-Evangeliums.* (SANT, 10; Munich: Kösel-Verlag, 3rd edn, 1964).

Tuckett, C.M. (ed.), *Synoptic Studies. The Ampleforth Conferences of 1982 and 1983* (Sheffield: JSOT Press, 1984).

van Tilborg, S., *The Jewish Leaders in Matthew* (Leiden: Brill, 1972).

van der Kwaak, H. 'Die Klage Über Jerusalem (Matth. xxiii 37-39)', *NovT* 8 (1966), pp. 156-70.

Viviano, B.T., 'Social World and Community Leadership: The Case of Matthew 23.1-12, 34', *JSNT* 39 (1990), pp. 3-21.

von Dobschütz, E., 'Matthäus als Rabbi und Katechet', *ZNW* 27 (1928), pp. 338-48. (ET in G.N. Stanton [ed.], *Interpretation of Matthew*, pp. 19-29).

Wagner, G., *An Exegetical Bibliography of the New Testament* (Macon, GA: Mercer University Press, 1983).

Wenham, D., *The Rediscovery of Jesus' Eschatological Discourse* (Gospel Perspectives, 4; Sheffield: JSOT Press, 1984).

Westerholm, S., *Jesus and Scribal Authority* (Lund: Gleerup, 1978).

White, W.C., *Chinese Jews: A Compilation of Matters Relating to the Jews of K'ai fêng Fu* (Toronto: University of Toronto Press, 2nd edn, 1966).

Wink, W., Review of *Synopse des Quatre Evangiles*, by M.-E. Boismard, *CBQ* 35 (1973), pp. 223-25.

Winter, B.W., The Messiah as the Tutor: The Meaning of καθηγητὴς in Matthew 23.10', *TynBul* 42 (1991), pp. 152-57.

Wissowa, G. (ed.), *Paulys Real-Encyclopädie der Classichen Altertumswissenschaft*, I (Stuttgart: J.B. Metzerscher Verlag, 1894).

Yadin, Y., *Judean Desert Studies: Finds from the Bar Kochba Period in the Cave of Letters* (Jerusalem: Israel Exploration Society, 1963).

—*Jerusalem Revealed: Archaeology in the Holy City 1968–74* (Jerusalem: Israel Exploration Society, 1975).

Zeitlin, S., 'A Reply [to H. Shanks]', *JQR* 53 (1963), pp. 345-49.

—'The Title Rabbi in the Gospels is Anachronistic', *JQR* 59 (1969), pp. 158-60.

INDEXES

INDEX OF REFERENCES

b. Men.		b. Šab.		b. Taan.	
43a	89	137b	105	24a	138
43b	89				
44a	89	b. Soṭ.		j. Ḥag.	
		22a	89	77b	77

JOSEPHUS

Ant.		18.23-25	97	War	
4.213	86			2.162-63	112
10.8	81	Apion		2.162	162
10.14	81	2.123	99	4.7	109
13.21	109	2.282	99	4.9	109
13.288-98	112			5.119	109
13.399-415	112	Life		5.147	109
14.9	99	191	112	5.55	109
18.12-15	112				

INDEX OF AUTHORS

JOURNAL FOR THE STUDY OF THE NEW TESTAMENT

Supplement Series